P9-DMQ-609

BLACK SUN

EUROPEAN PERSPECTIVES
A Series of the Columbia University Press

Other works by Julia Kristeva
published by Columbia

Desire in Language: A Semiotic Approach
to Literature and Art

Powers of Horror: An Essay on Abjection

Revolution in Poetic Language

The Kristeva Reader

Tales of Love

In the Beginning Was Love: Psychoanalysis and Faith

Language: The Unknown: An Initiation Into Linguistics

Strangers to Ourselves

The Samurai

Nations Without Nationalism

Proust and the Sense of Time

The Old Man and the Wolves

New Maladies of the Soul

Julia Kristeva

BLACK SUN

DEPRESSION AND MELANCHOLIA

Translated by Leon S. Roudiez

COLUMBIA UNIVERSITY PRESS

NEW YORK

COLUMBIA UNIVERSITY PRESS
New York   Chichester, West Sussex

Soleil Noir: Dépression et mélancolie, copyright © Editions Gallimard 1987;
English translation copyright © Columbia University Press 1989

Library of Congress Cataloging-in-Publication Data

Kristeva, Julia, 1941–
[Soleil noir. English]
Black sun : depression and melancholia / Julia Kristeva ;
translated by Leon S. Roudiez.
p. cm. — (European perspectives)
Translation of: Soleil noir.
Bibliography: p/
Includes index.
ISBN 0-231-06706-2
1. Depression, Mental.
2. Melancholy.
3. Melancholy in literature.
I. Title.   II. Series.
RC537.K7513   1980
616.85′27—dc20
89-7230
CIP

Casebound editions of Columbia University Press Books are printed on
permanent and durable acid-free paper

Printed in the United States of America

c 10 9 8 7 6 5 4 3
p 10 9 8 7 6 5 4

Why so downcast, my soul,
    why do you sigh within me?

Psalms 42:5 & 11

Man's greatness resides in his knowing himself to be
wretched.

Pascal, *Thoughts*, 165

That is perhaps what we seek throughout life, that and noth-
ing more, the greatest possible sorrow so as to become fully
ourselves before dying.

Céline, *Journey to the End of the Night*

CONTENTS

BLACK SUN

1

Psychoanalysis— A Counterdepressant

For those who are racked by melancholia, writing about it would have meaning only if writing sprang out of that very melancholia. I am trying to address an abyss of sorrow, a noncommunicable grief that at times, and often on a long-term basis, lays claims upon us to the extent of having us lose all interest in words, actions, and even life itself. Such despair is not a revulsion that would imply my being capable of desire and creativity, negative indeed but present. Within depression, if my existence is on the verge of collapsing, its lack of meaning is not tragic—it appears obvious to me, glaring and inescapable.

Where does this black sun come from? Out of what eerie galaxy do its invisible, lethargic rays reach me, pinning me down to the ground, to my bed, compelling me to silence, to renunciation?

The wound I have just suffered, some setback or other in my love life or my profession, some sorrow or bereavement affecting my relationship with close relatives—such are often the easily spotted triggers of my despair. A betrayal, a fatal illness, some accident or handicap that abruptly wrests me away from what seemed to me the normal category of normal people or else falls on a loved one with the same radical effect, or yet . . . What more could I mention? An infinite number of misfortunes weigh us down every day . . . All this suddenly gives me another life. A life that is unlivable, heavy with daily sorrows, tears held back or shed, a total despair, scorching at times, then wan and empty. In short, a devitalized existence that, although occasionally fired by the effort I make to prolong it, is ready at any moment for a plunge into death. An avenging death or a liberating death, it is henceforth the inner threshold of my despondency, the impossible meaning of a life whose burden constantly seems unbearable, save for those moments when I pull myself together and face up to the disaster. I live a living death, my flesh is wounded, bleeding, cadaverized, my rhythm slowed down or interrupted, time has been erased or bloated, absorbed into sorrow . . . Absent from other people's meaning, alien, accidental with respect to naive happiness, I owe a supreme, metaphysical lucidity to my depression. On the frontiers of life and death, occasionally I have the arrogant feeling of being witness to the meaninglessness of Being, of revealing the absurdity of bonds and beings.

My pain is the hidden side of my philosophy, its mute sister. In the same way, Montaigne's statement "To philosophize is to learn how to die" is inconceivable without the melancholy combination of sorrow and hatred—which came to a head in Heidegger's *care* and the disclosure of our "being-for-death." Without a bent for melancholia there is no psyche, only a transition to action or play.

Nevertheless, the power of the events that create my depression is often out of proportion to the disaster that suddenly overwhelms me. What is more, the disenchantment that I experience here and now, cruel as it may be, appears, under scrutiny, to awaken echoes of old traumas, to which I realize I have never been able to resign myself. I can thus discover antecedents to my current breakdown in a loss, death, or grief over someone or something that I once loved. The disappearance of that essential being continues to deprive me of what is most worthwhile in me; I live it as a wound or deprivation, discovering just the same that my grief is but the deferment of the hatred or desire for ascendency that I nurture with respect to the one who betrayed or abandoned me. My depression points to my not knowing how to lose—I have perhaps been unable to find a valid compensation for the loss? It follows that any loss entails the loss of my being—and of Being itself. The depressed person is a radical, sullen atheist.

Melancholia—Somber Lining of Amatory Passion

A sad voluptuousness, a despondent intoxication make up the humdrum backdrop against which our ideals and euphorias often stand out, unless they be that fleeting clear-mindedness shredding the amorous hypnosis that joins two persons together. Conscious of our being doomed to lose our loves, we grieve perhaps even more when we glimpse in our lover the shadow of a long lost former loved one. Depression is the hidden face of Narcissus, the face that is to bear him away into death, but of which he is unaware while he admires himself in a mirage. Talking about depression will again lead us into the marshy land of the Narcissus myth.[1] This time, however, we shall not encounter the bright and fragile amatory idealization; on the contrary, we shall see the shadow cast on the fragile self, hardly dissociated from the other, precisely by the *loss* of that essential other. The shadow of despair.

Rather than seek the meaning of despair (it is either obvious or metaphysical), let us acknowledge that there is

meaning only in despair. The child king becomes irre-
deemably sad before uttering his first words; this is because he has been irrevocably, desperately separated from
the mother, a loss that causes him to try to find her again,
along with other objects of love, first in the imagination,
then in words. Semiology, concerned as it is with the zero
degree of symbolism, is unavoidably led to ponder over
not only the amatory state but its corollary as well, melancholia; at the same time it observes that if there is no
writing other than the amorous, there is no imagination
that is not, overtly or secretly, melancholy.

Thought—Crisis—Melancholia

Nevertheless, melancholia is not French. The rigor of
Protestantism or the matriarchal weight of Christian orthodoxy admits more readily to a complicity with the
grieving person when it does not beckon him or her into
delectatio morosa. While it is true that the French Middle
Ages rendered sadness by means of delicate tropes, the
Gallic, renascent, enlightened tone tended toward levity,
eroticism, and rhetoric rather than nihilism. Pascal, Rous-
seau, and Nerval cut a sorry figure—and they stand as
exceptions.

For the speaking being life is a meaningful life; life is
even the apogee of meaning. Hence if the meaning of life
is lost, life can easily be lost: when meaning shatters, life
no longer matters. In his doubtful moments the depressed
person is a philosopher, and we owe to Heraclitus, Socra-
tes, and more recently Kierkegaard the most disturbing
pages on the meaning or lack of meaning of Being. One
must, however, go back to Aristotle to find a thorough
reflection on the relationship philosophers have maintained with melancholia. According to the *Problemata* (30,
I), attributed to Aristotle, black bile *(melaina kole)* saps

great men. The (pseudo-)Aristotelian reflection focuses on
the *ethos-peritton,* the exceptional personality, whose distinctive characteristic would be melancholia. While relying on the Hippocratic notions of four humors and tem-
peraments, Aristotle breaks new ground by removing
melancholia from pathology and locating it in nature but
also and mainly by having it ensue from *heat,* considered
to be the regulating principle of the organism, and *mesotes,*
the controlled interaction of opposite energies. This Greek
notion of melancholia remains alien to us today; it assumes
a "properly balanced diversity" *(eukratos anomalia)* that is
metaphorically rendered by froth *(aphros),* the euphoric
counterpoint to black bile. Such a white mixture of air
(pneuma) and liquid brings out froth in the sea, wine, as
well as in the sperm of man. Indeed, Aristotle combines
scientific statement with mythical allusions as he links
melancholia to spermatic froth and eroti, with explicit references to Dionysus and Aphrodite (953b, 31–
32). The melancholia he evokes is not a philosopher's
disease but his very nature, his *ethos.* It is not what strikes
the first Greek melancholy hero, Bellerophon, who is thus
portrayed in the *Iliad* (VI, 200–3): "Bellerophon gave of-
fense to the gods and became a lonely wanderer on the
Aleian plain, eating out his heart and shunning the paths
of men." Self-devouring because forsaken by the gods,
exiled by divine decree, this desperate man was condemned not to mania but to banishment, absence, void
. . . With Aristotle, melancholia, counterbalanced by genius, is coextensive with man's anxiety in Being. It could
be seen as the forerunner of Heidegger's anguish as the
Stimmung of thought. Schelling found in it, in similar
fashion, the "essence of human freedom," an indication of
"man's affinity with nature." The philosopher would thus
be "melancholy on account of a surfeit of humanity."[2]

This perception of melancholia as an extreme state and

as an exceptionality that reveals the true nature of Being undergoes a profound transformation during the Middle Ages. On the one hand, medieval thought returned to the cosmologies of late antiquity and bound melancholia to Saturn, the planet of spirit and thought.[3] Dürer's *Melancholia* (1514) was a masterful transposition into graphic art of theoretical speculations that found their highest expression with Marsilio Ficino. Christian theology, on the other hand, considered sadness a sin. Dante set "the woeful people who have lost the good of the intellect" in "the city of grief" (*Inferno,* III). They are "wretched souls" because they have lost God, and these melancholy shadows constitute "the sect of the wicked displeasing both to God and to His enemies"; their punishment is to have "no hope of death." Those whom despair has caused to turn violent against themselves, suicides and squanderers, are not spared either; they are condemned to turn into trees (*Inferno,* XIII). Nevertheless, medieval monks did promote sadness: as mystical ascesis *(acedia)* it became essential as a means toward paradoxical knowledge of divine truth and constituted the major touchstone for faith.

Changing in accordance with the religious climate, melancholia asserted itself, if I may say so, in religious doubt. There is nothing more dismal than a dead God, and Dostoyevsky himself was disturbed by the distressing sight of the dead Christ in Holbein's painting, contrasted with the "truth of resurrection." The periods that witness the downfall of political and religious idols, periods of crisis, are particularly favorable to black moods. While it is true that an unemployed worker is less suicidal than a deserted lover, melancholia does assert itself in times of crisis; it is spoken of, establishes its archeology, generates its representations and its knowledge. A written melancholia surely has little in common with the institutionalized stupor that bears the same name. Beyond the confusion in terminology that I have kept alive up to now (What is melancholia? What is depression?), we are confronted with an enigmatic paradox that will not cease questioning us: if loss, bereavement, and absence trigger the work of the imagination and nourish it permanently as much as they threaten it and spoil it, it is also noteworthy that the work of art as fetish emerges when the activating sorrow has been repudiated. The artist consumed by melancholia is at the same time the most relentless in his struggle against the symbolic abdication that blankets him . . . Until death strikes or suicide becomes imperative for those who view it as final triumph over the void of the lost object . . .

Melancholia/Depression

I shall call *melancholia* the institutional symptomatology of inhibition and asymbolia that becomes established now and then or chronically in a person, alternating more often than not with the so-called manic phase of exaltation. When the two phenomena, despondency and exhilaration, are of lesser intensity and frequency, it is then possible to speak of neurotic depression. While acknowledging the difference between melancholia and depression, Freudian theory detects everywhere the same *impossible mourning for the maternal object*. Question: impossible on account of what paternal weakness? Or what biological frailty? Melancholia—we again encounter the generic term after having demarcated psychotic and neurotic symptomatologies —admits of the fearsome privilege of situating the analyst's question at the intersection of the biological and the symbolical. Parallel series? Consecutive sequences? A dangerous crossing that needs to be clarified, another relationship that needs to be thought up?

The terms melancholia and depression refer to a composite that might be called melancholy/depressive, whose borders are in fact blurred, and within which psychiatrists ascribe the concept of "melancholia" to the illness that is irreversible on its own (that responds only to the administration of antidepressants). Without going into details about various types of depression ("psychotic" or "neurotic," or, according to another classification, "anxious," "agitated," "retarded," or "hostile"), or concerning myself with the promising but still imprecise field in which one studies the exact effects of antidepressants (monoamine oxidase inhibitors, tricyclics, and heterocyclics) or thymic stabilizers (lithium carbonates), I shall examine matters from a *Freudian point of view*. On that basis, I shall try to bring out, from the core of the melancholy/depressive composite, blurred as its borders may be, what pertains to a common experience of *object loss* and of a *modification of signifying bonds*. These bonds, language in particular, prove to be unable to insure, within the melancholy/depressive composite, the autostimulation that is required in order to initiate given responses. Instead of functioning as a "rewards system," language, on the contrary, hyperactivates the "anxiety-punishment" pair, and thus inserts itself in the slowing down of thinking and decrease in psychomotor activity characteristic of depression. If temporary sadness or mourning on the one hand, and melancholy stupor on the other are clinically and nosologically different, they are nevertheless supported by *intolerance for object loss* and *the signifier's failure* to insure a compensating way out of the states of withdrawal in which the subject takes refuge to the point of inaction (pretending to be dead) or even suicide. Thus I shall speak of depression and

[*10*]

melancholia without always distinguishing the particularities of the two ailments but keeping in mind their common structure.

The Depressive Person: Full of Hatred or Wounded, Mourned "Object" and Mourned "Thing"

According to classic psychoanalytic theory (Abraham, Freud, and Melanie Klein),[4] depression, like mourning, conceals an aggressiveness toward the lost object, thus revealing the ambivalence of the depressed person with respect to the object of mourning. "I love that object," is what that person seems to say about the lost object, "but even more so I hate it; because I love it, and in order not to lose it, I imbed it in myself; but because I hate it, that other within myself is a bad self, I am bad, I am non-existent, I shall kill myself." The complaint against oneself would therefore be a complaint against another, and putting oneself to death but a tragic disguise for massacring an other. Such logic presupposes, as one can imagine, a stern superego and a whole complex dialectic of idealization and devalorization of self and other, the aggregate of these activities being based on the mechanism of *identification*. For my identification with the loved-hated other, through incorporation-introjection-projection, leads me to imbed in myself its sublime component, which becomes my necessary, tyrannical judge, as well as its subject component, which demeans me and of which I desire to rid myself. Consequently, the analysis of depression involves bringing to the fore the realization that the complaint against oneself is a hatred for the other, which is without doubt the substratum of an unsuspected sexual desire. Clearly such an advent of hatred within transference entails risks for the analysand as well as the analyst, and the therapy of depression (even the one called neurotic) verges on schizoid fragmentation.

Melancholy cannibalism, which was emphasized by Freud and Abraham and appears in many dreams and fantasies of depressed persons (see chapter 3), accounts for this passion for holding within the mouth (but vagina and anus also lend themselves to this control) the intolerable other that I crave to destroy so as to better possess it alive. Better fragmented, torn, cut up, swallowed, digested . . . than lost. The melancholy cannibalistic imagination[5] is a repudiation of the loss's reality and of death as well. It manifests the anguish of losing the other through the survival of self, surely a deserted self but not separated from what still and ever nourishes it and becomes transformed into the self—which also resuscitates—through such a devouring.

Nevertheless, the treatment of narcissistic individuals has led modern analysts to understand another form of depression.[6] Far from being a hidden attack on an other who is thought to be hostile because he is frustrating, sadness would point to a primitive self—wounded, incomplete, empty. Persons thus affected do not consider themselves wronged but afflicted with a fundamental flaw, a congenital deficiency. Their sorrow doesn't conceal the guilt or the sin felt because of having secretly plotted revenge on the ambivalent object. Their sadness would be rather the most archaic expression of an unsymbolizable, unnameable narcissistic wound, so precocious that no outside agent (subject or agent) can be used as referent. For such narcissistic depressed persons, sadness is really the sole object; more precisely it is a substitute object they become attached to, an object they tame and cherish for lack of another. In such a case, suicide is not a disguised act of war but a merging with sadness and, beyond it,

[*12*]

with that impossible love, never reached, always else-where, such as the promises of nothingness, of death.

Thing and Object

The depressed narcissist mourns not an Object but the Thing.[7] Let me posit the "Thing" as the real that does not lend itself to signification, the center of attraction and repulsion, seat of the sexuality from which the object of desire will become separated.

Of this Nerval provides a dazzling metaphor that sug-gests an insistence without presence, a light without rep-resentation: the Thing is an imagined sun, bright and black at the same time. "It is a well-known fact that one never sees the sun in a dream, although one is often aware of some far brighter light."[8]

Ever since that archaic attachment the depressed person has the impression of having been deprived of an unname-able, supreme good, of something unrepresentable, that perhaps only devouring might represent, or an *invocation* might point out, but no word could signify. Conse-quently, for such a person, no erotic object could replace the irreplaceable perception of a place or preobject confin-ing the libido or severing the bonds of desire. Knowingly disinherited of the Thing, the depressed person wanders in pursuit of continuously disappointing adventures and loves; or else retreats, disconsolate and aphasic, alone with the unnamed Thing. The "primary identification" with the "father in individual prehistory"[9] would be the means, the link that might enable one to become reconciled with the loss of the Thing. Primary identification initiates a compensation for the Thing and at the same time secures the subject to another dimension, that of imaginary adherence, reminding one of the bond of faith, which is just what disintegrates in the depressed person.

With those affected by melancholia, primary identification proves to be fragile, insufficient to secure other identifications, which are symbolic this time, on the basis of which the *erotic Thing* might become a captivating *Object of desire* insuring continuity in a metonymy of pleasure. The melancholy Thing interrupts desiring metonymy, just as it prevents working out the loss within the psyche.[10] How can one approach the place I have referred to? Sublimation is an attempt to do so: through melody, rhythm, semantic polyvalency, the so-called poetic form, which decomposes and recomposes signs, is the sole "container" seemingly able to secure an uncertain but adequate hold over the Thing.

I have assumed depressed persons to be atheistic—deprived of meaning, deprived of values. For them, to fear or to ignore the Beyond would be self-deprecating. Nevertheless, and although atheistic, those in despair are mystics—adhering to the preobject, not believing in Thou, but mute and steadfast devotees of their own inexpressible container. It is to this fringe of strangeness that they devote their tears and jouissance. In the tension of their affects, muscles, mucous membranes, and skin, they experience both their belonging to and distance from an archaic other that still eludes representation and naming, but of whose corporeal emissions, along with their automatism, they still bear the imprint. Unbelieving in language, the depressive persons are affectionate, wounded to be sure, but prisoners of affect. The affect is their thing.

The Thing is inscribed within us without memory, the buried accomplice of our unspeakable anguishes. One can imagine the delights of reunion that a regressive daydream promises itself through the nuptials of suicide.

The looming of the Thing summons up the subject's life force as that subject is in the process of being set up; the premature being that we all are can survive only if it clings to an other, perceived as supplement, artificial extension, protective wrapping. Nevertheless, such a life drive is fully the one that, *at the same time,* rejects me, isolates me, rejects him (or her). Never is the ambivalence of drive more fearsome than in this beginning of otherness where, lacking the filter of language, I cannot inscribe my violence in "no," nor in any other sign. I can expel it only by means of gestures, spasms, or shouts. I impel it, I project it. My necessary Thing is also and absolutely my enemy, my foil, the delightful focus of my hatred. The Thing falls from me along the outposts of signifiance[11] where the Word is not yet my Being. A mere nothing, which is a cause, but at the same time a fall, before being an Other, the Thing is the recipient that contains my dejecta and everything that results from *cadere* [Latin: to fall]—it is a waste with which, in my sadness, I merge. It is Job's ashpit in the Bible.

Anality is summoned during the process of setting up this Thing, one that is our own and proper Thing as much as it is improper, unclean. The melancholy person who extols that boundary where the self emerges, but also collapses in deprecation, fails to summon the anality that could establish separations and frontiers as it does normally or as a bonus with obsessive persons. On the contrary, the entire ego of those who are depressed sinks into a dieroticized and yet jubilatory anality, as the latter becomes the bearer of a jouissance fused with the archaic Thing, perceived not as a significant object but as the self's borderline element. For those who are depressed, the Thing like the self is a downfall that carries them along into the invisible and unnameable. *Cadere.* Waste and cadavers all.

The Death Drive as Primary Inscription of Discontinuity (Trauma or Loss)

Freud's postulate of a *primary masochism* is consonant with aspects of narcissistic melancholia in which the dying out of all libidinal bonds appears not to be a simple matter of turning aggressiveness toward the object back into animosity against the self but is asserted as previous to any possibility of object positioning.

Brought up by Freud in 1915,[12] the notion of "primary masochism" became established in his work after the "death drive" turned up, particularly in "The Economic Problem of Masochism" (1924).[13] Having observed that living beings appeared later than the nonliving, Freud thought that a specific drive must reside in them, which tended toward "a return to an earlier state."[14] After *Beyond the Pleasure Principle* (1920), which established the notion of the death drive as a tendency to return to the inorganic state and homeostasis, in opposition to the erotic principle of discharge and union, Freud postulated that one part of the death or destructive drive is directed toward the outside world, notably through the muscular system, and is changed into a purely destructive drive, one of ascendency or strong willpower. In the attendance of sexuality it constitutes sadism. Freud points out nevertheless that *"Another portion does not share in this transposition outwards: it remains inside . . . and becomes libidinally bound there. It is in this portion that we have to recognize the original, erotogenic masochism."*[15] Since hatred of the other was already considered "older than love,"[16] would such a masochistic withdrawal of hatred point to the existence of a yet more archaic hatred? Freud seems to imply that: indeed, he considers the death drive as an intrapsychic manifestation of a phylogenetic inheritance going back to inorganic matter. Nevertheless, aside from those conjectures that most analysts since Freud do not endorse, it is possible to note if not the anteriority at least the strength of the disintegration of bonds within several psychic structures and manifestations. Furthermore, the frequency of masochism, the presence of negative therapeutic reaction, and also various pathologies of early childhood that seem to precede the object relation (infantile anorexia, merycism, some forms of autism) prompt one to accept the idea of a death drive that, appearing as a biological and logical inability to transmit psychic energies and inscriptions, would destroy movements and bonds. Freud refers to it thus:

> If we take into consideration the total picture made up of the phenomena of masochism immanent in so many people, the negative therapeutic reaction and the sense of guilt found in so many neurotics we shall no longer be able to adhere to the belief that mental events are exclusively governed by the desire for pleasure. These phenomena are unmistakable evidence of the presence of a power in mental life which we shall call the aggression or destruction drive, and which we trace back to the original death drive of living matter.[17]

Narcissistic melancholia would display such a drive in its state of disunity with the life drive. The melancholy person's superego appears to Freud as "a cultivation of death drive."[18] And yet the problem remains: is this melancholy diserotization opposed to the pleasure principle? Or is it, on the contrary, implicitly erotic? This would mean that the melancholy withdrawal would always be an overturning of the object relation, a metamorphosis of the hatred against the other. The work of Melanie Klein, who attached the greatest importance to the death drive, seems to have it depend, for the most part, on object relation, masochism and melancholia appearing then as imagos of the internalized bad object. Nevertheless, the Kleinian argument acknowledges situations in which erotic bonds are severed, without clearly stating whether they have never existed or have been broken off (in the latter case it would be the projection's introjection that would lead to such a withdrawal of erotic cathexis).

We shall take note particularly of the Kleinian definition of splitting introduced in 1946. On the one hand it moves backward from the depressive position toward a more archaic, paranoid, schizoid position. On the other, it distinguishes a binary splitting (the distinction between "good" and "bad" object insuring the unity of the self) and a parcellary splitting—the latter affecting not only the object but, in return, the very self, which literally "falls into pieces."

Integration/Nonintegration/Disintegration

For our purpose it is absolutely essential to note that such falling into pieces may be caused either by a drive-related *nonintegration* impeding the cohesion of the self, or by a disintegration accompanied by anxieties and provoking the schizoid splitting.[19] In the first hypothesis, which seems to have been borrowed from Winnicott, nonintegration results from biological immaturity; if it is possible to speak of Thanatos in this situation, the death drive appears as a biological unfitness for sequentiality and integration (no memory). In the second hypothesis, that of a disintegration of the self consequent to reversing the death drive, we observe "a Thanatic reaction to a threat that is in itself Thanatic."[20] Rather close to Ferenczi's concept, this one emphasizes the human being's tendency toward fragmentation and disintegration as an expression of the death drive. "The early ego largely lacks cohesion, and a tendency towards integration alternates with a tendency towards disintegration, a falling into bits . . . the anxiety of being destroyed from within remains active. It seems to me in keeping with the lack of cohesiveness that under the pressure of this threat the ego tends to fall into pieces."[21] If schizoid fragmentation is a radical, paroxysmal manifestation of parceling, melancholy inhibition (psychomotor retardation, deficiency in sequentiality) can be considered another manifestation of the disintegration of bonds. How so?

Following upon the deflection of the death drive, the *depressive affect* can be interpreted as a defense against parceling. Indeed, sadness reconstitutes an affective cohesion of the self, which restores its unity within the framework of the affect. The depressive mood constitutes itself as a narcissistic support, negative to be sure,[22] but nevertheless presenting the self with an integrity, nonverbal though it might be. Because of that, the depressive affect makes up for symbolic invalidation and interruption (the depressive's "that's meaningless") and at the same time protects it against proceeding to the suicidal act. That protection, however, is a flimsy one. The depressive denial that destroys the meaning of the symbolic also destroys the act's meaning and leads the subject to commit suicide without anguish of disintegration, as a reuniting with archaic non-integration, as lethal as it is jubilatory, "oceanic."

Hence, schizoid parceling is a defense against death—against somatization or suicide. Depression, on the other hand, does without the schizoid anguish of fragmentation. But if depression is not fortunate enough to rely on a certain *erotization of suffering* it cannot act as a defense against the death drive. The relief that precedes some

[*19*]

suicides perhaps translates the archaic regression by means of which the act of a denied or numbed consciousness turns Thanatos back on the self and reclaims the nonintegrated self's lost paradise, one without others or limits, a fantasy of untouchable fullness.

The speaking subject can thus react to trouble not only through defensive parceling but also through slowing down— inhibition, denial of sequentiality, neutralization of the signifier. Some immaturization or other neurobiological features tending toward nonintegration may condition such behavior. Is it a defensive one? Depressed persons do not defend themselves against death but against the anguish prompted by the erotic object. Depressive persons cannot endure Eros, they prefer to be with the Thing up to the limit of negative narcissism leading them to Thanatos. They are defended against Eros by sorrow but without defense against Thanatos because they are wholeheartedly tied to the Thing. Messengers of Thanatos, melancholy people are witness/accomplices of the signifier's flimsiness, the living being's precariousness.

Less skillful than Melanie Klein in presenting a new repertory of drives, the death drive in particular, Freud nevertheless seems drastic. As he sees it, the speaking being, beyond power, desires death. At this logical extreme, desire no longer exists. Desire becomes dissolved in a disintegration of transmission and a disintegration of bonds. Be it biologically predetermined, following upon preobject narcissistic traumas, or quite simply caused by inversion of aggresiveness, the phenomenon that might be described as a *breakdown of biological and logical sequentiality* finds its radical manifestation in melancholia. Would the death drive be the primary (logically and chronologically) inscription of that breakdown?

Actually, if the death drive remains a theoretical speculation, the experience of depression confronts the observer as much as the patient with the enigma of mood.

Is Mood a Language?

Sadness is the fundamental mood of depression, and even if manic euphoria alternates with it in the bipolar forms of that ailment, sorrow is the major outward sign that gives away the desperate person. Sadness leads us into the enigmatic realm of *affects*—anguish, fear, or joy.[23] Irreducible to its verbal or semiological expressions, sadness (like all affect) is the *psychic representation of energy displacements* caused by external or internal traumas. The exact status of such psychic representations of energy displacements remains, in the present state of psychoanalytic and semiological theories, very vague. No conceptual framework in the relevant sciences (particularly linguistics) has proven adequate to account for this apparently very rudimentary representation, presign and prelanguage. The "sadness" mood triggered by a stimulation, tension, or energy conflict within a psychosomatic organism is not a *specific* answer to a release mechanism (I am not sad as a response to or sign for X and only X). Mood is a "generalized transference" (E. Jacobson) that stamps the *entire* behavior and all the sign systems (from motor functions to speech production and idealization) without either identifying with them or disorganizing them. We are justified in believing that an archaic *energy signal* is involved, a phylogenetic inheritance, which, within the psychic space of the human being, is *immediately* assumed by verbal representation and consciousness. Nevertheless, such an "assumption" is not related to what occurs when the energies that Freud calls "bonded" lend themselves to verbalization, association, and judgment. Let us say that representations germane to

[*21*]

affects, notably sadness, are *fluctuating* energy cathexes: insufficiently stabilized to coalesce as verbal or other signs, acted upon by primary processes of displacement and condensation, dependent just the same on the agency of the ego, they record through its intermediary the threats, orders, and injunctions of the superego. Thus moods are *inscriptions,* energy disruptions, and not simply raw energies. They lead us toward a modality of signifiance that, on the threshold of bioenergetic stability, insures the preconditions for (or manifests the disintegration of) the imaginary and the symbolic. On the frontier between animality and symbol formation, moods—and particularly sadness—are the ultimate reactions to our traumas, they are our basic homeostatic recourses. For if it is true that those who are slaves to their moods, beings drowned in their sorrows, reveal a number of psychic or cognitive frailties, it is equally true that a diversification of moods, variety in sadness, refinement in sorrow or mourning are the imprint of a humankind that is surely not triumphant but subtle, ready to fight, and creative . . .

Literary creation is that adventure of the body and signs that bears witness to the affect—to sadness as imprint of separation and beginning of the symbol's sway; to joy as imprint of the triumph that settles me in the universe of artifice and symbol, which I try to harmonize in the best possible way with my experience of reality. But that testimony is produced by literary creation in a material that is totally different from what constitutes mood. It transposes affect into rhythms, signs, forms. The "semiotic" and the "symbolic"[24] become the communicable imprints of an affective reality, perceptible to the reader (I like this book because it conveys sadness, anguish, or joy) and yet dominated, set aside, vanquished.

Symbolic Equivalents/Symbols

Assuming that affect is the most archaic inscription of inner and outer events, how does one reach the realm of signs? I shall accept Hanna Segal's hypothesis, according to which, beginning with separation (let us note that a "lack" is necessary for the *sign* to emerge), the child produces or uses objects or vocalizations that are the *symbolic* equivalents of what is lacking. Later, and beginning with the so-called depressive position, it attempts to signify the sadness that overwhelms it by producing within its own self elements alien to the outer world, which it causes to correspond to such a lost or shifted outerness; we are then faced with *symbols* properly speaking, no longer with equivalencies.[25]

Let me add the following to Hanna Segal's position: what makes such a triumph over sadness possible is the ability of the self to identify no longer with the lost object but with a third party—father, form, schema. A requirement for a denying or manic position ("no, I haven't lost; I evoke, I signify through the artifice of signs and for myself what has been parted from me"), such an identification, which may be called phallic or symbolic, insures the subject's entrance into the universe of signs and creation. The supporting father of such a symbolic triumph is not the oedipal father but truly that "imaginary father," "father in individual prehistory" according to Freud, who guarantees primary identification. Nevertheless, it is imperative that this father in individual prehistory be capable of playing his part as oedipal father in symbolic Law, for it is on the basis of that harmonious blending of the two facets of fatherhood that the abstract and arbitrary signs of communication may be fortunate enough to be tied to the affective meaning of prehistorical identifications, and the dead language of the potentially depressive person can arrive at a live meaning in the bond with others.

Under the totally different circumstances of literary creation, for instance, the manic position as sheathing of depression—an essential moment in the formation of the symbol—can be manifested through the establishment of a symbolic lineage. We may thus find a recourse to proper names linked to a subject's real or imaginary history, with that subject declaring itself their heir or equal; what they truly memorialize, beyond paternal weakness, is nostalgic dedication to the lost mother (see chapter 6 on Nerval).

At the outset we have objectal depression (implicitly aggressive), and narcissistic depression (logically previous to the libidinal object relation)—an affectivity struggling with signs, going beyond, threatening, or modifying them. Starting from such a setting, the line of questioning that I shall pursue could be summed up as follows: aesthetic and particularly literary creation, and also religious discourse in its imaginary, fictional essence, set forth a device whose prosodic economy, interaction of characters, and implicit symbolism constitute a very faithful semiological representation of the subject's battle with symbolic collapse. Such a literary representation is not an *elaboration* in the sense of "becoming aware" of the inter- and intrapsychic causes of moral suffering; that is where it diverges from the psychoanalytic course, which aims at dissolving this symptom. Nevertheless, the literary (and religious) representation possesses a real and imaginary effectiveness that comes closer to catharsis than to elaboration; it is a therapeutic device used in all societies throughout the ages. If psychoanalysts think they are more efficacious, notably through strengthening the subject's cognitive possibilities, they also owe it to themselves to enrich their practice by paying greater attention to these sublimatory solutions to our crises, in order to be lucid counterdepressants rather than neutralizing antidepressants.

Is Death Nonrepresentable?

Having posited that the unconscious is ruled by the pleasure principle, Freud very logically postulated that there is no representation of death in the unconscious. Just as it is unaware of negation, the unconscious is unaware of death. Synonymous with absence of jouissance, imaginary equivalent of phallic dispossession, death could not possibly be seen. It is, perhaps, for that very reason that it opens the way to speculation.

And yet, as clinical experience led Freud to the notion of narcissism, ending in the discovery of the death drive and the second topography,[26] he compelled us to recognize a vision of the psychic apparatus in which Eros is threatened with domination by Thanatos and where, consequently, the possibility of representing death should be examined from a different standpoint.

Castration fear, glimpsed until then as underlying the conscious death anguish, does not disappear but is overshadowed by the *fear of losing the object* or *losing oneself as object* (etiology of melancholia and narcissistic psychoses).

Such an evolution in Freudian thought leaves us with two problems that have been emphasized by André Green.[27]

First, what about the *representation* of the death drive? Unknown to the unconscious, it is, with the "second Freud," a "cultivation of the superego," as one might put it in turning Freud's phrase around. The death drive splits the very ego into one component that is unaware of such drive while being affected by it (that is, its unconscious component) and another component that struggles against it (that is, the megalomaniac ego that negates castration and death and fantasizes immortality).

More basically, however, does not such a splitting cut across all discourse? The symbol is established through a negation *(Verneinung)* of the loss, but a disavowal *(Verleugnung)* of the symbol produces a physic inscription as close as one can get to hatred and a hold over the lost object (see chapter 2). That is what one deciphers in the blanks of discourse, vocalizations, rhythms, syllables of words that have been devitalized and need to be restored by the analyst on the basis of an apprehended depression.

Thus, if the death drive is not represented in the unconscious, must one invent another level in the psychic apparatus where—simultaneously with jouissance—the being of its nonbeing would be recorded? It is indeed a production of the split ego, made up of fantasy and fiction—in short, the level of the imagination, the level of writing—which bears witness to the hiatus, blank, or spacing that constitutes death for the unconscious.

Dissociations of Forms

Imaginary constructions change the death drive into eroticized aggression against the father or terrified loathing of the mother's body. We know that at the same time as he discovered the power of the death drive Freud shifted his interest not only from the theoretical model of the first topography (conscious/preconscious/unsconscious) toward that of the second topography, but especially, and thanks to the shift, turned toward the analysis of imaginary productions (religions, arts, literature). He found in them a kind of representation of death anxiety.[28] Does this mean that dread of dying—which henceforth is not summed up in castration fear but includes it and adds to it the wounding and perhaps even the loss of integrity of the body and the self—finds its representations in formations that are called "transconscious" in the imaginary constructions of the split subject, according to Lacan? Doubtless so.

The fact remains that another reading of the unconscious itself might locate within its own fabric, such as certain dreams disclose it for us, that nonrepresentative spacing of representation that is not the *sign* but the *index* of death drive. Dreams of borderline patients, schizoid personalities, or those undergoing psychedelic experiments are often "abstract paintings" or cascades of sounds, intricacies of lines and fabrics, in which the analyst deciphers the dissociation—or a nonintegration—of psychic and somatic unity. Such indices could be interpreted as the ultimate imprint of the death drive. Aside from the images of the death drive, necessarily displaced on account of being eroticized, the work of death as such, at the zero degree of psychicism, can be spotted precisely in the *dissociation of form* itself, when form is distorted, abstracted, disfigured, hollowed out: ultimate thresholds of inscribable dislocation and jouissance . . .

Furthermore, the unrepresentable nature of death was linked with that other unrepresentable—original abode but also last resting place for dead souls, in the beyond—which, for mythical thought, is constituted by the female body. The horror of castration underlying the anguish of death undoubtedly accounts in large part for the universal partnership with death of the penis-lacking feminine. Nevertheless, the death drive hypothesis compels a different reasoning.

Death-Bearing Woman

For man and for woman the loss of the mother is a biological and psychic necessity, the first step on the way to becoming autonomous. Matricide is our vital necessity, the sine-qua-non condition of our individuation, provided that it takes place under optimal circumstances and can be eroticized—whether the lost object is recovered as erotic object (as is the case for male heterosexuality or female homosexuality), or it is transposed by means of an unbelievable symbolic effort, the advent of which one can only admire, which eroticizes the *other* (the other sex, in the case of the heterosexual woman) or transforms cultural constructs into a "sublime" erotic object (one thinks of the cathexes, by men and women, in social bonds, intellectual and aesthetic productions, etc.). The lesser or greater violence of matricidal drive, depending on individuals and the milieu's tolerance, entails, when it is hindered, its inversion on the self; the maternal object having been introjected, the depressive or melancholic putting to death of the self is what follows, instead of matricide. In order to protect mother I kill myself while knowing—phantasmatic and protective knowledge—that it comes from her, the death-bearing she-Gehenna . . . Thus my hatred is safe and my matricidal guilt erased. I make of Her an image of Death so as not to be shattered through the hatred I bear against myself when I identify with Her, for that aversion is in principle meant for her as it is an individuating dam against confusional love. Thus the feminine as image of death is not only a screen for my fear of castration, but also an imaginary safety catch for the matricidal drive that, without such a representation, would pulverize me into melancholia if it did not drive me to crime. No, it is She who is death-bearing, therefore I do not kill myself in order to kill her but I attack her, harass her, represent her. . .

For a woman, whose specular identification with the mother as well as the introjection of the maternal body and self are more immediate, such an inversion of matricidal drive into a death-bearing maternal image is more difficult, if not impossible. Indeed, how can She be that bloodthirsty Fury, since I am She (sexually and narcissistically), She is I? Consequently, the hatred I bear her is not oriented toward the outside but is locked up within myself. There is no hatred, only an implosive mood that walls itself in and kills me secretly, very slowly, through permanent bitterness, bouts of sadness, or even lethal sleeping pills that I take in smaller or greater quantities in the dark hope of meeting . . . no one, unless it be my imaginary wholeness, increased with my death that accomplishes me. The homosexual shares the same depressive economy: he is a delightful melancholy person when he does not indulge in sadistic passion with another man.

The fantasy of feminine immortality perhaps has its basis in the feminine germinal transmission, capable of parthenogenesis. Furthermore, the new techniques of artificial reproduction endow the female body with unsuspected reproductive possibilities. If that feminine "all-mightiness" in the survival of the species can be undermined through other technical possibilities that, or so it seems, might make man pregnant as well, it is likely that this latter eventuality could attract only a small minority, even though it fulfills the androgynous fantasies of the majority. Nevertheless, the essential component of the feminine conviction of being immortal in and beyond death (which the Virgin Mary so perfectly embodies) is rooted less in those biological possibilities, where it is hard to discern the "bridge" to the psyche, than in "negative narcissism."

In its climax, the latter weakens the aggressive (matricidal) affect toward the other as well as the despondent affect within oneself and substitutes what one might call an "oceanic void." It is a feeling and fantasy of pain, but anestheticized, of jouissance, but in suspense, of an expectation and a silence as empty as they are fulfilled. In the midst of its lethal ocean, the melancholy woman is the dead one that has always been abandoned within herself and can never kill outside herself (see chapter 3). Modest, silent, without verbal or desiring bonds with others, she wastes away by striking moral and physic blows against herself, which, nevertheless, do not give her sufficient pleasures. Until the fatal blow—the definitive nuptials of the Dead Woman with the Same, whom she did not kill.

One cannot overemphasize the tremendous psychic, intellectual, and affective effort a woman must make in order to find the other sex as erotic object. In his philogenetic musings, Freud often admires the intellectual accomplishment of the man who has been (or when he is) deprived of women (through glaciation or tyranny on the part of the father of the primal horde, etc.). If the discovery of her invisible vagina already imposes upon woman a tremendous sensory, speculative, and intellectual effort, shifting to the symbolic order *at the same time* as to a sexual object of a sex other than that of the primary maternal object represents a gigantic elaboration in which a woman cathexes a psychic potential greater than what is demanded of the male sex. When this process is favorably carried out, it is evidenced by the precocious awakening of girls, their intellectual performances often more brilliant during the school years, and their continuing female maturity. Nevertheless, it has its price in the constant tendency to extol the problematic mourning for the lost object . . . not so fully lost, and it remains, throbbing, in the "crypt" of feminine ease and maturity. Unless a massive introjection of the ideal succeeds, at the same time, in satisfying narcissism with its negative side *and* the longing to be present in the arena where the world's power is at stake.

2

Life and Death of Speech

Let us keep in mind the speech of the depressed—repetitive and monotonous. Faced with the impossibility of concatenating, they utter sentences that are interrupted, exhausted, come to a standstill. Even phrases they cannot formulate. A repetitive rhythm, a monotonous melody emerge and dominate the broken logical sequences, changing them into recurring, obsessive litanies. Finally, when that frugal musicality becomes exhausted in its turn, or simply does not succeed in becoming established on account of the pressure of silence, the melancholy person appears to stop cognizing as well as uttering, sinking into the blankness of asymbolia or the excess of an unorderable cognitive chaos.

The Shattered Concatenation: A Biological Hypothesis

Inconsolable sadness often conceals a real predisposition for despair. It is perhaps biological in part: too much speed or too much slowing down of neural flow unquestionably depends on given chemical substances that are present in each one of us in varying degrees.[1]

It has been medically attested that the succession of emotions, gestures, actions, or words considered normal because statistically prevalent becomes hampered during depression. The rhythm of overall behavior is shattered, there is neither time nor place for acts and sequences to be carried out. If in the nondepressive state one has the ability to concatenate, depressive persons, in contrast, riveted to their pain, no longer concatenate and, consequently, neither act nor speak.

"Psychomotor Retardation": Two Models

There are many who have emphasized the psychomotor, affective, and ideational retardation that is characteristic of the melancholy/depressive state.[2] Even psychomotor agitation and delirious mania or more generally the depressive mood appear to be indissociable from simple retardation.[3] Language retardation partakes of the same pattern: speech delivery is slow, silences are long and frequent, rhythms slacken, intonations become monotonous, and the very syntactic structures—without evidencing disturbances and disorders such as can be observed in schizophrenics—are often characterized by nonrecoverable elisions (objects or verbs that are omitted and cannot be restored on the basis of the context).

Many models have been suggested in order to think out the processes underlying the depressive retardation state. One of them "learned helplessness," is based on the following observation: when all escape routes are blocked, animals as well as men learn to withdraw rather than flee or fight. The retardation or inactivity, which one might call depressive, would thus constitute a learned defense reaction to a dead-end situation and unavoidable shocks. Tricyclic antidepressants apparently restore the ability to flee, and this leads one to assume that learned inactivity is linked to noradrenergic depletion or cholinergic hyperactivity.

According to another model, all behavior would be governed by an autostimulation system, based on reward, that would condition the inception of responses. One ends up with the notion of "positive or negative intensification systems" and, assuming that the latter would be disturbed during the depressive state, one studies the structures and transmitters that are involved. One succeeds in putting forward a dual explanation for the disturbance. Since the intensification structure, the telencephalon's median network, having a noradrenergic transmission role, is responsible for the response, the depressive retardation and withdrawal would be caused by its dysfunctioning. In similar fashion, a hyperfunctioning of the preventricular "punishment" systems with a cholinergic transmission role would be the source of anxiety.[4] The role of the *locus coeruleus* of the telencephalon's median network would be essential to noradrenergic autostimulation and transmission. In experiments involving the suppression of a response in expectation of punishment, serotonin, in contrast, would increase. Antidepressive treatment would then call for a noradrenergic increase and a serotinergic decrease.

The *locus coeruleus'* essential role is emphasized by many as being

> a relay center for an "alarm" system inducing "normal" fear or anxiety. . . . The LC receives innervations directly from pain pathways throughout the body, and the LC shows sustained responses to repeated presentations of "noxious" stimulati even in anesthetized animals. . . . In addition, there are pathways to and from the cerebral cortex which provide feed-back loops that

explain the apparent influence that the *meaning or relevance of a stimulus* may exercise on the response. These same feed-back loops provide access to areas that may underlie *the cognitive experience of the emotional state (or states).*[5]

Language as "Stimulation" and Reinforcement"

At the current stage of attempts to think out the two channels—psychic and biological—of affects, it is again possible to formulate the question of language's central importance to human beings.

Within the experience of separation without resolution, or unavoidable shocks, or again pursuits without result, and unlike animals whose only recourse is in behavior, the child can find a fighting or fleeing solution in psychic representation and in language. The child imagines, thinks out, utters the flight or the fight and a full intermediate gamut as well, and this can be a deterrent from withdrawal into inactivity or playing dead, wounded by irreparable frustrations or harms. Nevertheless, for this nondepressive solution to the melancholy dilemma, *flight/fight: learned helplessness,* to be worked out, the child needs a *solid implication* in the symbolic and imaginary code, which, then and only then, becomes stimulation and reinforcement. In that case, responses to a given action are generated, and they are also implicitly symbolic, oriented by language or within the working of language alone. If, on the contrary, the symbolic dimension proves to be insufficient, subjects find themselves back at the dead-end of a helplessness leading to inaction and death. In other words, language in its heterogeneity (primary *and* secondary processes, ideational and emotional carrier of desire, hatred, conflicts) is a powerful factor that, through unknown mediations, has an activating (as well as, conversely, an inhibiting) effect on neurobiological networks. Within that perspective, several points are still unclear.

Is the symbolic breakdown one notices in depressed persons one component among others of a psychomotor retardation, which is clinically observable, or does it appear among its essential prerequisites? Is it conditioned by a dysfunction of the neuronal and endocrinal network that underlies (but in what fashion?) psychic representations and, particularly, word representations, and also the channels that link them to hypothalamic nuclei? Or still is it an inadequacy of symbolic impact that would be due merely to the family and social environment?

Without excluding the first hypothesis, the psychoanalyst will be concerned with shedding light on the second. We shall thus ask ourselves what *mechanisms erase symbolic impact* within the subject, who nevertheless has achieved an adequate symbolic ability, often apparently consonant with social norms, remarkably effective at times. I shall try, by means of the cure's dynamics and a specific economy of interpretation, to give its optimal power back to the imaginary and symbolic dimension of the heterogeneous set constituted by the speaking body. That will lead me to consider the problem of the depressed's *denial of the signifier* and also the role of primary processes in depressive as well as in interpretative speech as "imaginary and symbolic graft" through the agency of primary processes. Finally, I shall ponder the importance of *narcissistic recognition* and *idealization* for the purpose of facilitating, in the patient, an anchoring of the symbolic dimension, and this often amounts to a new acquisition of communication as parameter of desire and conflict, and even hatred.

To mention one last time the problem of "biological

limit," which I shall henceforth put aside, I shall posit that the register of psychic and, particularly, linguistic representation is neurologically transferred to the physiological occurrences of the brain, in the last instance through the hypothalamus' multiple networks. (The hypothalamic nuclei are connected to the cerebral cortex whose functioning underlies *meaning*—but how?—and also to the limbic lobe of the brain stem whose functioning underlies *affects*.) At present we don't know *how* this transfer takes place, but clinical experience allows us to think that it does *actually* take place (for instance, one will recall the exciting or sedative, "opiatic," effect of certain words). Finally, numerous illnesses—and depressions—whose origins can be traced to neurophysiological disturbances triggered by symbolic breakdowns remain set in registers that cannot be affected by language. The facilitating effect of antidepressants is then required in order to reconstitute a minimal neurophysiological base upon which psychotherapeutic work can begin, analyzing symbolic deficiencies and knots and reconstituting a new symbol system.

Other Possible Transfers Between Meaning and Cerebral Functioning

Interruptions in linguistic sequentiality and even more so their replacement with suprasegmental operations (rhythms, melodies) in depressive discourse can be interpreted as deficiencies in the left hemisphere, which controls linguistic generation, leading to domination—temporary as it may be—by the right hemisphere, which controls affects and emotions as well as their "primary," "musical," nonlinguistic inscriptions.[6] Moreover, to those observations should be added the model of a dual cerebral functioning: neuronal, electrical or wired, and digital; and also endocrinal, humoral, fluctuating, and analogical.[7] Certain chemical substances in the brain, even certain neurotransmitters, seem to operate in dual fashion—sometimes "neuronal," sometimes "endocrinal." Eventually, and in view of this cerebral duality where passions mainly find their anchoring in the humoral, it is possible to speak of a "fluctuating central state." If one grants that language, within its own register, must also translate that "fluctuating state," it follows that one must locate, in language functioning, those levels that seem closer to the "neuronal brain" (such as grammatical and logical sequentiality) and those that seem closer to the "glandular brain" (the suprasegmental components of discourse). One might thus be able to think out the "symbolic disposition" of signifiance in relation to the left hemisphere and the neuronal brain, and the "semiotic disposition" in relation to the right hemisphere and the glandular brain.

And yet there is nothing today that allows one to set up any relation whatsoever—aside from a leap—between the biological substratum and the level of *representations,* be they tonal or syntactic, emotional or cognitive, semiotic or symbolic. Nevertheless one should not ignore the possible ways of linking the two levels, attempting to provoke reverberations, aleatory and unpredictable to be sure, between the one and the other and, with all the more reason, modifications of the one by the other.

To conclude, if a dysfunction of noradrenalin and serotonin or of their reception hampers the synapses' conductivity and *can* condition the depressive state, the role of those few synapses, within the star-like structure of the brain, cannot be absolute.[8] Such inadequacy may be compensated for by other chemical phenomena and also by other external actions (symbolic ones included) on the brain, which adapts to them through biological modifications. Indeed, the experience of the relationship to the other, its violence or its delights, eventually puts its imprint on this biological terrain and completes the well-known picture of depressive behavior. Without refusing chemical action in the fight against melancholia, analysts have (or will have) at their disposal a wide range of verbalizations concerning that state and going beyond it. While remaining heedful of such interferences, they will confine themselves to the specific changes of depressive discourse as well as to the construction of their own consequent interpretative words.

The psychoanalysts' confrontation with depression thus leads them to ponder the position of the subject with respect to meaning as well as the heterogeneous dimensions of language that are liable to different psychic imprints; the latter, on account of such diversity, would have an increased number of access paths to the multiple aspects of cerebral functioning and hence to the organism's activity. Finally, seen from that standpoint, the imaginative experience will come to light both as evidence of a person's struggle against the symbolic abdication that is germane to depression, and as a range of means likely to enrich interpretative discourse.

The Psychoanalytic Leap: To Concatenate and Transpose

From the analyst's point of view, the possibility of concatenating signifiers (words or actions) appears to depend upon going through mourning for an archaic and indispensable object—and on the related emotions as well. Mourning for the Thing—such a possibility comes out of transposing, beyond loss and on an imaginary or symbolic level, the imprints of an interchange with the other articulated according to a certain order.

Relieved of the primal object, semiotic imprints are first organized in *series,* according to primary processes (displacement and condensation), then in phrases and sentences, according to the secondary processes of grammar and logic. There is agreement in all branches of linguistics today in recognizing that discourse is *dialogue:* its organization, rhythmic and intonational as well as syntactical, requires two speakers in order to be completed. To that fundamental precondition, which already implies the necessary separation between one subject and another, the following fact must nevertheless be added: verbal sequences turn up only if a trans-position is substituted for a more or less symbiotic primal object, this trans-position being a true reconstitution that retroactively gives form and meaning to the mirage of the primal Thing. That critical task of *transposition* consists of two facets: the mourning gone through for the object (and in its shadow the mourning for the archaic Thing), and the subject's acceptance of a set of signs (signifying precisely because of the absence of object) only thus open to serial organization. Evidence for this can be found in the child's acquisition of language, when that intrepid wanderer leaves the crib to meet the mother in the realm of representations. Depressed persons also provide evidence, contrariwise, when they give up signifying and submerge in the silence of pain or the spasm of tears that celebrates reunion with the Thing.

To transpose corresponds to the Greek *metaphorein,* to transport; language is, from the start, a translation, but on a level that is heterogeneous to the one where affective loss, renunciation, or the break takes place. If I did not agree to lose mother, I could neither imagine nor name her. The psychotic child is acquainted with that drama: such a child, being ignorant of metaphor, is an incompetent translator. As for the discourse of the depressed, it is the "normal" surface of a psychotic risk: the sadness that overwhelms us, the retardation that paralyzes us are also a shield—sometimes the last one—against madness.

Would the fate of the speaking being consist in ceaselessly transposing, always further beyond or more to the side, such a transposition of series or sentences testifying to our ability to work out a fundamental mourning and successive mournings? Our gift of speech, of situating ourselves in time for an other, could exist nowhere except beyond an abyss. Speaking beings, from their ability to endure in time up to their enthusiastic, learned, or simply amusing constructions, demand a break, a renunciation, an unease at their foundations.

The negation of that fundamental loss opens up the realm of signs for us, but the mourning is often incomplete. It drives out negation and revives the memory of signs by drawing them out of their signifying neutrality. It loads them with affects, and this results in making them ambiguous, repetitive or simply alliterative, musical or sometimes nonsensical. At that point, translation—our fate as speaking beings—stops its vertiginous course toward metalanguages or foreign languages, which are like many sign systems distant from the site of the pain. It seeks to become alien to itself in order to discover, in the mother tongue, a *"total word, new, foreign to the language"* (Mallarmé), for the purpose of capturing the unnameable. The excess of affect has thus no other means of coming to the fore than to produce new languages—strange concatenations, idiolects, poetics. Until the weight of the primal Thing prevails, and all translatability become impossible. Melancholia then ends up in asymbolia, in loss of meaning: if I am no longer capable of translating or metaphorizing, I become silent and I die.

The Denial of Negation

Listen again for a few moments to depressive speech, repetitive, monotonous, or empty of meaning, inaudible even for the speaker before he or she sinks into mutism. You will note that, with melancholy persons, meaning appears to be arbitrary, or else it is elaborated with the help of much knowledge and will to mastery, but seems secondary, frozen, somewhat removed from the head and body of the person who is speaking. Or else it is from the very beginning evasive, uncertain, deficient, quasi mutistic: "one" speaks to you already convinced that the words are wrong and therefore "one" speaks carelessly, "one" speaks without believing in it.

Meaning, however, is arbitrary; linguistics asserts it for all verbal signs and for all discourse. Is not the signifier LAF completely unmotivated with respect to the meaning of "laugh," and also, and above all, with respect to the act of laughing, its physical production, its intrapsychic and interreactional value? Here is the evidence: I call the same meaning and act *rire* in French, *smeyatsya* in Russian, and so forth. Now every "normal" speaker learns to take that artifice seriously, to cathex it or forget it.

Signs are arbitrary because language starts with a *negation (Verneinung)* of loss, along with the depression occasioned by mourning. "I have lost an essential object that happens to be, in the final analysis, my mother," is what the speaking being seems to be saying. "But no, I have found her again in signs, or rather since I consent to lose her I have not lost her (that is the negation), I can recover her in language."

Depressed persons, on the contrary, *disavow the negation:* they cancel it out, suspend it, and nostalgically fall back on the real object (the Thing) of their loss, which is just what they do not manage to lose, to which they remain painfully riveted. The *denial (Verleugnung) of negation* would thus be the exercise of an impossible mourning, the setting up of a fundamental sadness and an artificial, unbelievable language, cut out of the painful background that is not accessible to any signifier and that intonation alone, intermittently, succeeds in inflecting.

What Should Be Understood by Denial and Negation?

I shall call *denial* the rejection of the signifier as well as semiotic representatives of drives and affects. *Negation* will be understood as the intellectual process that leads the repressed to representation on the condition of denying it and, on that account, shares in the signifier's advent.

According to Freud, *denial* or *disavowal (Verleugnung)* refers to the psychic reality he deemed to be within the realm of perception. Such a denial would be common in children but becomes the starting point of a psychosis with adults since it focuses on external reality.[9] Ultimately, however, denial finds its prototype in denial of castration and becomes specific as it sets up fetishism.[10]

My broadening the scope of Freud's *Verleugnung* doesn't alter its function of effecting a splitting in the subject: on the one hand it denies archaic representations of traumatic perceptions; on the other it symbolically acknowledges their impact and tries to draw the conclusions.

Nonetheless, my conception modifies the object of the denial. Denial focuses on the *intrapsychic (semiotic and symbolic) inscription of the want,* be it fundamentally an object want or later eroticized as woman's castration. In other words, denial focuses on signifiers liable to inscribe semiotic traces and transpose them in order to produce meaning in the subject for another subject.

It will be noted that the disavowed value of the depressive signifier translates an impossibility to give up the object and is often accompanied by the fantasy of a phallic mother. Fetishism appears as a solution to depression and its denial of the signifier; with fetishists, fantasy and acting out replace the denial of psychic pain (of pain's psychic representatives) following upon the loss of biopsychic balance due to object loss.

The denial of the signifier is shored up by a denial of the father's function, which is precisely to guarantee the establishment of the signifier. Maintained in his function of ideal father or imaginary father, the depressive's father is deprived of phallic power, now attributed to the mother. Attractive or seductive, fragile and engaging, such a father holds the subject within suffering but does not allow the possibility of a way out by means of idealizing the symbolic. When this takes place, idealization relies on the maternal father and follows the path to sublimation.

Negation (Verneinung), whose ambiguities Freud maintains and emphasizes in his essay *Die Verneinung,*[11] is a process that inserts an aspect of desire and unconscious idea into consciousness. "The outcome of this is a kind of intellectual acceptance of the repressed, while at the same time what is essential to the repression persists." "With the help of the symbol of negation, thinking frees itself from the restrictions of repression. . . ." "Thus the content of a repressed image or idea can make its way into consciousness, on condition that it is *negated."* This psychic process, which can be observed in patients' defenses against their unconscious desires ("no, I don't love him or her" would signify an acknowledgment of that love in a precisely denied fashion), would be the same as the one that produces the logical and linguistic symbol.

I deem negativity to be coextensive with the speaking being's psychic activity. Its various dispositions, such as *negation, denial,* and *repudiation* (which can produce or modify repression, resistance, defense, or censorship), distinct as one might be from another, influence and condition one another. There is no "symbolic gift" without splitting, and verbal ability is potentially a bearer of fetishism (if only that of symbols themselves) and psychosis (even when remitted).

Nevertheless, the various psychic structures are diversely dominated by the negativity process. If *repudiation (Verwerfung)* were to prevail over negation the symbolic framework would collapse and erase reality itself: that is the pattern of psychosis. The melancholy person who can go as far as repudiation (melancholy psychosis) is, during the illness' mild development, characterized by the prevalence of *denial* over *negation.* The semiotic foundations (affect and drive representatives of loss and castration) underlying linguistic signs are denied, and the intrapsychic value of the latter for creating sense for the subject is consequently annihilated. The result is that traumatic memories (the loss of a loved relative during childhood, some other, more recent wound) are not repressed but constantly evoked as the *denial of negation* prevents the work of repression, at least of its representative part. As a consequence, that evocation, that representation of the repressed does not lead to the loss' symbolic *elaboration,* for signs are unable to pick up the intrapsychic primary inscriptions of the loss and to dispose of it through that very elaboration; on the contrary, they keep turning it over, helplessly. Depressed people know that their moods determine them thoroughly but do not allow such moods to pass into their speech. They know they suffer because they are separated from their narcissistic motherly coating but ceaselessly maintain their omnipotence over a hell that is not to be lost. They know their mothers have no penis but at the same time they have it displayed not only in daydreams but in their "liberated," "shameless" speech, neutral in fact, and in competition, often a death-bearing one, with that phallic power.

At the level of the sign, splitting separates the *signifier* from the *referent* as well as from the drive-related (semiotic) *inscriptions* and devalorizes all three.

At the narcissistic level splitting maintains the omnipotence at the same time as the destructiveness and the anguish of annihilation.

At the level of oedipal desire it wavers between the fear of castration and the fantasy of phallic omnipotence for the other as for the self.

Everywhere denial effects splittings and *devitalizes* representations and behaviors as well.

Unlike what happens with psychotics, however, those who are depressed maintain a paternal signifier that is disowned, weakened, ambiguous, devalorized, but nevertheless persistent until asymbolia shows up. Until they are wrapped up in that shroud and both father and subject are carried away into the solitude of mutism, depressed persons do not forget how to use signs. They keep them, but the signs seem absurd, delayed, ready to be extinguished, because of the splitting that affects them. For instead of bonding the affect caused by loss, the depressed sign disowns the affect as well as the signifier, thus admitting that the depressed subject has remained prisoner of the nonlost object (the Thing).

The Affective Perverseness of the Depressed

If the *denial of the signifier* with depressed persons reminds one of the process of perversion, two remarks seem necessary.

First, in depression, denial has a greater power than perverse denial and affects *subjective identity* itself, not only the *sexual identity* called into question by inversion (homosexuality) or perversion (fetishism, exhibitionism, etc.). Denial annihilates even the introjections of depressive persons and leaves them with the feeling of being worthless, "empty." By belittling and destroying themselves, they exhaust any possibility of an object, and this is also a roundabout way of preserving it . . . elsewhere, untouchable. The only traces of object constancy that depressive people maintain are in affects. The affect is the partial object of depressive persons; it is their "perversion," in the sense of a drug that allows them to insure a narcissistic homeostasis by means of a nonverbal, unnameable (hence untouchable and omnipotent) hold over a nonobjectal Thing. Thus the depressive affect—and its verbalization in analyses and also in works of art—is the perverse display of depressed persons, their ambiguous source of pleasure that fills a void and evicts death, protecting the subject from suicide as well as from psychotic attack.

In similar fashion, the various perversions appear, from this standpoint, as the other facet of depressive denial. Both depression and perversion, according to Melanie Klein, avoid elaborating the "depressive position."[12] Nevertheless, inversions and perversions seem borne by a denial that doesn't affect subjective identity while disturbing sexual identity and allowing for the creation (comparable to a fictional production) of a narcissistic libidinal homeostasis through recourse to autoeroticism, homosexuality, fetishism, exhibitionism, and so forth. Such acts and relations with partial objects preserve the subject and its object from total destruction and provide, with narcissistic homeostasis, a vitality that thwarts Thanatos. Depression is thus bracketed but at the cost of a dependency on perverse theater, often experienced as atrocious; on that stage one sees a parade of omnipotent relations and objects that prevent a confrontation with castration and shield from the pain of pre-oedipal separation. The weakness of the fantasy that is supplanted by acting out bears witness to the continuousness of the denial of the signifier at the level of mental operations in perversions. That feature is at one with the symbolic weakness as experienced by depressive persons as well as manic excitement through acts that become wild only if they are deemed insignificant.

The alternation of perverse and depressive behavior within the neurotic realm of the melancholy/depressive set is frequent. It points to the articulation of the two structures in a same operation (that of denial) having varied intensities bearing on different elements of the subjective structure. Perverse denial has not affected autoeroticism and narcissism. The latter can therefore be mobilized to oppose emptiness and hatred. Depressive denial, on the other hand, affects even the possibilities of a *representation of narcissistic coherence,* hence depriving the subject of its autoerotic exultation, of its "jubilatory assumption." At that point there remains only the masochistic domination of narcissistic folds by a mediationless superego who condemns the affect to remain without object, even a partial one, and display itself to consciousness only as widowed, plunged into mourning, full of pain. Such affective pain, resulting from denial, is *meaning without signification,* but it is used as a shield against death. When that shield also gives way, what remains as the only possible concatenation or act is the act of severance, of un-concatenation, which imposes the non-meaning of death; this constitutes a *challenge* to the others thus rediscovered as rejects or a narcissistic *strengthening* of the subject that one acknowledges (because the fateful act has been carried out) as having always been outside the parental symbolic pact, that is, located where denial (be it parental or its own) had pinned it.

Thus the denial of negation that was seen to be central to the avoidance of the "depressive position" with depressed persons does not necessarily endow that affection with a perverse coloring. The depressed are nonconscious perverts; it is even to their advantage to be nonconscious, for their taking action, which no symbolization appears to satisfy, can be so paroxysmal. True, the delights of suffering can lead to a morose suffering not unfamiliar to monks and that Dostoyevsky, closer to us in time, has exalted.

It is mainly in its manic phase, characteristic of bipolar forms of depression, that *denial* takes on its full strength and appears in broad daylight. Admittedly, it has always been there, but secretly: as sorrow's underhanded, consoling companion, the denial of negation constructed a dubious meaning and turned dismal language into an unbelievable seeming. It called attention to its existence in the detached speech of depressed persons who have at their disposal a trick they do not know how to handle: beware of still waters and overly obedient children . . . With manic persons, however, denial goes beyond the double repudiation that supports sadness: it walks on stage and becomes the tool that builds a shield against loss. Far from being satisfied with elaborating a false language, denial henceforth erects variegated arrays of substitutive erotic objects; we are familiar with widows' or widowers' erotomania, the orgiastic compensations for narcissistic wounds connected with disease or disability, and so forth. Aesthetic exultance, rising by means of ideal and artifice above ordinary constructions suitable to the standards of natural language and trivialized social code, can partake of this manic activity. If it remains at that level the work will stand revealed in its falsity—ersatz, imitation, or carbon copy. On the contrary, the work of art that insures the rebirth of its author and its reader or viewer is one that succeeds in integrating the artificial language it puts forward (new style, new composition, surprising imagination) and the unnamed agitations of an omnipotent self that ordinary social and linguistic usage always leave somewhat orphaned or plunged into mourning. Hence such a fiction, if it isn't an antidepressant, is at least a survival, a resurrection . . .

Arbitrary or Empty

Persons in despair become hyperlucid by nullifying negation. A signifying sequence, necessarily an arbitrary one, will appear to them as heavily, violently arbitrary; they will think it absurd, it will have no meaning. No word, no object in reality will be likely to have a coherent concatenation that will also be suitable to a meaning or referent.

The arbitrary sequence perceived by depressive persons as absurd is coextensive with a loss of reference. The depressed speak of nothing, they have nothing to speak of: glued to the Thing *(Res),* they are without objects. That total and unsignifiable Thing is insignificant—it is a mere Nothing, their Nothing, Death. The chasm that settles in between subject and signifiable objects is translated into the impossibility for concatenations to signify. Such an exile, however, reveals a chasm in the very subject. On the one hand, objects and signifiers, denied to the extent that they are identified with life, assume the value of nonmeaning: language and life have no meaning. On the other hand, on account of splitting, an intense, extravagant value is attributed to the Thing, to Nothing—to the unsignifiable and to death. Depressed speech, built up with absurd signs, slackened, scattered, checked sequences, conveys the collapse of meaning into the unnameable where it founders, inaccessible and delightful, to the benefit of affective value riveted to the Thing.

Denial of negation deprives the language signifiers of their role of making sense for the subject. While they have a signification in themselves, such signifiers are experienced by the subject as *empty*. That is because they *are not bound* to semiotic imprints (drive-related representatives and affect representations). It follows that such archaic psychic inscriptions, once they are set free, can be used in projective identification as quasi-objects. They give rise to acting out, which replaces language in depressive persons (see chapter 3). The surge of mood, up to the stupor that invades the body, is a return of acting out upon the very subject: such overwhelming mood is an action that is not taken on account of the denial that involves the signifier. Moreover, the feverish defensive activity that shrouds the disconsolate sadness of so many depressed persons, before and up to murder or suicide, is a projection of symbolization remainders; relieved of their meaning through denial, their actions are dealt with as quasi-objects that are expelled outward or turned back upon the self with the greatest indifference of a subject benumbed by denial.

The psychoanalytic hypothesis of the denial of the signifier with depressive persons, which does not exclude resorting to biochemical means to remedy neurological deficiencies, reserves the possibility of reinforcing the subject's cognitive capabilities. By analyzing—that is, by dissolving—the denial mechanism wherein depressive persons are stuck, analytic cure can implement a genuine "graft" of symbolic potential and place at the subject's disposal dual discursive strategies working at the intersection of affective and linguistic inscriptions, at the intersection of the semiotic and the symbolic. Such strategies are real counterdepressant reserves that the optimal interpretation within analysis places at the disposal of the depressive patient. At the same time, considerable empathy is required between the analyst and the depressed patient. On that basis, vowels, consonants, or syllables may be extracted from the signifying sequence and put together again in line with the overall meaning of the discourse that identification with the patient has allowed the analyst to discover. This is an infra- and translinguistic level that must often be taken into consideration and linked with the "secret" and the unnamed affect of the depressive.

Dead Language and the Thing Buried Alive

The spectacular collapse of meaning with depressive persons—and, at the limit, the meaning of life—allows us to assume that they experience difficulty integrating the universal signifying sequence, that is, language. In the best of cases, speaking beings and their language are like one: is not speech our "second nature"? In contrast, the speech of the depressed is to them like an alien skin; melancholy persons are foreigners in their maternal tongue. They have lost the meaning—the value—of their mother tongue for want of losing the mother. The dead language they speak, which foreshadows their suicide, conceals a Thing buried alive. The latter, however, will not be translated in order that it not be betrayed; it shall remain walled up within the *crypt* of the inexpressible affect, anally harnessed, with no way out.[13]

A woman patient, prone to frequent bouts of melancholia, came to our first meeting wearing a brightly colored blouse on which the word "house" was printed countless times. She spoke to me of her worries concerning her apartment, her dreams of buildings made of heterogeneous materials, and an African house, the heavenly abode of her childhood, lost by the family under dramatic circumstances. "You are in mourning for a house," I told her.

"A house," she answered, "I don't understand, I don't see what you mean, words fail me!"

Her speech became voluble, brisk, feverish, but tense with cold, abstract excitement. She never ceased using language: "My job as teacher," she said, "forces me to talk continuously, but I explain other people's lives, I'm not involved; and even when I speak of my own, it's as if I spoke of a stranger." The object of her sadness is inscribed in the pain of her skin and her flesh, even in the silk of her tight-fitting blouse. It does not, however, work its way into her mental life, it flees her speech, or rather, Anne's speech has abandoned sorrow and her Thing in order to build up its logic and un-affected, split coherence. As one flees suffering by throwing oneself headlong into a job that is as successful as it is unsatisfactory.

The abyss that, with depressive persons, separates language from affective experience reminds one of a precocious narcissistic trauma. It might have drifted into psychosis, but the superego's protection has in fact stabilized it. A rather unusual intelligence and secondary identification with paternal or symbolic agency have contributed to that stability. Consequently, the depressed are lucid observers, watching day and night over their misfortunes and discomforts, and such an inspective obsession leaves them perpetually dissociated from their affective life during the "normal" times between bouts of melancholia. Just the same, they do give the impression that their symbolic armor hasn't been integrated, their defensive shell not introjected. Their speech is a mask—a beautiful facade carved out of a "foreign language."

The Tone That Calls the Song

Nevertheless, if depressive speech avoids sentential *signification,* its *meaning* has not completely run dry. It occasionally hides (as will be seen in the following example) in the tone of the voice, which one must learn to understand in order to decipher the *meaning* of affect. Research on tonal modulations of depressed speech already does and will in the future teach us a great deal about some depressive persons who, in their discourse, appear unaffected but, on the contrary, maintain a strong, variegated emotionalism concealed in their intonation; or else it teaches us about others, whose "flattening of affect" even reaches the tonal level that stays (at the same time as the sentence sequence that is broken up into "nonrecoverable elisions") monotonous and weighed down with silences.[14]

In the analytic cure, the importance of speech's suprasegmental level (intonation, rhythm) should lead the analyst, on the one hand, to interpret the voice, and on the other, to disarticulate the signifying sequence that has become banal and lifeless—the purpose being to extract the infrasignifying meaning of depressive discourse that is hidden in fragments of lexical items, in syllables, or in phonic groups yet strangely semanticized.

During analysis Anne complains of states of despondency, despair, of losing the taste for life; this frequently leads her to withdraw for entire days to her bed, refusing to speak or to eat (anorexia can alternate with bulimia), often ready to swallow a vial of sleeping pills—and yet she has never taken that fateful step. This intellectual woman, perfectly integrated in a team of anthropologists, nevertheless always underrates her profession and accomplishments, describing herself as "incompetent," "useless," "unworthy," and so forth. At the very outset of the cure I analyzed the conflictual relationship with her mother and noted that the patient effected a true swallowing of the hated maternal object thus preserved deep within herself and changed into a source of rage against herself and of a feeling of inner emptiness. Nonetheless, I had the impression, or as Freud says, the countertransferential conviction that our verbal exchange led to a rationalization of the symptoms but not to a working through (Durcharbeitung). Anne confirmed me in that conviction: "I speak," she would often say, "as if at the edge of words, and I have the feeling of being at the edge of my skin, but the bottom of my sorrow remains unreachable."

I may have interpreted those words as a hysterical refusal of the castrating exchange with me. That interpretation, however, did not seem sufficient, considering the intensity of the depressive complaint and the extent of the silence that either settled in or broke up her speech in "poetic" fashion, making it, at times, undecipherable. I said, "At the edge of words, but at the heart of the voice, for your voice is uneasy when you talk about that incommunicable sadness." This interpretation, whose seductive value one clearly perceives, may have, in the case of a depressive patient, the sense of going through the defensive, empty exterior of the linguistic signifier and looking for mastery (Bemachtigung) over the archaic object (the preobject, the Thing) on the level of vocal inscriptions. Now, it so happens that this patient, in the early years of her life, suffered form serious skin diseases and was probably deprived of the contact with her mother's skin and identification with the mother's face in the mirror. I continued: "Since you couldn't touch your mother you hid beneath your skin, 'at the edge of the skin'; and in that hiding place you enclosed your desire and hatred of her in the sound of your voice, since you heard hers from afar."

We are here in the area of primary narcissism where the image of the self is built up and where, precisely, the image of the depressive future does not succeed in knitting itself into verbal representation. That is because the mourning for the object is not accomplished in such a representation. On the contrary, the object is as if buried—and dominated—by jealously kept affects, finally concealed in vocalizations. I believe the analyst can and must, through interpretation, reach that vocal level of discourse without fearing to be intrusive. By giving a meaning to affects that were kept secret on account of the mastery over the archaic preobject, interpretation recognizes *that affect as well as the secret language the depressive patient endows it with (in this instance, vocal modulation), thus opening up a channel for it at the level of words and secondary processes. The latter—hence language—considered empty up to this point because cut off from affective and vocal inscriptions, are revitalized and may become a space of desire, that is, of meaning for the subject.*

Another example taken from the speech of the same patient will show the extent to which an apparent destruction of the signifying sequence removes it from the denial in which the depressed patient was locked and endows it with the affective inscriptions that she is dying to keep secret. Upon returning from a vacation in Italy, Anne related a dream to me. There was a trial, like [Klaus] *Barbie's trial: I handled the prosecution, everyone was convinced. Barbie was found guilty. She felt relieved, as if she herself had been freed of possible torture on the part of some torturer or other, but she wasn't there, she was elsewhere, it all seemed hollow to her, she preferred to sleep, founder, die, never wake up, in a grief-laden dream that nonetheless attracted her irresistibly, "without any image". . . . I hearkened to the manic excitement surrounding torture that took hold of Anne in her relationship with her mother and sometimes with her partners in between her depressions. But I also heard, "I am elsewhere, a dream of sweetness and pain without image," and I thought of her depressive complaint of being ill, of being barren. I said: "On the surface there are torturers* [tortionnaires]. *Further away, however, or elsewhere, where your sorrow lies, there is perhaps:* Torse-io–naître/pas naître [torso-I-to be born/ not to be born]."

I broke up the word tortionnaire *into its component parts— I tortured it, so to speak, I inflicted upon it the violence that I heard buried in the often devitalized, neutral speech of Anne herself. Nevertheless, the torture that I revealed in the full daylight of words came from my collusion with her pain—from what I believe to be my close, tonic, rewarding listening to her unnamed discomforts, those black holes of pain of which Anne knows the affective meaning but not the significance. The torso is undoubtedly her own but is coiled up with her mother's in the passion of unconscious fantasy; two torsos that didn't touch when Anne was a baby and now unwind in a rage of words during the two women's quarrels. She—Io—wants to be born through analysis, to give herself another body. But joined without verbal representation to her mother's torso, she cannot name that desire, she does not grasp the significance of that desire. Now, if one does not know the significance of a desire, this means that one is without that very desire. It means one is the prisoner of affect, of the archaic Thing, of the primary inscriptions of affects and emotions. That is precisely where ambivalence holds sway and hatred for the mother-Thing is at once changed into self-depreciation . . . Anne went on to confirm my interpretation: she abandoned the manic problematics of torture and persecution in order to speak of the source of her depression. At that time she was overcome by the fear of being barren and the underlying desire to give birth to a girl: "I dreamt that a little girl came out of my body, the spitting image of my mother, while I have often told you that when I close my eyes I can't bring her face to mind, as if she had died before I was born and carried me along into that death. And now here I am giving birth and it is she who lives again. . . ."*

Acceleration and Diversity

Nevertheless, the sequence of linguistic representations, dissociated as it might be from drive-related and affective representatives, can assume with depressed persons considerable associative originality, in keeping with the cycles' rapidity. The psychomotor retardation of depressive persons may be accompanied, contrary to appearances of passivity, by an accelerated, creative cognitive process—witness the studies bearing on the very singular and inventive associations made by depressed persons starting from word lists submitted to them.[15] Such hyperactivity with signifiers reveals itself particularly by connecting distant semantic fields and recalls the puns of hypomanics. It is coextensive with the cognitive hyperlucidity of depressed persons, but also with the manic-depressive's inability to decide or to choose.

Lithium treatment, mastered in the sixties by the Danish doctor Hans Jacob Schou, stabilizes the basic mood and also verbal association and, while maintaining, or so it seems, the originality of the creative process, slows it down and makes it less productive.[16] One might thus agree with those who have conducted those experiments and say that lithium interrupts the diversity process and holds the subject within a word's semantic field, ties him to a significance, and perhaps stabilizes him around an object-referent. On the other hand, one could deduce from those experiments (note that they are limited to depressions that respond to lithium treatment) that certain forms of depression are bouts of associative accelerations that destabilize the subject and afford it an escape route away from confrontation with a stable signification or a steady object.

[*59*]

A Past That Does Not Pass By

As the time in which we live is the time of our discourse, the alien, retarded, or vanishing speech of melancholy people leads them to live within a skewed time sense. It does not pass by, the before/after notion does not rule it, does not direct it from a past toward a goal. Massive, weighty, doubtless traumatic because laden with too much sorrow or too much joy, *a moment* blocks the horizon of depressive temporality or rather removes any horizon, any perspective. Riveted to the past, regressing to the paradise or inferno of an unsurpassable experience, melancholy persons manifest a strange memory: everything has gone by, they seem to say, but I am faithful to those bygone days, I am nailed down to them, no revolution is possible, there is no future . . . An overinflated, hyperbolic past fills all the dimensions of psychic continuity. Such a fancy for ephemeral memory is also undoubtedly a means for capitalizing on the narcissistic object, of brooding over it within the enclosure of an exitless personal vault. This particularity of melancholy temporization is the essential datum on the basis of which concrete disturbances of nychthemeral rhythm can develop, as well as the precise dependency of bouts of depression on the specific biological rhythm of a given subject.[17]

Let us remember that the idea of viewing depression as dependent on a *time* rather than a *place* goes back to Kant. Considering the specific variant of depression constituted by nostalgia, Kant asserted that nostalgic persons did not desire the place of their youth but their youth itself; their desire is a search for the *time* and not for the *thing* to be recovered.[18] The Freudian notion of *psychic object,* to which depressive persons would be riveted, partakes of the same concept: the psychic object is a memory event, it belongs to lost time, in the manner of Proust. It is a subjective construct, and as such it falls within the realm of a memory, elusive to be sure and renewed in each current verbalization, that nevertheless is from the start located not within a physic space but within the imaginary and symbolic space of the psychic system. When I say that the object of my grief is less the village, the mother, or the lover that I miss here and now than the blurred representation that I keep and put together in the darkroom of what thus becomes my psychic tomb, this at once locates my ill-being in the imagination. A dweller in truncated time, the depressed person is necessarily a dweller in the imaginary realm.

Such a linguistic and temporal phenomenology discloses, as I have often emphasized, an unfulfilled mourning for the maternal object.

Projective Identification or Omnipotence

In order better to account for it, we must come back to the notion of *projective identification* suggested by Melanie Klein. The study of very young children, and also the dynamics of psychosis, leads one to conjecture that the most archaic psychic processes are the projections of the good and bad components of a not-yet self onto an object not yet separated from it, with the aim less of attacking the other than of gaining a hold over it, an omnipotent possession. Such oral and anal omnipotence is perhaps the more intense as certain biopsychological particularities hamper the ideally wished for autonomy of the self (psychomotor difficulties, auditory or visual disorders, various illnesses, etc.). The behavior of mothers and fathers, overprotective and uneasy, who have chosen the child as a narcissistic artificial limb and keep incorporating that child as a restoring element for the adult psyche intensifies the infant's tendency toward omnipotence.

Now, the semiotic means through which this omnipotence expresses itself is a preverbal semiology—gestural, motor, vocal, olfactory, tactile, auditory. Primary processes govern that expression of archaic domination.

Omnipotent Meaning

The subject of a *meaning* is already there, even if the subject of linguistic *signification* has not yet been constructed and awaits the depressive position in order to come into being. The meaning that is already there (one can assume it to be supported by a precocious and tyrannical superego) is made up of gestural, acoustic, phonatory rhythms and devices where pleasure is articulated along sensory series that constitute a first differentiation from the Thing, which is exciting as well as threatening, and from autosensual confusion. Thus the continuum of the body, which is in the process of becoming "one's own and proper body," is articulated as an organized discontinuity, exercising a precocious and primary mastery, flexible yet powerful, over the erotogenic zones, blended with the preobject, the maternal Thing. What appears on the psychological level as omnipotence *is the power of semiotic rhythms, which convey an intense presence of meaning in a presubject still incapable of signification.*

What we call meaning is the ability of the *infans* to record the signifier of parental desire and include itself therein in his own fashion; he does so by displaying the semiotic abilities he is endowed with at that moment of his development and which allow him a mastery, on the level of primary processes, of a "not yet other" (of the

Thing) included in the erotogenic zones of such a semi-otizing *infans*. Nevertheless, the omnipotent meaning remains a "dead letter" if it is not invested in signification. It will be the task of analytic interpretation to search for depressive meaning in the vault where sadness has locked it up with the mother, and tie it to the signification of objects and desires. Such an interpretation overthrows the omnipotence of meaning and amounts to working through the depressive position that was denied by the subject having a depressive structure.

It will be recalled that separation from the object starts the so-called depressive phase. Upon losing mother and relying on negation, I retrieve her as sign, image, word.[19] Nevertheless, the omnipotent child does not give up the ambiguous delights of the paranoid-schizoid position of a former projective identification during which all psychic impulses were located within an undissociated, fusional other. Or else the child refuses separation and mourning and, instead of tackling the depressive position and language, takes refuge in a passive position, in fact a schizo-paranoid one, dominated by projective identification—the refusal to speak that underlies a number of language retardations is in fact an assertion of omnipotence and thus of primary ascendancy over the object. Or else, still, the child discovers a compromise in *denial* of the negation, which generally leads to working through mourning by establishing a symbolic system (particularly language). The subject then freezes his unpleasant affects like all others and preserves them in a *psychic inside* thus constituted once and for all as distressed and inaccessible. This painful inerness, put together with semiotic markings but not with signs,[20] is the invisible face of Narcissus, the secret source of his tears. The wall of the *denial of negation* then separates the stirrings of the subject from the symbolic makeups that he nonetheless acquires, often even brilliantly, thanks precisely to the repeated negation. Melancholy persons, with their despondent, secret insides, are potential exiles but also intellectuals capable of dazzling, albeit abstract, constructions. With depressive people, *denial of the negation* is the logical expression of omnipotence. Through their empty speech they assure themselves of an inaccessible (because it is "semiotic" and not "symbolic") ascendency over an archaic object that thus remains, for themselves and all others, an enigma and a secret.

Sadness Holds Back Hatred

A symbolic construct acquired in such fashion, a subjectivity erected on that basis can easily collapse when the experience of new separations, or new losses, revives the object of primary denial and upsets the omnipotence that had been preserved at the cost of the denial. The linguistic signifier, which was a seeming, is then swept away by the disturbances like a sea wall by ocean breakers. As primary inscription of the loss that persists beyond denial, the affect swamps the subject. My sadness affect is the ultimate yet *mute* witness to my having, in spite of all, lost the archaic Thing of omnipotent ascendancy. That sadness is the final filter of aggressiveness, the narcissistic restraint of a hatred that is unacknowledged not because of simple moral or superego decency, but because in sadness the self is yet joined with the other, it carries it within, it introjects its own omnipotent projection—and joys in it. Sadness would thus be the negative of omnipotence, the first and primary indication that the other is getting away from me, but that the self, nevertheless, does not put up with being abandoned.

The surge of affect and primary semiotic processes comes

into conflict, in depressive persons, with the linguistic armor (which I have called alien or "secondary"), as well as with symbolic constructs (apprenticeships, ideologies, beliefs). Retardations or accelerations turn up, expressing the rhythm of the normally controlled primary processes and, undoubtedly, biophysiological rhythm. Discourse no longer has the capacity to break and even less so to change that rhythm, but on the contrary allows itself to be changed by affective rhythm to the extent of fading into muteness (through too much retardation, or too much acceleration, making the choice of action impossible). When the struggle between imaginary creation (art, literature) and depression is carried out precisely on that frontier of the symbolic and the biological we see indeed that the narrative or the argument is ruled by primary processes. Rhythms, alliterations, condensations shape the transmission of message and data. That being the case, would *poetry* and, more generally, the style that bears its secret imprint bear witness to a (for the time being) conquered depression?

We are thus led to take at least three parameters into consideration in order to describe psychic and, particularly, depressive modifications: *symbolic processes* (the grammar and logic of discourse) and *semiotic processes* (displacement, condensation, alliterations, vocal and gestural rhythms, etc.) along with the supports constituted by *biophysiological rhythms* of transmission and stimulation. Whatever endogenous factors may condition the latter, and however powerful the pharmacological means of effecting an optimal transmission of nerve stimulation may be, the problem of primary and above all secondary integration of stimulation remains.

It is precisely at this place that psychoanalytic treatment comes in. Identifying pleasure and displeasure in their minute meanderings—and this at the very heart of the transference position, which replicates the primitive conditions of omnipotence and the simulated separation from the object—remains our only means of access to melancholia, that paradoxical formation of the subject. Paradoxical indeed, for the subject, at the cost of a *negation,* had opened up the doors of the symbolic only to shut them through its *denial,* keeping for himself the unnameable jouissance of an omnipotent affect. There is perhaps a chance, then, for analysis to transform such subjectivation and endow discourse with a modifying power over the fluctuations of primary processes and even bioenergetic transmissions, by favoring a better integration of semiotic agitation within the symbolic fabric.

The Western Fate of Conveyance

To posit the existence of a primal object, or even of a Thing, which is to be conveyed through and beyond a completed mourning—isn't that the fantasy of a melancholy theoretician?

Certainly the primal object, the "in-itself" that always remains to be conveyed, the ultimate cause of conveyability, exists only for and through discourse and the already constituted subject. Because what is conveyed is already there, the conveyable can be imagined and posited as in excess and incommensurable. Positing the existence of that other language and even of an other of language, indeed of an outside-of-language, is not necessarily setting up a preserve for metaphysics or theology. The postulate corresponds to a psychic requirement that Western metaphysics and theory have had, perhaps, the good luck and audacity to represent. That psychic requirement is certainly not universal; Chinese civilization, for instance, is not a civilization of the conveyability of the thing in itself;

it is rather one of sign repetition and variation, that is to say, of transcription.

The obsession with the primal object, the object to be conveyed, assumes a certain appropriateness (imperfect, to be sure) to be considered possible between the sign and not the referent but the nonverbal experience of the referent in the interaction with the other. I am able to name truly. The Being that extends beyond me—including the being of affect—may decide that its expression is suitable or nearly suitable. The wager of conveyability is also a wager that the primal object can be mastered; in that sense it is an attempt to fight depression (due to an intrusive preobject that I cannot give up) by means of a torrent of signs, which aims precisely at capturing the object of joy, fear, or pain. Metaphysics, and its obsession with conveyability, is a discourse of the pain that is stated and relieved on account of that very statement. It is possible to be unaware of, to deny the primal Thing, it is possible to be unaware of pain to the benefit of signs that are written out or playful, without innerness and without truth. The advantage of those civilizations that operate on the basis of such a model is that they are able to mark the immersion of the subject within the cosmos, its mystical immanence with the world. But, as a Chinese friend recognized, such a culture is without means for facing the onset of pain. Is that lack an advantage or a weakness?

Westerners, on the other hand, are convinced they can convey the mother—they believe *in her,* to be sure, but in order to convey her, that is, to betray her, transpose her, be free of her. Such melancholy persons triumph over the sadness at being separated from the loved object through an unbelievable effort to master signs in order to have them correspond to primal, unnameable, traumatic experiences.

Even more so and finally the belief in conveyability

[67]

("mother is nameable, God is nameable") leads to a strongly individualized discourse, avoiding stereotypes and clichés, as well as to the profusion of personal styles. But in that very practice we end up with the perfect *betrayal* of the unique and in-itself Thing (the *Res divina*): if all the fashions of naming it are allowable, does not the Thing postulated in itself become dissolved in the thousand and one ways of naming it? The posited conveyability ends up with a multiplicity of possible conveyances. The Western subject, as potential melancholy being, having become a relentless conveyor, ends up a confirmed gambler or potential atheist. The initial belief in conveyance becomes changed into a belief in stylistic performance for which the near side of the text, its other, primal as it might be, is less important than the success of the text itself.

3

Illustrations of Feminine Depression

The following fragments do not open up the universe of clinical melancholia; rather, they lead us into neurotic regions of the melancholy/depressive set. What one notices there is the alternation between depression and anxiety, depression and perverse action, loss of object and meaning of speech and sadomasochistic domination over them. Being caught in woman's speech is not merely a matter of chance that could be explained by the greater frequency of feminine depressions—a sociologically proven fact. This may also reveal an aspect of feminine sexuality: its addiction to the maternal Thing and its lesser aptitude for restorative perversion.

CANNIBALISTIC SOLITUDE

The Body as Tomb or the Omnipotent Devouring

From the time of her birth Helen suffered from serious motor problems that had required several surgical operations and confined her to bed until she was three. The little girl's brilliant intellectual development, however, enabled her to have an equally brilliant professional career, all the more so since nothing remains of her earlier motor deficiencies or of the family context that, quite obviously, fostered them.

Nothing, that is, aside from frequent instances of serious depression that did not seem triggered by the current reality, a rather prosperous one, of Helen's life. A number of situations (speaking with more than one person, being in a public place, defending a position shared by none of the people present) produced in her a state of stupor. "I find myself glued to the spot, as if paralyzed, I lose the ability to speak, my mouth fills with chalk, my mind is completely empty." She was overcome with a sense of total incapacity, quickly followed by utter dejection that separated Helen from the world, caused her to withdraw into her room, dissolve into tears, and remain speechless, thoughtless for days on end. "As if I were dead but I do not even think of killing myself, nor do I desire to do so, it is as if it had already been done."

In such circumstances, "being dead" meant a physical experience for Helen, an unspeakable one at first. When she later tried to find words to describe it, she spoke of states of artificial weightiness, of swept-out dryness, of absence against a backdrop of dizziness, of emptiness cut out into black lightning . . . But those words still seemed to her too imprecise for what she experienced as a total paralysis of psyche and body, an irremediable dissociation between herself and everything else, and also within what should have been "she." An absence of sensations, a loss of pain or hollowing out of sorrow—an absolute, mineral, astral numbness, which was nevertheless accompanied by the impression, also an almost physical one, that this "being dead," physical and sensory as it might be, was also a thought nebula, an amorphous imagination, a muddled representation of some implacable helplessness. The reality and fiction of death's being. Cadaverization and artifice. An absolute impotence that was, nevertheless, secretly all powerful. The artifice of maintaining herself alive, but . . . "beyond it all." Beyond castration and disintegration; being *as if* she were dead, *playing* dead seemed for Helen when she could talk about it, therefore after the event, like a "poetics" of survival, an inverted life, coiled around imaginary and real disintegration to the extent of embodying death *as if* it were real. In that world-view, swallowing a vial of barbiturates is not a choice but a gesture that is imperative on the basis of an elsewhere— a non-act, or rather a sign of completion, a near-aesthetic harmonization of its fictious fullness, "beyond."

A total oceanic death would engulf the world and He-len's being in a prostrate, mindless, motionless passivity. Such a lethal flood could settle down for days and weeks on end, allowing neither interest in nor access to any exteriority. When an object's image or a person's face managed to crystallize in it, they were at once perceived as precipitates of hatred, as hurtful or hostile elements, both disintegrating and agonizing, which she could face in no other way except by killing them. Putting those aliens to death was then a substitute for being dead, and the lethal flood changed into torrents of anguish. Neverthe-less, it was anguish that kept Helen alive. It was her vital dance, following and in addition to morbid stupor. Cer-tainly painful and insufferable, anguish just the same gave her access to an extent of reality. The faces to be killed were mainly the faces of children. That unbearable temp-tation horrified her and gave her the impression of being monstrous, and yet *being*—emerging out of nothingness.

Faces of the disabled child that she was and henceforth

[*73*]

wanted to be finished with? It would seem, rather, that the desire to kill was triggered only when the world of others, previously taken over by the lethal self in its almighty helplessness, succeeded in becoming free from the confinement where dreamlike melancholia had trapped her. Then confronted with others without seeing them as such, the depressed Helen continued to project onto them: "I am not killing my frustraters or my tyrants, I am killing *their* baby, which they have dropped."

Like an Alice in distressland, the depressed woman cannot put up with mirrors. Her image and that of others arouse within her wounded narcissism, violence, and the desire to kill—from which she protects herself by going through the looking glass and settling down in that other world where, by limitlessly spreading her constrained sorrow, she regains a hallucinated completedness. Beyond the grave, Proserpina survives as a blind shade. Her body is already elsewhere, absent, a living corpse. It often happens that she does not feed it or else, on the contrary, she stuffs it the better to get rid of it. Through her fuzzy, tearmisted gaze that sees neither you nor herself, she savors the bitter sweetness of being forsaken by so many absent ones. Concerned with brooding, within her body and her psyche, over a physical and moral distress, Helen nevertheless strolls among the others—when she leaves her graveyard bed—like an extraterrestrial, the inaccessible citizen of the magnificent land of Death, of which no one could ever deprive her.

At the start of her analysis Helen was warring with her mother—inhuman, artificial, nymphomaniac, incapable of any feeling, and having thoughts only, so said the patient, for money or for seduction. Helen remembered her mother's "bursting into" her room as "a desecration, a forcible entry, a rape," or her overly intimate, overly explicit remarks—"in fact, I thought them obscene"—made in the presence of friends, which made her blush with shame . . . and pleasure.

Behind that veil of erotic aggressiveness, however, we uncovered another relationship between the handicapped child and her mother. "As much as I try to imagine her face, nor or at the time of my childhood, I don't see it. I am sitting on someone who holds me, perhaps on her lap, but actually it isn't anybody. A person would have a face, a voice, a glance, a head. The fact is that I perceive nothing of the sort, merely a support, that's all, nothing else." I venture an interpretation: "As to the other, you have perhaps assimilated her into yourself, you wanted her support, her legs, but as for everything else, *she* was perhaps *you*."—"I had a dream," Helen went on, "I was climbing your stairs, they were covered with bodies that looked like the people on my parents' wedding photo. I myself had been invited to that wedding, it was a cannibalistic meal, I was supposed to eat those bodies, those scraps of bodies, those heads, my mother's head also. It was ghastly."

Orally assimilating the mother who gets married, who has a man, who flees. Possessing her, holding her within oneself so as never to be separated from her. Helen's almightiness shows through the mask of aggressiveness and shores up the other's nonexistence in her daydream as well as the difficulty she experiences in deciding who she is when facing a person different from herself, separated from herself, in actual life.

The thought of a minor surgical operation distresses Helen so much that she is willing to run the risk of aggravating her condition rather than confronting anesthesia. "It's too dismal, being put to sleep, I don't think I could stand it. They are going to go through me, of course, but that isn't what frightens me. It's strange, I have the feeling that I'm going to end up being frightfully alone. Even so, that's preposterous, because in fact, people will never have taken care of me so much." She perhaps feels that the surgical "operation" (I refer to my own interpretational "operations") will take away someone close, some indispensible person, whom she imagines she has locked up within herself and constantly keeps her company? "I don't see who that might be. I've already told you, I think of no one, for me there is no other one, I see no one by my side as far back as I can remember . . . I forgot to tell you, I've had sex and I was nauseated. I vomited and I saw, as if I were in between sleep and wakefulness, something like the head of a child falling into the washbasin while a voice called me from a distance, but mistakenly calling me by my mother's name." Helen thus confirmed my interpretation—she had locked up a fantasy, the representation of her mother, within her body. And she reeled as she spoke of it, as if she were disconcerted by having to relinquish, if only by words, the object that was imprisoned within herself, and which, if she happened to miss it, would plunge her into a bottomless grief. Punctual and remarkably regular, she forgot, for the first time during her analysis, the time of her ensuing appointment. At the next meeting, she confessed that she remembered nothing about the meeting previous to the one she missed: everything was void, blank, she felt drained and frightfully sad, nothing meant anything, she was once more back in those states of stupor that are so painful . . . Had she tried to lock me within herself instead of the mother we had flushed out? To confine me in her body so that, the one blended with the other, we could no longer meet, since she had for a time incorporated, ingested, buried me in her imaginary tomb-like body, as she had done with her mother?

Perverse and Frigid

Helen often complained that her words, with which she hoped to "touch" me, were actually hollow and dry, "far removed from true feeling": "It is possible to say anything, it may be a piece of information, but it has no meaning, at any rate not for me." That description of her speech reminded her of what she called her "orgies." Beginning with her teens and up to the start of her analysis she alternated between states of prostration and "erotic feasts": "I did everything and anything, I was man, woman, beast, whatever was called for, it created a sensation, and me, it made me come, I think, but it wasn't really me. It was pleasant, but it was someone else."

Omnipotence and disavowal of loss led Helen on a feverish quest for gratification: she could do everything, she was almightiness. A narcissistic and phallic triumph, such a maniacal attitude finally turned out to be exhausting, since it blocked all possibility of symbolization for the negative affects—fear, sorrow, pain . . .

Nonetheless, when the analysis of omnipotence gave those affects access to speech, Helen went through a period of frigidity. The maternal object, necessarily erotic, which had first been captured in order to be annihilated in Helen, once it was recovered and named during the course of analysis did probably, and for a time, fulfill the patient. "I have her within me," the frigid woman seemed to say, "she doesn't leave me, but no one else can take her place, I am impenetrable, my vagina is dead." Frigidity, which is essentially vaginal and can be partly compensated for with clitoral orgasm, betrays an imaginary capture by the frigid woman of a maternal figure anally imprisoned and transferred to the cloaca-vagina. Many women know that in their dreams their mothers stand for lovers or husbands and vice versa, and they keep settling with them, without satisfaction, accounts of anal possession. Such a mother, who is imagined as indispensable, fulfilling, intrusive, is for that very reason death-bearing: she devitalizes her daughter and leaves her no way out. What is more, since she has been imagined as monopolizing the jouissance her daughter had given her, but without returning anything in its stead (without getting her pregnant), such a mother cloisters the frigid woman in an imaginary solitude that is affective as well as sensory. The partner would need to be imagined, in turn, as "more-than-a-mother," in order to act the part of both "Thing" and "Object," in order not to fall short of the narcissistic request, but also and fore-most in order to dislodge that request and lead the woman to cathex her autoeroticism in a jouissance of the other (separate, symbolic, phallic).

Two forms of jouissance thus seem possible for a woman. On the one hand there is phallic jouissance—competing or identifying with the partner's symbolic power—which mobilizes the clitoris. On the other hand, there is an *other jouissance* that fantasy imagines and carries out by aiming more deeply at psychic space, and the space of the body as well. That other jouissance requires that the melancholy object blocking the psychic and bodily interior literally be liquefied. Who is capable of doing it? An imagined partner able to dissolve the mother imprisoned within myself by giving me what she could and above all what she could not give me, while remaining in a different place—no longer the mother's but that of the person who can obtain for me the major gift she was never able to offer: a new life. A partner who acts neither the father's part, ideally rewarding his daughter, nor the symbolic stallion's that one is supposed to obtain through a manly competition.

The feminine interior (meaning the psychic space and, at the level of bodily experience, the vagina-anus combination) can then cease being the crypt that encloses the dead woman and conditions frigidity. Putting to death the death-bearing mother within me endows the partner with the appeal of a life-giver, precisely of one who is "more-than-a-mother." He is not a phallic mother but rather a restoration of the mother by means of a phallic violence that destroys the bad but also bestows and honors. The so-called vaginal jouissance that follows is symbolically dependent, as can be seen, on a relation to the Other no longer imagined as part of a phallic outbidding, but as an invigorator of the narcissistic object and able to insure its *outward* displacement—by giving a child, by himself becoming the link between the mother-child bond and phallic power, or else by furthering the beloved woman's symbolic life.

There is no evidence that the other jouissance is absolutely necessary for a woman's psychic fulfillment. Very often, either phallic, professional, or maternal compensation, or else clitoral pleasure are frigidity's hermetic veil. Just the same, if men and women endow the *other jouissance* with nearly sacred value, it is perhaps because it is the language of the female body that has temporarily triumphed over depression. It is a triumph over death, surely not as the individual's ultimate fate, but over the imaginary death where the premature human being is permanently at stake if abandoned, neglected, or misunderstood by the mother. Within feminine fantasy such a jouissance assumes a triumph over the death-bearing mother, in order for the interior to become a source of rewards while eventually becoming a source of biological life, childbearing, and motherhood.

TO KILL OR TO KILL ONESELF:
THE ENACTED WRONGDOING

The Act Would Be Merely Reprehensible

Feminine depression is occasionally concealed by a feverish activity that gives the depressed person the appearance
of a practical woman, at ease with herself, who thinks
only of being useful. To such a mask, which many women
wear either deceitfully or unwittingly, Marie-Ange adds a
cold urge for revenge, a true death-bearing plot, of which
she herself is surprised to be the brain and the weapon,
and which brings her suffering because she experiences it
as a serious wrongdoing. Having discovered that her husband deceived her, Marie-Ange succeeds in identifying her
rival and indulges in a series of more or less childish or
diabolical schemings in order simply to eliminate the in-
truder, who happens to be a friend and colleague. It mainly
amounts to pouring sleeping drugs and other harmful
products into coffee, tea, and other drinks that Marie-
Ange offers her freely. But it also goes as far as slashing
her car's tires, disabling the brakes, and so forth.

A kind of rapture seizes Marie-Ange when she under-
takes such retaliations. She forgets her jealousy and her
wound and, even though ashamed of what she is doing,
she comes close to feeling gratified. To be at fault causes
her to suffer because being at fault gives her joy, and vice
versa. Hurting her rival, disorienting her or even killing
her, does that not also amount to inserting herself into the
other woman's life, giving her jouissance unto death? Marie-
Ange's violence endows her with a phallic power that
makes up for humiliation and, even more so, gives her the
feeling of being more powerful than her husband—more

authoritative, so to speak, over his mistress' body. The complaint against the husband's adultery is but a trivial coating. While wounded by her spouse's "wrongdoing," what rouses Marie-Ange's suffering and avenging mood is neither moral castigation nor the complaint about the narcissistic wound inflicted by her guilty husband.

In more primary fashion, *any possibility for action* would appear to be seen by her fundamentally as a transgression, as a wrongdoing. Acting would amount to compromising herself, and when the depressive retardation underlying inhibition hampers any other possibility of realization, the only act that is possible for such a woman becomes the major wrongdoing—to kill or to kill oneself. One may imagine an intense oedipal jealousy with respect to the parents' "primal act," doubtless perceived and thought of always as reprehensible; or a precocious harshness on the part of the superego, a fierce hold on the Thing-Object of archaic homosexual desire . . . "I do not act, or if I do it is abominable, it must be reprehensible."

In the manic phase, the paralysis of action takes on the appearance of insignificant activity (and for that very reason hardly culpable), hence possible, or else it aspires to the major wrongdoing.

A Blank Perversion

Loss of the erotic object (unfaithfulness or desertion by the lover or husband, divorce, etc.) is felt by the woman as an assault on her genitality and, from that point of view, amounts to castration. At once, such a castration starts resonating with the threat of destruction of the body's integrity, the body image, and the entire psychic system as well. As a result, feminine castration, rather than being diseroticized, is concealed by narcissistic anguish, which

[*81*]

masters and protects eroticism as a *shameful secret.* Even though a woman has no penis to lose, it is her entire being —body and especially soul—that she feels is threatened by castration. *As if her phallus were her psyche,* the loss of the erotic object breaks up and threatens to empty her whole psychic life. The outer loss is immediately and depressively experienced as an inner void.

This means that the psychic void[1] and the painful affect that constitutes its minute yet intense expression settle in place instead of the shameful loss. Depressive behavior develops on the basis of and within such a void. Blank activity, lacking meaning, may just as well follow a death-bearing course (killing the rival who steals the partner) or an innocuous one (wearing herself out doing housework or checking the children's homework). She remains constantly restrained by an aching psychic wrapping, anesthetized, as if "dead."

In the early stages of analysis for depressive women their emptiness as living dead is honored and respected. Only through friendly collusion, free from superego tyranny, does analysis allow shame to be spoken out and death to find its orbit as the death wish. Marie-Ange's desire to cause (the other's) death so as not to pretend to be dead (herself) can then be narrated as a sexual desire to joy in her rival or to give her jouissance. For that reason, depression appears as the veil of a *blank perversion*—one that is dreamed of, desired, even thought through, but unmentionable and forever impossible. The depressive course precisely avoids carrying out the perverse act: it hollows out the painful psyche and stands in the way of experienced sex as shameful. Melancholia's unbounded activity, which is somewhat hypnoidal, secretely cathexes perversion in the most inflexible feature of the law—constraint, duty, destiny, and even the fatality of death.

[*82*]

By revealing the sexual (homosexual) secret of the depressive course of action that causes the melancholy person to *live with death,* analysis gives back its place to desire within the patient's psychic territory (the death drive is not the death wish). It thus marks off a psychic territory that becomes able to integrate *loss* as signifiable as well as erogenetic. The separation henceforth appears no longer as a threat of disintegration but as a *stepping stone* toward some other—conflictive, bearing Eros and Thanatos, open to both meaning and nonmeaning.

Don Juan's Wife—Sorrowful or Terrorist

Marie-Ange has an elder sister and several younger brothers. She has always been jealous of that elder sister, the father's favorite, but she retains from her childhood the certainty that she was abandoned by her mother, whose many successive pregnancies claimed all her attention. No hatred toward her sister or her mother seems to have been shown in the past, any more than at present. Marie-Ange, on the contrary, comported herself like a well-behaved child, sad, always withdrawn. She was afraid of going out, and when her mother went shopping she would wait for her by the window, worried. "I stayed in the house as if I were there in her stead, I preserved her fragrance, I imagined her presence, I kept her with me." Her mother deemed that such sadness was not normal. "That nun's expression is deceitful, she is hiding something," the matriarch would say disapprovingly, and those words would discourage the little girl even more as she withdrew to her inner hiding place.

It took Marie-Ange a long time to talk of her present depressive states. Under the surface of the always punctual, busy, and faultless teacher, a woman showed up who sometimes took extended sick leaves because she did not want to, could not, leave her house; in order to imprison what fleeing presence?

Nevertheless, she managed to control her states of total dereliction and paralysis by identifying with the maternal figure: either with the superactive housewife, or even—and this is how she came to take action against her rival—with a desired phallic mother whose homosexual passive partner she would like to be or, conversely, whose body she herself would like to arouse by putting her to death. So, Marie-Ange told me a dream that enabled her to glimpse the kind of passion that nourished her hatred for her rival. She manages to open the door of her husband's mistress' car to hide an explosive in it. But in fact it is not a car, it is her mother's bed; Marie-Ange is huddled against her, and she suddenly notices that this mother, who so generously breast-fed the swarm of little boys who came after Marie-Ange, owned a penis.

The heterosexual partner of a woman, when the relationship is satisfying from her point of view, often bears the attributes of her mother. The depressive woman goes against this rule only indirectly. Her favorite partner or her husband is a fulfilling although unfaithful mother. The desperate woman can then be dramatically, painfully, attached to her Don Juan. For, beyond the fact that he gives her the possibility of enjoying an unfaithful mother, Don Juan satisfies her eager thirst for other women. His own mistresses are her own mistresses. His exploits satisfy her own erotomania and provide her with an antidepressive, a feverish excitement beyond pain. If the sexual desire underlying that passion were repressed, murder might take the place of embrace and the depressed woman might change into a terrorist.

Taming sorrow, not fleeing sadness at once but allowing it to settle for a while, even to blossom, and in this way to wear itself out: that is what one of the temporary and yet indispensable phases of analysis might be. Could the wealth of my sadness be my way of protecting myself against death—the death of the desired/rejected other, the death of myself?

Marie-Ange had muffled within herself the distress and devalorization where the real or imaginary maternal neglect had left her. The idea of her being ugly, useless, and insignificant did not leave her, but it was more of an ambiance than an idea, nothing obvious, just the glum coloring of a dull day. On the other hand, the desire for death, for her own death (for want of avenging herself on the mother) filtered into her phobias: fear of falling out the window, from the elevator, off a rock, or off the slope of a mountain. Fear of finding herself in a void, of dying of the void. A permanent vertigo. Marie-Ange protected herself from it for the time being by displacing it onto her rival, who was supposed to be drowned in poison or vanish in a car going at breakneck speed. Her life was unharmed at the price of the other's sacrificed life.

The terrorism of such depressive hysteria is often expressed by aiming for the mouth. Many stories involving harems and other feminine jealousies have established the image of the poisoner as a privileged image of feminine Satanism. Poisoning drink or food nevertheless reveals, beyond the raging sorceress, a little girl deprived of the breast. And if it is true that little boys are also deprived, everyone knows that man recovers his lost paradise in the heterosexual relationship, but also and mainly through various roundabout means that lavish oral satisfactions on him or do so by means of orality.

Acting out, where a woman is concerned, is more inhibited, less developed, and consequently it can be, when

[85]

it takes place, more violent. For the loss of the object seems beyond remedy for a woman and its mourning more difficult, if not impossible. So, substitutive objects, perverse objects that should lead her to the father, seem derisory to her. She often reaches heterosexual desire by repressing archaic pleasures, even pleasure itself—she yields to heterosexuality in frigidity. Marie-Ange wants to keep her husband to herself, for herself but not for sexual pleasure. Access to jouissance is then effected only through man's perverse object: Marie-Ange's pleasure comes from the mistress, and when her husband does not have one he no longer interests her. The depressive woman's perversion is deceitful, it needs the go-between and screen of man's object-woman in order to seek the other sex. But once settled on that path, the tired-out desire of the melancholy woman knows no bounds: it wants everything, to the end, until death.

The sharing of that death-bearing secret with analysts is not merely a test of their reliability or of the difference between their discourse and the domain of law, condemnation, or repression. Such a trust ("I am having you share in my crime") is an attempt to win over the analyst into a common jouissance—the one that the mother declined, that the mistress steals. By pointing out that the trust is an attempt to gain ascendency over the analyst as erotic object, the interpretation maintains the patient in the truth of her desire and her attempts at manipulation. But in abiding by an ethics that does not merge with that of punitive legislation the analyst recognizes the reality of the depressive stance, and asserting the symbolic legitimacy of its distress, allows the patient to seek out other means, symbolic or imaginary, of working out her suffering.

A VIRGIN MOTHER

"Black Hole"

To her it seemed as if conflicts with, desertions by, separations from her lovers did not affect her, she experienced no grief. No more than when her mother died . . . This did not imply an indifference that would be based on self-control and mastery of the situation or else (and this is most frequently the case) on hysterical repression of sadness and desire. When Isabel, during sessions, attempted to piece together such states, she would speak of "anesthetized wounds," "numbed sorrow," or "a blotting out that holds everything in check." I had the impression that she had fitted in her psychic space one of those "crypts" Maria Torok and Nicolas Abraham talk about, in which there was nothing, but the whole depressive identity was organized around this nothingness. Such nothingness was an absolute. Grief, humiliating by dint of having been kept secret, unnameable, and unspeakable, had turned into a *psychic silence* that did not repress the wound but took its place and, what is more, by condensing it, gave it back an exorbitant intensity, imperceptible by sensations and representations.

Melancholy mood, with her, amounted only to mental blanks, evasiveness, distraught and seemingly hallucinated gazings on what may have been grief, but which Isabel's superego dignity at once transformed into inaccessible hypertrophy. A nothingness that is neither repression nor simply the mark of the affect but condenses into a *black hole*—like invisible, crushing, cosmic antimatter—the sensory, sexual, fantasy-provoking ill-being of abandonments and disappointments. Narcissistic wounds and castration, sexual dissatisfaction and fantasy-laden dead-ends become telescoped into a simultaneously killing and irretrievable burden that organizes her subjectivity; within, she is nothing but bruises and paralysis; outside, all that was left to her was acting out or sham activism.

Isabel needed that "black hole" of her melancholia in order to construct her living motherhood and activities outside it, just as others organize themselves around repression or splitting. It was her own thing, her home, the narcissistic center where she foundered as much as she replenished herself.

Isabel decided to have a child at the darkest moment of one of her depressive periods. Disappointed by her husband, distrustful of what appeared to be her lover's "childish inconsistency," she wanted to have her child "for herself." Knowing who fathered it mattered little to her. "I want the child, not the father," the "virgin mother" reflected. She had to have a "reliable companion," "Someone who would need me, we would be accomplices, we would never leave each other, well, almost never. . . ."

The child conceived as antidote against depression is destined to bear a heavy burden. The indeed virginal calmness of the pregnant Isabel—no period in her life had ever seemed so euphoric to her as her pregnancy—concealed a bodily tension that any heedful observer would have detected at the beginning of this analysis. Isabel did not manage to relax on the couch but, her neck muscles tensed and her feet on the ground ("so as not to damage your belongings," she said), she seemed ready to leap forward and confront some threat or other. That of being made pregnant by the analyst? Some unweaned babies' hyperkinesia no doubt conveys their mothers' unnamed, unconscious, utmost physical and psychic tension.

Living for the Sake of Dying

Anxiety over deformity in the fetus, common in most pregnant women, reached a suicidal peak with Isabel. She imagined that her baby would die during delivery or be born with a serious congenital defect. She would then kill it, before killing herself, mother and child becoming united again, inseparable in death as in pregnancy. The much hoped for birth changed into a burial, and the vision of the funeral exalted the patient, as if she had desired her child for death alone. She would give birth for death's sake. The brutal stopping of the life she was preparing to give, and of her own as well, was destined to spare her all worry, to relieve her of the troubles of life. Birth destroyed the future and the project.

Desire for a child was revealed as narcissistic desire for lethal fusion—it was a death of desire. Thanks to her child Isabel would elude the risks of erotic ordeals, the surprises of pleasure, the uncertainties of the other's discourse. Once she had become a mother she would be able to remain a virgin. Deserting the child's father in order to live as a single woman (or else as an imaginary couple with her analyst?), alone with her daydreams, needing no one and threatened by none, she entered motherhood as one enters a convent. Isabel was getting ready to gaze upon herself complacently in that living being destined for death that her child was to be, like a painful shadow of herself that she would at last be able to care for and bury, whereas no one would be capable of doing it "properly" for herself. The depressive mother's selflessness is not without a modicum of paranoid smugness.

When little Alice was born, Isabel felt as if she were bombarded by reality. The baby's neonatal jaundice and the first childhood illnesses that were inordinately serious threatened to change the death fantasy into an unbearable fact. Undoubtedly with the help of analysis, Isabel was not swallowed up by postpartum blues. Her depressive inclination was transformed into a fierce struggle to save the life of her daughter, whose development she hence- forth followed with great tenderness, albeit with the temptation to be overprotective.

Smug Abnegation

The initial melancholia was devoured by "Alice's prob- lems." Nevertheless, without disappearing, it acquired an- other aspect. It was transformed into total ascendancy, both oral and anal, over the girl's body, and her develop- ment was thus set back. Feeding Alice, controlling her meals, weighing her, weighing her again, supplementing the diet prescribed by some doctor or other by drawing from the advice found in such-and-such a book . . . Checking Alice's stools until she started school and after- ward, her constipations, her diarrheas, giving her enemas . . . Watching over her sleep—what is the normal length of sleep for a two-year-old? And a three-year-old? A four- year-old? And is not this babble rather an abnormal cry? The obsessive anxiety of the "typical" worried mother was multiplied by Isabel. As an unwed mother wasn't she responsible for everything? Wasn't she all that this "poor Alice" had in the world? Her mother, father, aunt, grand- father, grandmother? The grandparents, having deemed that this birth was not very orthodox, had stood aloof from the "virgin mother" and unwittingly given Isabel an additional excuse in her need to be all-powerful.

A depressive person's pride is immeasurable, and this is something one must take into account. Isabel is ready to take on any labor, worry, duty, trouble, even defect (if someone chanced to find any), rather than to admit her suffering. Alice has become a new speech inhibitor in the already not-so-talkative world of her mother. For the sake of the daughter's well-being, the mother had to "hold out": facing up to things, not appearing to be an inadequate person or a loser.

How long can this last, this delightful, smug imprisonment by the sadness of being alone, the sorrow *of not being?* With some women, it lasts until the child no longer needs her, has sufficiently grown up, and leaves her. They then find themselves abandoned once more, downcast, this time without being able to resort to another childbirth. Pregnancy and motherhood turned out to be a parenthesis within the depression, a new negation of that impossible loss.

Isabel, for her part, did not wait that long. She had the verbal and erotic recourse of transference. She could cry and break down before her analyst, trying to come to life again not beyond but this time *through* the mourning of the analysis, ready to hear a wounded speech. Once solitude has been named, we are less alone if words succeed in infiltrating the spasm of tears—provided they can find an addressee for an overflow of sorrow that had up to then shied away from words.

Aroused Father and Ideal Father

Isabel's dreams and fantasies might suggest that she had been the victim of a precocious seduction on the part of her father or some other adult among their acquaintances. No precise memory clearly surfaced from Isabel's discourse, either to confirm or deny it; the hypothesis was suggested by an oneiric, repetitive sequence where Isabel is alone in a closed room with an older man who is irrationally pushing her against the wall; or one in her father's office where again the two of them are alone, with her shaking less from fear than from emotion, blushing and perspiring, such an incomprehensible state filling her with shame. Was this true seduction or a desire to be seduced? Isabel's father appears to have been an uncommon character. A poor farmer who became the manager of a firm, he aroused the admiration of his employees, friends, and children, and particularly that of Isabel. And yet this man, aiming at success, had frightful, sudden changes of mood, especially under the influence of alcohol, which he indulged in more and more as he grew older. Isabel's mother would conceal that emotional instability; at the same time she compensated for it and held it in contempt. As far as the child was concerned, such contempt meant that mother disapproved of the father's sexuality, his excessive fire, his lack of composure. A father, in short, who was both desired and condemned. He might have been, to a certain extent, an identifying solution for his daughter, a support in her rivalry with and disappointment in the mother, the genitor who was always distracted by another baby. But beyond an intellectual and social attraction, that father was also a disappointing figure. "From my point of view he was immediately demystified, I could not believe in him as outsiders did, he was my mother's creation, her biggest baby. . . ."

Her father's symbolic existence doubtless helped Isabel in erecting her professional armor, but the erotic man, the imaginary father, the loving, giving, and gratifying one had become unbelievable. He displayed emotions, passions, and pleasures from the angle of crisis and anger—fascinating, but how dangerous and destructive. The link between pleasure and symbolic dignity that is insured by an imaginary father, as he leads his child from primary to secondary identification, no longer existed for Isabel.

She then had a choice between a paroxysmal sexual life and . . . "virginity"—between perversion and abnegation. The experience of the former had filled her years as a teenager and a young woman. Such excesses, or "overflows" as she called them, punctuated the end of her depressive episodes. "It was as if I were drunk, and afterwards I ended up vacuous. Perhaps I am like my father. But his constant fluctuation between high and low—that, I don't want. I prefer serenity, stability, sacrifice if you wish. The sacrifice for my daughter, however, is it really a sacrifice? It is a moderate joy, a permanent joy. . . . Well, a well-tempered joy, like the clavier."

Isabel gave a child to her ideal father—not the father who displayed a drunken body but the father with the absent body, therefore a dignified father, a master, a leader. The masculine body, the aroused and drunken body, that is the mother's object: Isabel leaves it to that deserting rival, for in the competition with her mother's presumed perversion, the daughter at once admitted she was a minor, a loser. As for her, she chose the prestigious name, and it is precisely as a celibate, unwed mother that she will succeed in preserving it in its untouchable perfection, dissociating it from the "overly" aroused masculine body, which is manipulated by the other woman.

If it be true that such a paternity largely conditions Isabel's depression, forcing her back toward the mother from whom she could not be separated without risks (of stimulation, of imbalance), it is also true that, through his ideal aspect, his symbolic success, such a father also provides his daughter with a few means, admittedly ambiguous, to pull herself through. In becoming the mother *and* the father Isabel has finally reached an absolute. But does the ideal father exist anywhere other than in the abnegation of his own daughter as celibate, unwed mother?

When all is said and done, however, and even if it is only with one child, Isabel manages much better than her mother. For is it not true that if she does not produce many children, she does everything for a single one? Nevertheless, that overtaking the mother in the imagination is only a temporary solution to depression. Mourning still remains impossible under the guise of a masochistic triumph. The real work remains to be done, through separation from the child and, finally, through separation from the analyst, so that a woman might try to face the void within the meaning that is produced and destroyed in all its connections and all its objects . . .

4

Beauty:
The Depressive's Other
Realm

Fulfilling the Beyond Here and Now

Naming suffering, exalting it, dissecting it into its smallest components—that is doubtless a way to curb mourning. To revel in it at times, but also to go beyond it, moving on to another form, not so scorching, more and more perfunctory . . . Nevertheless, art seems to point to a few devices that bypass complacency and, without simply turning mourning into mania, secure for the artist and the connoisseur a sublimatory hold over the lost Thing. First by means of prosody, the language beyond language that inserts into the sign the rhythm and alliterations of semiotic processes. Also by means of the polyvalence of sign and symbol, which unsettles naming and, by building up a plurality of connotations around the sign, affords the subject a chance to imagine the nonmeaning, or the true meaning, of the Thing. Finally by means of the psychic organization of forgiveness: identification of the speaker with a welcoming, kindly ideal, capable of removing the guilt from revenge, or humiliation from narcissistic wound, which underlies depressed people's despair.

Can the beautiful be sad? Is beauty inseparable from the ephemeral and hence from mourning? Or else is the beautiful object the one that tirelessly returns following destructions and wars in order to bear witness that there is survival after death, that immortality is possible?

Freud touches on those matters in a brief essay, "On Transience" (1915–1916), inspired by a discussion during a stroll with two melancholy friends, one of whom was a poet.[1] To the pessimist who depreciated the beautiful on the ground that its ephemeral fate led to a decrease in value Freud retorted, "On the contrary, an increase!" The sadness that the ephemeral gives rise to, however, seemed to him unfathomable. "To the psychologist, mourning is a great riddle. . . . But why is it that this detachment of the libido from its objects should be such a painful process is a mystery to us and we have not hitherto been able to frame any hypothesis to account for it."

Shortly afterwards, in *Mourning and Melancholia* (1917), he offered an explanation for melancholia, which, following the model of mourning, would be caused by the introjection of the lost object, both loved and hated, that I discussed earlier (see chapter 1). Here, however, in the essay "On Transience," by linking the themes of mourning, transience, and beauty, Freud suggested that sublimation might be the counterpoise of the loss, to which the libido so enigmatically fastens itself. Enigma of mourning or enigma of the beautiful? And what is their relationship?

Admittedly invisible until mourning for the object of love takes place, beauty nevertheless remains and, even more so, enthralls us. "Our high opinion of the riches of civilization has lost nothing from our discovery of their fragility." There might thus be something that is not affected by the universality of death: beauty?

Might the beautiful be the ideal object that never disappoints the libido? Or might the beautiful object appear as the absolute and indestructible restorer of the deserting object? That could be due to its having placed itself at once on a different level of the libidinal territory, so enigmatically clinging and disappointing, where the ambiguity of the "good" and "bad" object is displayed. In the place of death and so as not to die of the other's death, I bring forth—or at least I rate highly—an artifice, an ideal, a "beyond" that my psyche produces in order to take up a position outside itself—*ek-stasis*. How beautiful to be able to replace all perishable psychic values.

Since then, however, analysts have asked themselves an additional question: by means of what psychic process, through what alteration in signs and materials, does beauty succeed in making its way through the drama that is being played out between the *loss* and the *mastery* over the self's loss/devalorization/execution?

Sublimation's dynamics, by summoning up primary processes and idealization, weaves a *hypersign* around and with the depressive void. This is *allegory,* as lavishness of that which *no longer is,* but which regains for myself a higher meaning because I am able to remake nothingness, better than it was and within an unchanging harmony, here and now and forever, for the sake of someone else. Artifice, as sublime meaning for and on behalf of the underlying, implicit nonbeing, replaces the ephemeral. Beauty is consubstantial with it. Like feminine finery concealing stubborn depressions, beauty emerges as the admirable face of loss, transforming it in order to make it live.

A denial of loss? It can be so; such beauty is then perishable and vanishes into death, unable to check the artist's suicide, or else fading away from memory at the very moment of its appearance. But not only that.

When we have been able to go through our melancholia to the point of becoming interested in the life of signs, beauty may also grab hold of us to bear witness for someone who grandly discovered the royal way through which humanity transcends the grief of being apart: the way of speech given to suffering, including screams, music, silence, and laughter. The grandiose would even be the impossible dream, the depressive's other world, fulfilled here below. Outside the depressive space, is the grandiose anything but a game?

Sublimation alone withstands death. The beautiful object that can bewitch us into its world seems to us more worthy of adoption than any loved or hated cause for wound or sorrow. Depression recognizes this and agrees to live within and for that object, but such adoption of the sublime is no longer libidinal. It is already detached, dissociated, it has already integrated the traces of death, which is signified as lack of concern, absentmindedness, carelessness. Beauty is an artifice; it is imaginary.

Might the Imaginary Be Allegorical?

There is a specific economy of imaginary discourses as they have been produced within Western tradition (heir to Greek and Roman antiquity, Judaism, and Christianity); they are constituently very close to depression and at the same time show a necessary shift from depression to possible meaning. Like a tense link between Thing and Meaning, the unnameable and the proliferation of signs, the silent affect and the ideality that designates and goes beyond it, the *imaginary* is neither the objective description that will reach its highest point in science nor theological idealism that will be satisfied with reaching the symbolic uniqueness of a beyond. The experience of *nameable melancholia* opens up the space of a necessarily heterogeneous subjectivity, torn between the two co-necessary and co-present centers of opacity and ideal. The opacity of things, like that of the body untenanted by meaning—a depressed body, bent on suicide—is conveyed to the work's meaning, which asserts itself as at the same time absolute and corrupt, untenable, impossible, to be done all over again. A subtle alchemy of signs then compels recognition—musicalization of signifiers, polyphony of lexemes, dislocation of lexical, syntactic, and narrative units—and this is *immediately* experienced as a psychic transformation of the speaking being between the two limits of nonmeaning and meaning, Satan and God, Fall and Resurrection.

Nonetheless, maintaining those two extreme thematics results in a breathtaking orchestration in the imaginary economy. While necessary to the latter, they fade away during times of value crisis that affect the very foundations of civilization, leaving as the only place where melancholia can unfurl nothing save the signifier's ability to be filled with meaning as well as to be reified into nothing (see chapters 5 and 8).

Although intrinsic to the dichotomous categories of Western metaphysics (nature/culture, body/spirit, lowly/elevated, space/time, quantity/quality . . .) the imaginary world as signified sadness but also, the other way around, as nostalgic signifying jubilation over a fundamental, nutritive nonmeaning is nevertheless the very universe of the *possible*. Possibility of evil as perversion and of death as ultimate non-meaning. Furthermore, and on account of the meaning maintained during the fading away period, there is the infinite possibility of ambivalent, polyvalent resurrections.

According to Walter Benjamin, it is *allegory,* which was powerfully handled in Baroque art, particularly in the *Trauerspiel* (literally, mourning play, playing with mourning; actually, it refers to the tragic drama of the Baroque period), that best achieves melancholy tension.[3]

By shifting back and forth from the *disowned meaning,*

still present just the same, of the remnants of antiquity for instance (thus, *Venus,* or the "royal crown") to the *literal meaning* that the Christian spiritualist context attributes to all things, allegory is a tenseness of meanings between their depression/depreciation and their signifying exaltation (*Venus* becomes the allegory of Christian love). It endows the lost signifier with a signifying pleasure, a resurrectional jubilation even to the stone and corpse, by asserting itself as coextensive with the subjective experience of a named melancholia—of melancholy jouissance.

Nevertheless, allegorisis (the genesis of allegory)—through its fate in Calderon, Shakespeare, and down to Goethe and Hölderlin, through its antithetical essence, through its potential for ambiguity, and through the unsettled meaning it sets down beyond its aim to give a signified to silence and to mute things (to the ancient or natural *daimons*)—reveals that allegory's simple figure is perhaps a regional fixation, in time and space, of a broader dynamics—the dynamics of imagination. A temporary fetish, allegory does no more than clarify a number of historical and ideological components of the Baroque imagination. Beyond its concrete moorings, however, this rhetorical figure discovers what Western imagination basically owes to loss (to mourning) and its reversal into a threatened, fragile, spoiled enthusiasm (see chapters 6 and 7). Whether it reappears as such or vanishes from the imagination, allegory is inscribed in the very logic of the imagination, which its didactic oversimplicty has the privilege of revealing ponderously. Indeed, we sense the imaginary experience not as theological symbolism or secular commitment but as flaring-up of dead meaning with a surplus of meaning, in which the speaking subject first discovers the shelter of an ideal but above all the opportunity to play it again in illusions and disillusion . . .

The imaginative capability of Western man, which is fulfilled within Christianity, is the ability to transfer meaning to the very place where it was lost in death and/or nonmeaning. This is a survival of idealization—the imaginary constitutes a miracle, but it is at the same time its shattering: a self-illusion, nothing but dreams and words, words, words . . . It affirms the almightiness of temporary subjectivity—the one that knows enough to speak until death comes.

5

Holbein's Dead Christ

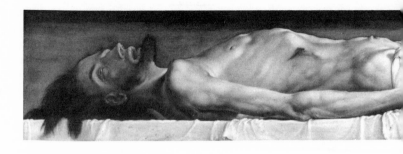

Hans Holbein the Younger, *The Body of the Dead Christ in the Tomb.*
Oeffentliche Kunstsammlung Basel, Kunstmuseum.

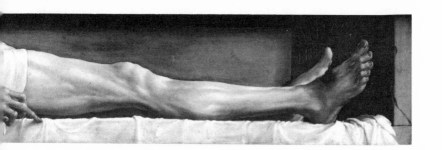

"Some May Lose Their Faith"

In 1522 (the underlying coat bears the date 1521) Hans
Holbein the Younger (1497–1543) painted a disturbing
picture, *The Body of the Dead Christ in the Tomb,* which
may be seen at the Basel museum and apparently made a
tremendous impression on Dostoyevsky. Prince Myshkin
attempted to speak of it, but to no avail, at the very outset
of *The Idiot;* only through a new polyphonic twist of the
plot did he see a reproduction of it at Rogozhin's house
and, "struck by a sudden thought," he exclaimed: "[look-
ing] At that picture! Why, some people may *lose their faith*
by looking at that picture!"[1] A little later Ippolit, a periph-
eral character who nevertheless seems in many respects to
be the narrator's and Myshkin's double, gave a striking
account of it:

> The picture depicted Christ, who has just been taken
> from the cross. I believe that painters are usually in the
> habit of portraying Christ, whether on the cross or
> taken down from it, as still retaining a shade of extraor-
> dinary beauty on his face, a beauty they strive to pre-
> serve even in his moments of greatest agony. In Rogo-

zhin's picture there was no trace of beauty. It was a faithful representation of the dead body of a man who had undergone unbearable torments before the crucifixion, been wounded, tortured, beaten by the guards, beaten by the people, when he carried the cross and fell under its weight, and, at last, suffered the agony of crucifixion, which lasted for six hours (according to my calculation, at least). Truly, this was the face of a man who had only *just* been taken from the cross—that is, still retaining a great deal of warmth and life; rigor mortis had not yet set in, so that there is still a look of suffering on the face of the dead man, as though he were still feeling it (that has been well caught by the artist); on the other hand, the face has not been spared in the least; it is nature itself, and, indeed, any man's corpse would look like that after such suffering.

I know that the Christian Church laid it down in the first few centuries of its existence that Christ really did suffer and that the Passion was not symbolical. His body on the cross was therefore fully and entirely subject to the laws of nature. In the picture the face is terribly smashed with blows, tumefied, covered with terrible, swollen, and bloodstained bruises, the eyes open and squinting; the large, open whites of the eyes have a sort of dead and glassy glint. But, strange to say, as one looks at the dead body of this tortured man, one cannot help asking oneself the peculiar, arresting question: if such a corpse (and it must have been just like that) was seen by all His disciples, by His future chief apostles, by the women who followed Him and stood by the cross, by all who believed in Him and worshipped Him, then how could they possibly have believed, confronted with such a sight, that this martyr would rise again? Here one cannot help being struck by

the idea that if death is so horrible and if the laws of
nature are so powerful, then how can they be overcome? How can they be overcome when even He did
not conquer them, He who overcame nature during His
lifetime and whom nature obeyed, who said *Talitha
cumi!* and the little girl arose, who cried, *Lazarus come
forth!* and the dead man came forth? Looking at that
picture, you get the impression of nature as some enormous, implacable, and dumb beast, or, to put it more
correctly, much more correctly, though it may seem
strange, as some huge engine of the latest design, *which
has senselessly seized, cut to pieces, and swallowed up—
impassively and unfeelingly—a great and priceless Being,* a
Being worth the whole of nature and all its laws, worth
the entire earth, which was perhaps created solely for
the coming of that Being!

The picture seems to give expression to the idea of a
dark, insolent, and senseless eternal power, to which
everything is subordinated, and which controls you in
spite of yourself. The people surrounding the dead man,
none of whom is shown in the picture, must have been
overwhelmed by a feeling of terrible anguish and dis-
may on that evening *which had shattered all their hopes
and almost all their beliefs in one fell blow.* They must have
parted in a state of the most dreadful terror, though
each of them carried away within him him a mighty
thought which would never be wrested from him. And
if, on the eve of the crucifixion, the Master could have
seen what He would look like when taken from the
cross, would he have mounted the cross and died as he
did? This question, too, you can't help asking yourself
as you look at the picture.[2]

The Man of Sorrows

Holbein's painting represents a corpse stretched out by itself on a slab covered with a cloth that is scarcely draped.[3] Life size, the painted corpse is seen from the side, its head slightly turned toward the viewer, the hair spread out on the sheet. The right arm is in full view, resting alongside the emaciated, tortured body, and the hand protrudes slightly from the slab. The rounded chest suggests a triangle within the very low, elongated rectangle of the recess that constitutes the painting's frame. The chest bears the bloody mark of a spear, and the hand shows the stigmata of the crucifixion, which stiffen the outstretched middle finger. Imprints of nails mark Christ's feet. The martyr's face bears the expression of a hopeless grief; the empty stare, the sharp-lined profile, the dull blue-green complexion are those of a man who is truly dead, of Christ forsaken by the Father ("My God, my God, why have you deserted me?") and without the promise of Resurrection.

The unadorned representation of human death, the well-nigh anatomical stripping of the corpse convey to viewers an unbearable anguish before the death of God, here blended with our own, since there is not the slightest suggestion of transcendency. What is more, Hans Holbein has given up all architectural or compositional fancy. The tombstone weighs down on the upper portion of the painting, which is merely twelve inches high, and intensifies the feeling of permanent death: this corpse shall never rise again.[4] The very pall, limited to a minimum of folds, emphasizes, through that economy of motion, the feeling of stiffness and stone-felt cold.

The viewer's gaze penetrates this closed-in coffin from

below and, following the painting from left to right, stops at the stone set against the corpse's feet, sloping at a wide angle toward the spectators.

What was the purpose of a painting with such peculiar dimensions? Does the *Dead Christ* belong to the altar that Holbein did for Hans Oberried in 1520–1521 in which the two outside wings depicted the Passion and the center was saved for the Nativity and the Adoration?[5] There is nothing to support such a hypothesis, which, however, is not implausible when one takes into account a few features it shares with the outside wings of the altar that was partially destroyed during iconoclastic outbursts in Basel.

Among the various interpretations given by critics, one stands out and seems today the most plausible one. The painting would have been done for a predella that remained independent and was to occupy a raised position with respect to visitors filing down frontally, from the side and the left (for instance, from the church's central nave toward the southern aisle). In the Upper Rhine region there are churches that contain funerary recesses where *sculptured* Christly bodies are displayed. Might Holbein's work be a painterly transposition of such recumbent statues? According to one hypothesis, this *Dead Christ* would have been the covering for a sacred tomb open only on Good Friday and closed the rest of the year. Finally, relying on X-rays of the painting, Fridtjof Zschokke has shown that the *Dead Christ* was initially located in a recess shaped in a semicircle, like the section of a tube. That location corresponds to the date inscribed next to the right foot and the signature: *H. H. DXXI*. One year later Holbein substituted the arched recess with a rectangular one and signed above the feet: *MDXXII H. H.*[6]

The biographical and professional context within which *The Dead Christ in the Tomb* was situated is also worth recalling. Holbein painted a series of Madonnas (between 1520 and 1522), among which is found the very fine *Enthroned Virgin and Child* known as the "Solothurn Madonna." In 1521 his first son, Philip, was born. This is also the time of a strong friendship with Erasmus, whose portrait Holbein did in 1523.

On the one hand, we have the birth of a child—and the threat of death weighing on him but especially on the painter as a father whom the coming generation would one day displace. On the other, there is the friendship with Erasmus and renunciation not only of fanaticism but also, with some humanists, of faith itself. A small diptych of the same period, Gothic in style and painted mostly in shades of brown, portrays *Christ as the Man of Sorrows* and the *Virgin as the Mater Dolorosa* (Basel, 1519–1520). The body of the man of sorrows, strangely athletic, brawny, and tensed, is shown seated under a colonnade; the right hand, curled up before the sexual organ, seems spasmic; the head alone, wearing a crown of thorns, together with the aching face with gaping mouth, expresses a morbid suffering beyond vague eroticism. From what passion did such a pain arise? Would the man-God be distressed, that is, haunted by death, *because* he is sexual, prey to sexual passion?

A Composition in Loneliness

Italian iconography embellishes, or at least ennobles, Christ's face during the Passion but especially surrounds it with figures that are immersed in grief as well as in the certainty of the Resurrection, as if to suggest the attitude we should ourselves adopt facing the Passion. Holbein, on the contrary, leaves the corpse strangely alone. It is perhaps that isolation—*an act of composition*—that endows the painting with its major melancholy burden, more so than delineation and coloring. To be sure, Christ's suffering is expressed through three components inherent in lines and colors: the head bent backwards, the contortion of the right hand bearing the stigmata, the position of the feet— the whole being bonded by means of a dark palette of grays, greens, and browns. Nevertheless, such realism, harrowing on account of its very parsimony, is emphasized to the utmost through the painting's composition and location: a body stretched out alone, situated above the viewers, and separated from them.

Cut off from us by its base but without any prospect toward heaven, for the ceiling in the recess comes down low, Holbein's *Dead Christ* is inaccessible, distant, but without a beyond. It is a way of looking at mankind from afar, even in death—just as Erasmus saw folly from a distance. It is a vision that opens out not on glory but on endurance. Another, a new morality resides in this painting.

Christ's dereliction is here at its worst: forsaken by the Father, he is apart from all of us. Unless Holbein, whose mind, pungent as it was, does not appear to have lead him across the threshold of atheism, wanted to include us, humans, foreigners, spectators that we are, forthrightly in this crucial moment of Christ's life. With no intermediary, suggestion, or indoctrination, whether pictorial or theological, other than our ability to imagine death, we are led to collapse in the horror of the caesura constituted by death or to dream of an invisible beyond. Does Holbein forsake us, as Christ, for an instant, had imagined himself forsaken? Or does he, on the contrary, invite us to change the Christly tomb into a living tomb, to participate in the painted death and thus include it in our own life, in order to live with it and make it live? For if the living body, in opposition to the rigid corpse, is a dancing body, doesn't our life, through identification with death, become a "danse macabre," in keeping with Holbein's other well-known depiction?

This enclosed recess, this well-isolated coffin simultaneously rejects us and invites us. Indeed, the corpse fills the entire field of the painting, without any labored reference to the Passion. Our gaze follows the slightest physical detail, it is, as it were, nailed, crucified, and is riveted to the hand placed at the center of the composition. Should it attempt to flee it quickly stops, locked in at the distressed face or the feet propped against the black stone. And yet such walling in allows two prospects.

On the one hand, there is the insertion of date and signature, *MDXXII H. H.,* at Christ's feet. Placing the painter's name, to which was often added that of the donor, in that position was common at the time. It is nevertheless possible that in abiding by that code Holbein inserted himself into the drama of the Dead body. A sign of humility: the artist throwing himself at God's feet? or a sign of equality? The painter's name is not lower than Christ's body—they are both at the same level, jammed into the recess, united in man's death, in death as the essential sign of humanity, of which the only surviving evidence is the ephemeral creation of a picture drawn here and now in 1521 and 1522!

We have, on the other hand, this hair and this hand that extend beyond the base as if they might slide over toward us, as if the frame could not hold back the corpse. The frame, precisely, dates from the end of the sixteenth century and includes a narrow edging bearing the inscription *Jesus Nazarenus Rex Judaeorum,* which encroaches upon the painting. The edging, which seems nonetheless always to have been part of Holbein's painting, includes, between the words of the inscription, five angels bearing the instruments of the martyrdom: the shaft, the crown of thorns, the scourge, the flogging column, the cross. Integrated afterwards in that symbolic framework, Holbein's painting recovers the evangelical meaning that it did not insistently contain in itself, and which probably legitimized it in the eyes of its purchasers.

Even if Holbein's painting had originally been conceived as a predella for an altarpiece, it remained alone; no other panel was added to it. Such isolation, as splendid as it is gloomy, avoided Christian symbolism as much as the surfeit of German Gothic style, which would combine painting and sculpture but also add wings to altarpieces, aiming for syncretism and the imparting of motion to figures. In the face of that tradition, which directly preceded him, Holbein isolated, pruned, condensed, reduced.

Holbein's originality lies then in a vision of Christly death devoid of pathos and Intimist on account of its very banality. Humanization thus reached its highest point: the point at which glory is obliterated by means of graphics. When the dismal brushes against the nondescript, the most disturbing sign is the most ordinary one. Contrasting with Gothic enthusiasm, humanism and parsimony were the inverted products of melancholia.

And yet such originality is affiliated with the Christian iconographic tradition that came out of Byzantium (see chapter 7).[7] Many depictions of the dead Christ were spread through central Europe, around 1500, under the influence of Dominican mystique, whose major representatives in Germany were Meister Eckart (c. 1260–1328), Johannes Tauler (c. 1300–1361), and especially Heinrich von Berg, who called himself Heinrich Suso (c. 1295–1366).[8]

Grünewald and Mantegna

Holbein's vision should also be confronted with that of Mathias Grünewald in his dead Christ of the *Isenheim Altarpiece* (1512–1515), which was removed to Colmar in 1794. The central panel representing the crucifixion shows Christ bearing the paroxysmal marks of martyrdom (the crown of thorns, the cross, the countless wounds), including even putrefaction of the flesh. Gothic expressionism here reached a peak in the exhibition of pain. Grünewald's Christ, however, is not reduced to isolation as was Holbein's. The human realm to which he belonged is represented by the Virgin who falls into the arms of John the Evangelist, by Mary Magdalene and John the Baptist who introduce compassion into the picture.[9]

Now the predella of the same Colmar altarpiece painted by Grünewald displays a Christ somewhat different from the one in the *Crucifixion*. It is an *Entombment* or *Lamentation*. Horizontal lines take the place of the *Crucifixion*'s verticalness, and the corpse appears more elegiac than tragical—it is a heavy, soothed body, dismal in its calm. Holbein might simply have inverted the body of Grünewald's dying Christ in placing the feet toward the right and erasing the likeness of the three mourners (Magdalene, the Virgin, and John). More sober than the *Crucifixion*, the *Lamentation* already suggests the possibility of Gothic art's transition toward Holbein. Certainly, however, Holbein goes much further than the temporary quieting down shown by the Colmar master. Doing something more poignant than Grünewald, with bare realism as his only means, all the more so amounts to a struggle against the father-painter, since it seems that Grünewald was very much inspired by Holbein the Elder, who had settled in

Isenheim where he died in 1526.[10] Holbein thoroughly quiets the Gothic upheaval, and while his art comes close to the emerging mannerism with which he is contemporary, it gives evidence of a classicism that avoids infatuation with an unballasted empty form. He forces upon the picture the weight of human grief.

Finally, Mantegna's famous *Cristo in scruto* (c. 1480, at the Brera Museum in Milan) may be considered the precursor of the quasi-anatomical vision of the dead Christ. With the soles of the feet turned toward the viewers the foreshortened perspective of the corpse compels recognition with a brutality that verges on the obscene. Nevertheless, the two women who appear in the top left-hand corner of Mantegna's painting introduce the grief and compassion that Holbein precisely puts aside by banishing them from sight or else creating them with no other mediator than the invisible appeal to our all-too-human identification with the dead Son. As if Holbein had integrated the Dominican-inspired Gothic grief, filtered through Suso's sentimentalism, such as Grünewald's expressionism displays it, freeing it of its excessiveness as well as of the divine presence that presses down with all its guilt-provoking, expiatory weight upon Grünewald's imagination. As if again Holbein had picked up the anatomical and pacifying lesson taught by Mantegna and Italian Catholicism, less sensitive to man's sin than to forgiving him and influenced more by the bucolic, embellishing ecstasy of the Franciscans than by Dominican dolorousness. And yet, always heedful of the Gothic spirit, Holbein maintains grief while humanizing it, without following the Italian path of negating pain and glorifying the arrogance of the flesh or the beauty of the beyond. Holbein belongs in another dimension: he makes commonplace the Passion of the crucified Christ in order to make it more accessible to

us. Such a humanizing gesture, which is not without a
modicum of *irony* toward transcendence, suggests a tremendous amount of mercy with respect to *our* death.
According to legend, the corpse of a Jew recovered from
the Rhine could have provided Holbein with a model . . .

The same half-ghoulish, half-ironical verve reached its
climax in what must now be termed pure grotesque when,
in 1524, Holbein was staying in the south of France and,
in Lyons, he was commissioned by the publishers Melchior and Gaspard Treschel to execute a *Danse Macabre* in
a series of woodcuts.[11] This dance of Death, drawn by
Holbein and cut by Hans Lützelburger, was published in
Lyons in 1538. It was reproduced and circulated throughout Europe, presenting renascent mankind with a picture
of itself that was both devastating and grotesque, taking
up François Villon's tone by means of images. From the
newborn and the lower classes to popes, emperors, bishops, abbots, noblemen, young wife and husband—all the
human species is in the hands of death. Clasped in the
arms of Death, no one escapes its grip, a fatal one to be
sure, but here anguish conceals its own depressive force
and displays defiance through sarcasm or the grimace of a
mocking smile, lacking triumphancy, as if, in the knowledge of being done for, laughter was the only answer.

Death Facing the Renaissance

We easily imagine Renaissance man as Rabelais depicted
him: imposing, perhaps somewhat funny like Panurge,
but boldly launched on the pursuit of happiness and the
wisdom of the divine bottle. Holbein, on the other hand,
proposes another vision—that of man subject to death,
man embracing Death, absorbing it into his very being,
integrating it not as a condition for glory or a consequence

of a sinful nature but as the ultimate essence of his desacralized reality, which is the foundation of a new dignity. For that very reason the picture of Christly and human death with Holbein is in intimate partnership with *In Praise of Folly* (1511) by Desiderius Erasmus, whose friend, illustrator, and portrayer he became in 1523. Because he acknowledges his folly and looks death in the face— but perhaps also because he faces his mental risks, the risks of psychic death—man achieves a new dimension. Not necessarily that of atheism but definitely that of a disillusioned, serene, and dignified stance. Like a picture by Holbein.

The Protestant Affliction

Did the Reformation influence such a concept of death, and more specifically such an emphasis on Christ's death to the detriment of any allusion to the Redemption and Resurrection? Catholicism is well known for its tendency to stress the "beatific vision" in Christ's death without dwelling on the torments of the Passion, underscoring that Jesus had always had the knowledge of his own Resurrection (Psalms 22:29ff.). Calvin, on the other hand, insists on the *formidabilis abysis* into which Jesus had been thrust at the hour of his death, descending to the depths of sin and hell. Luther had already described himself personally as a melancholy being under the influence of Saturn and the devil. "I, Martin Luther, was born under the most unfavorable stars, probably under Saturn," he wrote in 1532. "Where there lives a melancholy person, the devil has drawn his bath. . . . I have learned from experience how one must behave during temptation. Whoever is besieged with sadness, despair, or any other deep affliction, whoever harbors a serpent in his conscience must first hold to the consolation of the divine Word, and then when eating and drinking he will seek the company and conversation of pious and Christian people. In this manner things will be better with him."[12]

As early as his ninety-five *Theses* Against Indulgences Martin Luther formulated a mystical call for suffering as a means of access to heaven. And if the idea of man's generation through grace is to be found next to that immersion into pain, the fact remains nevertheless that the intensity of one's faith is geared to one's ability for contrition. Thus: "As long as hatred of self abides (i.e., true inward penitence) the penalty of sin abides, viz., until we enter the kingdom of heaven" (thesis 4); "God never remits guilt to anyone without, at the same time, making him humbly submissive to the priest, His representative" (thesis 7); "A truly contrite sinner seeks out, and loves to pay, the penalties of his sins; whereas the very multitude of indulgences dulls men's consciences, and tends to make them hate the penalties" (thesis 40); "Christians should be exhorted to be zealous to follow Christ, their Head, through penalties, deaths, and hells" (thesis 94).

Lucas Cranach the Elder became the Protestants' official painter, while Dürer sent Luther a series of religious engravings. But a humanist such as Erasmus was wary at first about the Reformer. Afterwards he became more and more reserved about the radical changes proposed in *On the Babylonian Captivity of the Church of God,* particularly with respect to Luther's thesis according to which human will was slave to God and the devil. Erasmus agreed with the Occamistic position that free will constituted a means of access to salvation.[13] In all likelihood, Holbein must have felt closer to his friend Erasmus than to Luther.

Iconoclasm and Minimalism

Theologians of the Reformation such as Andreas Karlstadt, Ludwig Haetzer, Gabriel Zwilling, Huldreich Zwingli, and others, including Luther himself although in more ambiguous fashion, began waging a real war against images and all representational forms or objects other than words or sounds.[14]

Basel, a commercial city but also a flourishing religious one, was overrun by the Protestant iconoclasm of 1521–1523. Reacting against what they thought were the papacy's materialistic, paganistic excesses and abuses, the Wittenberg reformers sacked churches, pillaged and destroyed images and all material representations of faith. In 1525 the Peasants' War provided the occasion for renewed destruction of art works. A great "idolomachy" took place in Basel in 1529. Although not a devout Catholic, Holbein was distressed by it as an artist, one who had, besides, painted wonderful Virgins: *The Adoration of the Shepherds* and *The Adoration of the Magi* (the two wings of the *Oberried Altarpiece,* Freiburg-im-Breisgau, Münster, 1520–1521), the so-called "Solothurn Madonna" (1521), and later the *Meyer Madonna,* also known as the "Darmstadt Madonna," painted for burgomaster Meyer (1526–1530). Basel's iconoclastic climate caused the painter to flee: he left for England carrying a letter from Erasmus (probably in 1526) that introduced him to Thomas More and contained the well-known statement: "Here the arts are cold: he goes to England in order to scrape together a few angelots."[15]

It will be noted, however, that in both camps — reformers and humanists — a tendency arose to intensify the confrontation between man and suffering and death, giving evidence of the truth of and challenge to the shallow mercantilism of the official Church.

Nevertheless, even more so than his illustrious friend Erasmus and contrary to the martyr of Catholic faith that Thomas More became at the end of his life, Holbein probably experienced a true revolution, even an erosion, of belief. While maintaining appearances, such a curbing of faith within the strict dispassionateness of his profession seems to have led him to integrate, in his own particular way, various aspects of the religious and philosophical currents of his time—from scepticism to rejection of idolatry—and remodel, for his own use, by means of art, a new vision of mankind. The stamp of suffering (as in *Portrait of His Wife and His Two Elder Children,* 1528, Basel Museum, or the Amerbach diptych—*Christ as the Man of Sorrows,* and *The Virgin as the Mater Dolorosa*—of 1519–1520) and even more so the unimaginable and invisible landscape of death ("The Ambassadors," 1533, includes the anamorphosis of a tremendous cranium in the lower part of the picture) compelled Holbein's attention as the main ordeal of the new man and undoubtedly of the artist himself. Nothing seems desirable anymore, values collapse, you are morose? Well, that state can be made beautiful, one can give desirability to the very withdrawal of desire, and as a consequence what might have appeared an abdication or a deadly dejection will henceforth be perceived as harmonious dignity.

From a painterly standpoint, we are facing a major test. The problem is to give form and color to the nonrepresentable—conceived not as erotic luxuriance (as it appears in Italian art even and most particularly in the representation of Christ's Passion); rather, it is the nonrepresentable conceived of as the dissipation of means of representation on the threshold of their extinction in death. Holbein's chromatic and compositional asceticism renders such a competition between form and a death that is neither dodged nor embellished but set forth in its minimal visibility, in its extreme manifestations constituted by pain and melancholia.

In 1530, having returned from England to Basel in 1528, Holbein became converted to the Protestant church after asking, as recorded in the Christian Recruitment registers, for "a better explanation of the Holy Communion before he would go." His conversion, founded on "reason and information," as Fritz Saxl noted,[16] is exemplary of the ties he maintained with Lutherans. Some of his drawings display a clear choice in favor of a spirit of reformation within the Church but without joining the fanaticism of the Reformer himself. Thus, in *Christ as the Light of the World,* in the diptych on Leo X, the cover of the first Lutheran bible published in Basel, and the illustrations for Luther's Old Testament, Holbein was expressing a personal opinion rather than illustrating an encompassing dogma. In a woodcut depicting Luther, the Reformer appears as a *Hercules Germanicus,* but the artist actually represents his fear, his horror, and an *atrocitas* of fanaticism.[17] Erasmus' world appears to suit him more than Luther's. The famous portrait that Holbein did of Erasmus in 1523 settled for posterity the definitive image of the humanist; when we think of the author of *In Praise of Folly,* do we not always give him the features that Holbein the Younger imprinted on him? Closer yet to my purpose, the intimacy of both men with death should be kept in mind.

"Mors Ultima Linea Rerum"

Holbein's famous series, which I have already mentioned, the *Danse Macabre,* explored with exceptional variety the seemingly limited theme of an individual's encounter with death. But what diversity there is, what vastness of space within those scaled-down miniatures and topic! Holbein took up again the same theme on a dagger's sheath, inserting the deathly dancers in a concave, bounded space. Likewise for the *Alphabet with the Dance of Death,* where each letter is accompanied by a human figure grappling with Death. It is difficult not to link such an obsessive and soothed presence of Death in Holbein with the fact that his friend Erasmus' patron saint was the Roman god *Terminus* and that the motto on his medal bearing that god's likeness read, *Terminus Concedo Nulli* or *Concedo Nulli Terminus,* meaning, "I yield to none," and also, in the medal's circumference, "Contemplate the End of a Long Life" (in Greek) and "Death is the Ultimate Boundary of Things" (in Latin). *Mors ultima linea rerum* might indeed be the motto of the *Dead Christ* of Basel—if it were not the motto of Horace and Erasmus.[18]

The coldness, the restraint, and even the unsophisticated appearance of Holbein's art have often been emphasized.[19] It is true that the change in the painter's status, in his time, governed a change in style characterized by a loosening of bonds within an atelier, concern for one's own career, a kind of biographical erosion to the benefit of a nascent mannerism that favored affectation, plane surfaces, and slopes that he was nevertheless able to link to his feeling for space. Protestant iconoclasm also left its mark. Holbein disapproved of it, he even fled from it when he left Basel for England; but without, for that matter, giving in to any form of exaltation, in fact he absorbed the spirit of his time—a spirit of deprivation, of leveling, of subtle minimalism. It would not be accurate to reduce the trend of the period to a personal choice of melancholia, even if the latter shows through the demeanor of figures from variegated countries or social circles that he was fond of painting. Nevertheless, such personality and period features converge: they end up locating representation on the ultimate threshold of representability, grasped with the utmost exactness and the smallest amount of enthusiasm, on the verge of indifference . . . In fact, neither in art nor in friendship was Holbein a committed person. The disgrace of his friend Thomas More did not bother him, and he stayed with Henry VIII. Erasmus himself was shocked by such cynicism, which was perhaps only an aesthetic and psychological aloofness: the coldness and emotional paralysis of the melancholy person. In the addendum to a letter to Boniface Amerbach dated March 22, 1533, Erasmus complained about those, including Holbein, who imposed upon his patronage, took advantage of their hosts, and disappointed those to whom he had recommended them.[20]

Cynical or Aloof

Was Holbein, the enemy of iconoclasts, one who had escaped the destruction of images during the Protestant fury in Basel, an iconoclast of ideals? Had the distant, aloof, accomplished ironist become a sort of amoralist out of loathing for any kind of pressure? Was he a devotee of disenchanted non-pressure *[dé-pression]*, including the extinction of all artifice at the heart of a gloomily, scrupulously mannered artifice? Appreciated in the nineteenth century, disappointing in the eyes of twentieth-century artists, he shall perhaps come closer to us in the part ironic, part gloomy, part desperate, part cynical light of his *Dead Christ*. Living with death and smiling about it in order to represent it was perhaps not the way to blaze the trail for a humanistic ethic of Goodness, neither did it lead to martyrdom for the Protestant faith; rather, it heralded more clearly the technician's amoralism without consideration for the beyond, one who sought a form of beauty somewhere between derprivation and profit. Paradoxically, out of this arid spot, out of this desert whence all beauty should be missing, he compacted distress into a masterpiece of colors, forms, spaces . . .

Indeed, his minimalism maintained a powerful, expressive seriousness that one understands readily when one contrasts it with the stately but haughty sadness, one that is incommunicable and somewhat artificial, of the Jansenist *Dead Christ* by Philippe de Champaigne (at the Louvre).[21]

In short, was he neither a Catholic, nor a Protestant, nor a humanist? A friend of Erasmus and Thomas More, but subsequently very much at ease with Henry VIII, their fierce, bloodthirsty foe. Fleeing the Protestants of Basel but also accepting their praise when he returned from his first trip to England, and perhaps a convert to Protestantism. Willing to stay in Basel but leaving again for England to become the official painter of a tyrannical king who had put to death a number of his former friends, whose portraits he had carefully made. When one follows these events, about which Holbein has left no biographical commentary (in contrast with Dürer, for instance), when one scrutinizes the stern faces of his models, gloomy and straightforward, treated without any complaisance, one seems to detect the character and the aesthetic position of a disenchanted verist.

Can Disenchantment Be Beautiful?

At the heart of a disrupted Europe the quest for moral truth was accompanied by excesses on both sides, while the realistic taste of a class of merchants, artisans, and navigators promoted the rule of strict discipline, but one already corruptible by gold. At such a world of simple and fragile truths, the artist refused to cast an embellishing gaze. If he embellished the setting or the clothing, he banished the illusion of having grasped the personality. A new idea was born in Europe, a paradoxical painterly idea —the idea that truth is severe, sometimes sad, often melancholy. Can such a truth also constitute beauty? Holbein's wager, beyond melancholia, is to answer, yes it can.

Disenchantment transformed into beauty is particularly perceptible in feminine portraits. The somewhat despondent serenity of the "Solothurn Madonna" whose prototype was the painter's wife was followed by the clearly distressed and downcast representation of the wife in the *Portrait of His Wife and His Two Elder Children* (Basel, 1528). The portraits of women done in England do not depart from the assumption of deprivation to the point of desolation. Certainly, the kingdom's tragic history under Henry VIII lends itself to it, but while the people simultaneously feared and adored their king, Holbein retained a gloomy vision of his time. Such indeed is the series of wives in which the delicacy of the features and the strength of character vary but all maintain an identical, somewhat frightened or doleful stiffness; see, for instance, the *Portrait of Queen Jane Seymour,* the *Portrait of Anne of Cleves,* the *Portrait of a Lady* [once thought to be Catherine Howard], as well as the *Portrait of Edward, Prince of Wales* (1539), whose lowered eyelids suffuse with held-back sorrow the swollen cheeks of a child's innocence. Alone, perhaps the slight mischievousness—or is there more irony than pleasure here?—of *Venus and Cupid* (Basel, 1526) and *Laïs of Corinth* (Basel, 1526), whose model may have been the painter's common-law wife, are free from such sternness, without for that matter leading Holbein's brush into the realm of jolly, carefree sensuality. Among the portraits of men, the gentleness of mind in the *Portrait of Erasmus of Rotterdam,* or exceptionally the elegance of aristocratic, thoroughly intellectual handsomeness in *Portrait of Bonifacius Amerbach* (Basel, 1519), the sensuality in *Portrait of Benedict von Hertenstein* (New York, Metropolitan Museum of Art, 1517) interrupt the continuous vision of a mankind always already entombed. You do not behold death? Try harder, it can be found in the lines of the drawing, in the composition, it is transformed into the volume of objects, faces, bodies; as with the anamorphosis of a skull at the feet of "The Ambassadors" *[Double Portrait of Jean de Dinteville and Georges de Selve]* (London, 1533).[22]

An Expenditure of Colors and Laid-Out Forms

It is not my point to maintain that Holbein was afflicted with melancholia or that he painted melancholy people. More profoundly, it would seem, on the basis of his oeuvre (including his themes and painterly technique), that a *melancholy moment* (an actual or imaginary loss of meaning, an actual or imaginary despair, an actual or imaginary razing of symbolic values, including the value of life) summoned up his aesthetic activity, which overcame the melancholy latency while keeping its trace. One has imagined for the young Holbein a secret and intense erotic activity, on the grounds of Magdalena Offenburg's having been the model for his Basel *Venus* (done earlier than 1526) and his *Laïs of Corinth,* and of the two illegitimate children he left in London. Charles Patin was the first to emphasize Holbein's dissipated life in his edition of Erasmus' *In Praise of*

Folly (Basel, 1676). Rudolf and Margot Wittkower endorsed that interpretation and made a spendthrift of him: he would have squandered the considerable sums he was assumed to have received at the court of Henry VIII buying wild, opulent clothing, so much that he left only a paltry legacy to his heirs . . .[23] There is no serious evidence either to prove or to disprove such biographical assumptions, except for the legend of Magdalena Offenburg's own dissipated life. The Wittkowers, moreover, insist on ignoring the painter's work and consider as unimportant that his pictures do not in any way reflect the erotic and financial extravagance they ascribe to him. From my point of view, that personality trait—assuming it is confirmed—in no way invalidates the depressive center the work reflects and overcomes. The economy of depression is supported by an omnipotent object, a monopolizing Thing rather than the focus of metonymical desire, which "might account for" the tendency to protect oneself from it through, *among other means,* a splurge of sensations, satisfactions, passions, one as elated as it is aggressive, as intoxicating as it is indifferent. It will be noted, nevertheless, that the common feature of those outlays is a *detachment*—getting rid ot it, going elsewhere, abroad, toward others . . . The possibility of unfolding primary processes, spontaneously and under control, artfully, appears, however, as the most efficacious way of overcoming the latent loss. In other words, the controlled and mastered "expenditure" of colors, sounds, and words is imperative for the artist-subject, as an essential recourse, similar to "Bohemian life," "criminality," or "dissoluteness" alternating with "miserliness," which one observes in the behavior of such skylarking artists. Hence, very much like personal behavior, artistic *style* imposes itself as a means of countervailing the loss of other and of meaning: a means more powerful than any other because more autonomous (no matter who his patron is, isn't the artist master of his work?) but, in fact and fundamentally, analogous with or complementary to behavior, for it fills the same psychic need to confront separation, emptiness, death. Isn't the artist's life considered, by himself to start with, to be a work of art?

The Death of Christ

A depressive moment: everything is dying, God is dying, I am dying.

But how is it possible for God to die? Let us briefly return to the evangelical meaning of Christ's death. Theological, hermetic, and doctrinal accounts of the "mystery of redemption" are numerous, complex, and contradictory. While the analyst cannot accept them, he or she might try, by examining them, to discover the meaning of the text as it unfolds within his or her hearing.

There are words of Christ that foretell his violent death without referring to salvation; others, however, seem at once to be pointing to, hence serving, the Resurrection.[24]

"Serving," which in Luke's context refers to "serving at the table," shifts to "giving his life," a life that is a "ransom" *(lytron)* in Mark's gospel.[25] Such a semantic shift clearly sheds light on the status of the Christly "sacrifice." He who provides food is the one who sacrifices himself and disappears so that others might live. His death is neither murder nor evacuation but a life-giving discontinuity, closer to nutrition than to the simple destruction of value or the abandonment of a fallen object. A change in the conception of sacrifice obviously takes place within those texts, one that claims to establish a link between men and God through the mediation of a donor. While it is true that giving implies deprivation on the part of the one who gives, who gives of *himself,* there is greater stress placed on the *bond,* on assimilation ("serving at the table"), and on the reconciliatory benefits of that process.

Indeed, the only rite that Christ handed down to his disciples and faithful on the basis of the last supper is the oral one of the Eucharist. Through it, sacrifice (and concomitantly death and melancholia) is *aufgehoben*—destroyed and superseded.[26] A number of commentators question René Girard's thesis, which postulates the abolition of sacrifice by Christ and in Christian thought, thus also bringing to an end the very notion of the sacred.[27]

The significance one can extract from the word "expiate" is in keeping with such a supersession: *expiare* in Latin, *hilaskomai* in Greek, *kipper* in Hebrew, which imply more of a reconciliation ("to be favorably disposed toward someone, to let God be reconciled with oneself") than the fact of "undergoing punishment." It is indeed possible to trace the meaning of "to reconcile" to the Greek *allasso* ("to make different," "to change with respect to someone"). This leads one to see in the Christian expiatory "sacrifice" the offering of an acceptable and accepted gift rather than the violence of shed blood. The generous change of the "victim" into a saving, mediating "offering" under the sway of a loving God is without doubt, in its essence, specifically Christian. It represents something new for the Greek and Judaic worlds, something of which they were unaware, or else they viewed it, in the light of their own worship, as scandalous.

Nevertheless, one should not forget that a whole ascetic, martyrizing, and sacrificial Christian tradition has magnified the victimized aspect of that offering by eroticizing both pain and suffering, physical as well as mental, as much as possible. Is that tradition no more than a simple medieval deviation that betrayed the "true meaning" of the Gospels? That would be setting little store by the anguish expressed by Christ himself, according to the Evangelists. How can we understand it when it is so powerfully asserted alongside the oblatory assurance of an oblatory gift made to a father who is also oblatory, equally present in the Gospels' text?

Hiatus and Identification

The break, brief as it might have been, in the bond linking Christ to his Father and to life introduces into the mythical representation of the Subject a fundamental and psychically necessary discontinuity. Such a caesura, which some have called a "hiatus,"[28] provides an image, at the same time as a narrative, for many separations that build up the psychic life of individuals. It provides image and narrative for some psychic cataclysms that more or less frequently threaten the assumed balance of individuals. Thus, psychoanalysis identifies and relates as an indispensable condition for autonomy a series of splittings (Hegel spoke of a "work of the negative"); birth, weaning, separation, frustration, castration. Real, imaginary, or symbolic, those processes necessarily structure our individuation. Their nonexecution or repudiation leads to psychotic confusion; their dramatization is, on the contrary, a source of exorbitant and destructive anguish. Because Christianity set that rupture at the very heart of the absolute subject— Christ; because it represented it as a Passion that was the solidary lining of his Resurrection, his glory, and his eternity, it brought to consciousness the essential dramas that are internal to the becoming of each and every subject. It thus endows itself with a tremendous cathartic power.

In addition to displaying a dramatic diachrony, the death

of Christ offers imaginary support to the nonrepresentable catastrophic anguish distinctive of melancholy persons. It is well known that the so-called "depressive" stage is essential to the child's access to the realm of symbols and linguistic signs. Such a depression—parting sadness as the necessary condition for the representation of any absent thing—reverts to and accompanies our symbolic activities unless exaltation, its opposite, reappropriates them. A suspension of meaning, a darkness without hope, a recession of perspective including that of life, then reawaken within the memory the recollection of traumatic partings and thrust us into a state of withdrawal. "Father, why have you deserted me?" Moreover, serious depression or paroxismal clinical melancholia represents a true hell for modern individuals, convinced as they are that they must and can realize all their desires of objects and values. The Christly dereliction presents that hell with an imaginary elaboration; it provides the subject with an echo of its unbearable moments when meaning was lost, when the meaning of life was lost.

The postulate according to which Christ died "for all of us" appears often in the texts.[29] *Hyper, peri, anti:* the words mean not only "because of us" but "in favor of us," "in our stead."[30] They go back to the "Songs of the Servant of Yahweh" (in the Book of the Consolation of Israel, a collection of prophecies included in the Book of Isaiah) and even earlier to the Hebraic notion of *ga'al:* "to free by purchasing back goods and people that have become alien property." Thus, *redemption* (repurchase, liberation) implies a substitution between the Savior and the faithful, which opened the way for many interpretations. One of these is a compelling one in the analyst's literal reading: the one that suggests an imaginary *identification*. Identification does not mean delegating sins or shifting their burden to the person of the Messiah. On the contrary, it calls for a total implication of the subjects in Christ's suffering, in the hiatus he experiences, and of course in his hope of salvation. On the basis of that identification, one that is admittedly too anthropological and psychological from the point of view of a strict theology, man is nevertheless provided with a powerful symbolic device that allows him to experience death and resurrection even in his physical body, thanks to the strength of imaginary identification— and of its actual effects—with the absolute Subject (Christ).

A true initiation is thus elaborated, at the very heart of Christian thought, which takes up again the deep intrapsychic meaning of initiatory rites that were anterior or alien to its domain, and gives them new meaning. Here as elsewhere, *death*—that of the old body making room for the new, death to oneself for the sake of glory, death of the old man for the sake of the spiritual body—lies at the center of the experience. But, if there be a Christian initiation, it belongs first and entirely within the imaginary realm. While opening up the entire gamut of complete identifications (real and symbolic), it allows for no ritualistic ordeal other than the words and signs of the Eucharist. From that standpoint, the paroxysmal and realistic manifestations of asceticism and "dolor" are indeed extreme positions. Beyond and above that, the implicitness of love and consequently of reconciliation and forgiveness completely transforms the scope of Christian initiation by giving it an aura of glory and unwavering hope for those who believe. Christian faith appears then as an antidote to hiatus and depression, along with hiatus and depression and starting from them.

Could it be superego voluntarism that maintains the image of an oblatory Father, or is it the commemoration of an archaic paternal figure arisen from the paradise of primary identifications? The forgiveness inherent in Redemption condenses *death and resurrection* and presents itself as one of the most interesting and innovative instances of trinitary logic. The key to the nexus seems to be primary identification: the oral and already symbolic oblatory gift exchanged between Father and Son.

For individual reasons, or else on account of the historical crushing of political or metaphysical authority, which is our social fatherhood, the dynamics of primary identification at the foundation of idealization can run into difficulty—it can appear as deprived of significance, illusory, false. The only thing then surviving is the meaning of the deeper workings represented by the cross: that of caesura, discontinuity, depression.

Did Holbein become the painter of such a Christian thought, stripped of its antidepressive carrier wave, and amounting to identification with a rewarding beyond? He leads us, at any rate, to the ultimate edge of belief, to the threshold of nonmeaning. The *form* (of art) alone gives back serenity to the waning of forgiveness, while love and salvation take refuge to the execution of the work. Redemption would simply be the discipline of a rigorous technique.

Representing "Severance"

Hegel brought to the fore the dual action of death in Christianity: on the one hand there is a natural death of the natural body; on the other, death is "infinite love," the "supreme renunciation of self for the sake of the Other." He sees in it a victory over the tomb, the *sheol,* a "death of death," and emphasizes the dialectic that is peculiar to such a logic. *"This negative movement, which belongs to Spirit only as Spirit,* is inner conversion and change . . . *the end being resolved in splendor, in the feast honoring the reception of the human being into the divine Idea.*"³¹ Hegel stresses the consequences of this action for representation. Since death is represented as being natural but realized only on condition that it be identified with its otherness, that is, divine Idea, one witnesses *"a marvellous union of these absolute extremes,"* "*a supreme alienation of the divine Idea. . . . 'God is dead, God himself is dead' is a marvellous, fearsome representation,* which offers to representation the deepest abyss of severance."³²

Leading representation to the heart of that severance (natural death *and* divine love) is a wager that one could not make without slipping into one or the other of two tendencies: Gothic art, under Dominican influence, favored a pathetic representation of natural death; Italian art, under Franciscan influence, exalted, through the sexual beauty of luminous bodies and harmonious compositions, the glory of the beyond made visible through the glory of the sublime. Holbein's *Body of the Dead Christ in the Tomb* is one of the rare if not a unique realization located at the very place of the severance of representation of which Hegel spoke. The Gothic eroticism of paroxysmal pain is missing, just as the promise of the beyond or the renascent exaltation of nature are lacking. What remains is the tight-rope—as the represented body—of an economical, sparing graphic rendition of pain held back within the solitary meditation of artist and viewer. To such a serene, disenchanted sadness, reading the limits of the insignificant, corresponds a painterly art of utmost sobriety and austerity. It presents no chromatic or compositional exultation but rather a mastery of harmony and measure.

Is it still possible to paint when the bonds that tie us to body and meaning are severed? Is it still possible to paint when *desire,* which is a bond, disintegrates? Is it still possible to paint when one identifies not with desire but with *severance,* which is the truth of human psychic life, a severance that is represented by death in the imagination and that melancholia conveys as symptom? Holbein's answer is affirmative. Between classicism and mannerism his minimalism is the metaphor of severance: between life and death, meaning and nonmeaning, it is an intimate, slender response of our melancholia.

Pascal confirmed, before Hegel and Freud, the sepulchre's invisibility. For him, the tomb would be Christ's hidden abode. Everyone looks at him on the cross but in the tomb he hides from his enemies' eyes, and the saints alone see him in order to keep him company in an agony that is peace.

> Christ was dead, but seen on the cross. He is dead and hidden in the sepulchre.
> Christ has been shrouded only by saints.
> Christ did not perform a single miracle in the sepulchre.
> Saints alone enter there.
> That is where Christ assumes a new life, not on the cross.
> It is the final mystery of the Passion and the Redemption.
> On earth Christ was able to rest nowhere but in the sepulchre.
> His enemies ceased working on him only in the sepulchre.[33]

Seeing the death of Christ is thus a way to give it meaning, to bring him back to life. But in the tomb at Basel Holbein's Christ is alone. Who sees him? There are no saints. There is of course the painter. And ourselves. To be swallowed up by death, or perhaps to see it in its slightest, dreadful beauty, as the limit inherent in life. *"Christ in grief . . . Christ being in agony and in the greatest sorrow, let us pray longer."*[34]

Painting as a substitute for prayer? Contemplating the painting might perhaps replace prayer at the critical place of its appearance—where the nonmeaning becomes significant, while death seems visible and livable.

Like Pascal's invisible tomb, death is not representable in Freud's unconscious. It is imprinted there, however, as noted earlier, by spacings, blanks, discontinuities, or destruction of representation (see chapter 1). Consequently, death reveals itself as such to the imaginative ability of the self in the isolation of signs or in their becoming commonplace to the point of disappearing: such is Holbein's minimalism. But as it grapples with the erotic vitality of the self and the jubilatory abundance of exalting or morbid signs conveying Eros's presence, death calls for a distant realism or, better, a grating irony: this brings forth the "danse macabre" and disenchanted profligacy inborn in the painter's style. The self eroticizes and signifies the obsessive presence of Death by stamping with isolation, emptiness, or absurd laughter its own imaginative assurance that keeps it alive, that is, anchored in the interplay of forms. To the contrary, images and identities—the carbon copies of that triumphant self—are imprinted with inaccessible sadness.

Our eyes having been filled with such a vision of the invisible, let us look once more at the people that Holbein has created: heroes of modern times, they stand straitlaced, sober, and upright. Secretive, too: as real as can be and yet indecipherable. Not a single impulse betraying jouissance. No exalted loftiness toward the beyond. Nothing but the sober difficulty of standing here below. They simply remain upright around a void that makes them strangely lonesome. Self confident. And close.

6

Gérard de Nerval, The Disinherited Poet

El Desdichado *(The Disinherited)*

(As published in *Le Mousquetaire* on December 10, 1853)

1 Je suis le ténébreux, le veuf, l'inconsolé,
2 Le prince d'Aquitaine à la tour abolie;
3 Ma seule étoile est morte, et mon luth constellé
4 Porte le soleil noir de la mélancolie.

5 Dans la nuit du tombeau, toi qui m'a consolé,
6 Rends-moi le Pausilippe et la mer d'Italie,
7 La fleur qui plaisait tant à mon cœur désolé,
8 Et la treille où le pampre à la vigne s'allie.

9 Suis-je Amour ou Phœbus, Lusignan ou Byron?
10 Mon front est rouge encor des baisers de la reine;
11 J'ai dormi dans la grotte où verdit la sirène.

12 Et j'ai deux fois vivant traversé l'Achéron,
13 Modulant et chantant sur la lyre d'Orphée
14 Les soupirs de la sainte et les cris de la fée.

1 *I am saturnine, bereft, disconsolate,*
2 *The Prince of Aquitaine whose tower has crumbled;*
3 *My lone star is dead, and my bespangled lute*
4 *Bears the black sun of melancholia.*

5 *In the night of the grave, you who brought me solace,*
6 *Give me back Posilipo and the sea of Italy,*
7 *The flower that so pleased my distressed heart,*
8 *And the arbor where vine and grape combine.*

9 *Am I Cupid or Phoebus, Lusignan or Byron?*
10 *My brow is still red from the kisses of the queen;*
11 *I have slept in the cave where the siren turns green,*

12 *I've twice, yet alive, been across the Acheron,*
13 *Modulating and singing on Orpheus' lyre*
14 *The sighs of the saint and the screams of the fay.*

El Desdichado *(The Disinherited)*

(as published in *Les Filles du feu,* 1854)

1 Je suis le ténébreux, — le veuf, — l'inconsolé,
2 Le prince d'Aquitaine à la tour abolie;
3 Ma seule *étoile* est morte, — et mon luth constellé
4 Porte le *Soleil noir* de la *Mélancolie.*

5 Dans la nuit du tombeau, toi qui m'a consolé,
6 Rends-moi le Pausilippe et la mer d'Italie,
7 La *fleur* qui plaisait tant à mon cœur désolé,
8 Et la treille où le pampre à la rose s'allie.

9 Suis-je Amour ou Phébus?. . . Lusignan ou Byron?
10 Mon front est rouge encor du baiser de la reine;
11 J'ai rêvé dans la grotte où nage la sirène . . .

12 Et j'ai deux fois vainqueur traversé l'Achéron:
13 Modulant tour à tour sur la lyre d'Orphée
14 Les soupirs de la sainte et les cris de la fée.

1 *I am saturnine — bereft — disconsolate,*
2 *The Prince of Aquitaine whose tower has crumbled;*
3 *My lone* star *is dead — and my bespangled lute*
4 *Bears the* Black Sun *of* Melancholia.

5 *In the night of the grave, you who brought me solace,*
6 *Give me back Posilipo and the sea of Italy,*
7 *The* flower *that so pleased my distressed heart,*
8 *And the arbor where grapevine and rose combine.*

9 *Am I Cupid or Phebus?. . . Lusignan or Byron?*
10 *My brow is still red from the kiss of the queen;*
11 *I have dreamt in the cave where the siren swims . . .*

12 *I've twice, as a conqueror, been across the Acheron;*
13 *Modulating by turns on Orpheus' lyre*
14 *The sighs of the saint and the screams of the fay.*

[*141*]

14

I am alone, I am bereft, and the night falls upon me
— Victor Hugo,
Booz

. . . it is melancholia that becomes his Muse
— Gérard de Nerval,
To Alexandre Dumas

"El Desdichado" and "Artémis," written in red ink, were sent to Alexandre Dumas by Nerval in a letter dated November 14, 1853. "El Desdichado" was first published in *Le Mousquetaire* on December 10, 1853, with an essay by Dumas serving as introduction. A second version appeared in *Les Filles du feu* in 1854. The manuscript of that poem, which belonged to Paul Eluard, bears the title *Le Destin* and is essentially the same as the *Les Filles du feu* version.

After his fit of madness of May 1853, Gérard de Nerval (1808–1855) set out for his native Valois (Chaalis Abbey, Senlis, Loisy, Mortefontaine) in order to seek nostalgic refuge and relief.[1] The tireless wanderer who never grew weary of crisscrossing Southern France, Germany, Austria, and the East, withdrew for a while into the crypt of a past that haunted him. In August the symptoms showed up again: there he was, like a threatened archeologist, visiting the osteology wing at the Jardin des Plantes, convinced, in the rain, that he was witnessing the Flood. Graves, skeletons, the irruption of death indeed continually haunted him. Within such a context, "El Desdichado" was his Noah's Ark. Albeit a temporary one, it nevertheless secured him a fluid, enigmatic, spellbinding identity. Orpheus, once again, retained victory over the Black Prince.

The title, "El Desdichado," at once points to the strangeness of the text that follows; its Spanish resonance, however, shrill and trumpeting beyond the word's woeful meaning, contrasts sharply with the shaded, discreet vowel pattern of the French language and appears to herald some triumph or other in the very heart of darkness.

Who is "El Desdichado"? On the one hand, Nerval might have borrowed the name from Walter Scott's *Ivanhoe* (chapter 8); it refers to one of King John's knights whom the king dispossessed of the castle that Richard Lion-Heart had bequeathed to him. The unfortunate, disinherited knight then decided to embellish his shield with the picture of an uprooted oak and the words "El Desdichado." On the other hand, a "French source for El Desdichado" has been suggested; this would be Don Blaz Desdichado, a character in Alain René Lesage's *Le Diable boiteux* [The Lame Devil] who goes mad because, lacking heirs, he is forced to return his wealth to his in-laws after his wife's death.[2] If it be true that for many French readers the Spanish "el desdichado" translates as "disinherited," an accurate, literal rendition of the word would be "wretched," "unfortunate," "pitiful." Nerval, however, appears to have been attached to "disinherited"—which was, moreover, Alexandre Dumas' choice in his translation of *Ivanhoe*. It is also the term Nerval used to refer to himself in another context ("Thus, myself, once a brilliant actor, an unknown prince, a mysterious lover, disinherited, excluded from happiness, handsome and saturnine. . . .").[3]

Lost "Thing" or "Object"

Disinherited of what? An initial deprivation is thus indicated at once; it is not, however, the deprivation of a "property" or "object" constituting a material, transferable heritage, but the loss of an unnameable domain, which one might, strangely enough, evoke or invoke, from a foreign land, from a constitutional exile. This "something" would be previous to the detectable "object": the secret and unreachable horizon of our loves and desires, it assumes, for the imagination, the consistency of an archaic mother, which, however, no precise image manages to encompass. The untiring quest for mistresses or, on the religious level, the accumulation of feminine divinities or mother goddesses that Eastern and particularly Egyptian religions lavish on the "subject," points to the elusive nature of that *Thing*—necessarily lost so that this "subject," separated from the "object," might become a speaking being.

If the melancholy person ceaselessly exerts an ascendency, as loving as it is hateful, over that Thing, the poet finds an enigmatic way of being both subordinate to it and . . . elsewhere. Disinherited, deprived of that lost paradise, he is wretched; writing, however, is the strange way that allows him to overcome such wretchedness by setting up an "I" that controls both aspects of deprivation—the darkness of disconsolation and the "kiss of the queen."

The "I" then asserts itself on the field of artifice: there is a place for the "I" only in play, in theater, behind the masks of possible identities, which are as extravagant, prestigious, mythical, epic, historical, and esoteric as they are incredible. Triumphant, but also uncertain.

This "I" that pins down and secures the first line, "I am

saturnine—bereft—disconsolate," points, with a knowledge as certain as it is illuminated with a hallucinatory
nescience, to the necessary condition for the poetic act. To
speak, to venture, to settle within the legal fiction known
as symbolic activity, that is indeed to lose the Thing.

Henceforth the dilemma can be stated as follows: will
the traces of that lost Thing sweep the speaker along, or
will he succeed in carrying them away—integrating them,
incorporating them in his discourse, which has become a
song by dint of seizing the Thing. In other words: is it the
bacchantes who tear Orpheus to pieces, or is it Orpheus
who carries the bacchantes away through his incantation,
as in a symbolic anthropophagy?

I Am That Which Is Not

The fluctuation will be permanent. After an unbelievable
assertion of presence and certainty, recalling Victor Hugo's self-confidence as a patriarch whom solitude does not
disturb but brings peace to ("I am alone, I am bereft, and
the night falls upon me"), we are once more amid misfortune. The qualities of that triumphant "I" are negative
ones; deprived of light, deprived of wife, deprived of
solace, he is that which *is not.* He is "saturnine," "bereft,"
"disconsolate."

Nerval's interest in alchemy and esoterica render perfectly plausible Georges Le Breton's interpretation, according to which the first lines of *El Desdichado* follow the
tarot cards' order (cards 15, 16, 17). "Saturnine" would
refer to hell's great demon (the fifteenth card of the tarot
is the devil's card); he also might well be Pluto the alche-
mist, who died celibate, whose deformity caused the goddesses to flee (hence he is bereft), and who figured the

earth at the bottom of a caldron where all alchemical processes have their source.[4]

Nonetheless, those references that make up Nerval's ideology are inserted into a poetic web—uprooted, transposed, they achieve a multivalency and a set of connotations, all of which are often undecidable. The polyvalency of symbolism within the new symbolic order structured by the poem, combined with the rigidity of symbols within esoteric doctrines, endow Nerval's language with a two fold advantage: on the one hand, insuring a stable meaning as well as a secret community where the disconsolate poet is heard, accepted, and, in short, solaced; on the other, slipping away from monovalent meaning and that same community in order to reach as closely as possible the specifically Nervalian object, sorrow—and this through the uncertainty of naming. Before attaining the level of erased meaning where poetic language accompanies the disappearance of the melancholy subject foundering in the lost object, let us follow those processes of Nerval's text that are logically easy to pin down.

Inversions and a Double

The qualifier "saturnine" [Nerval's word: *ténébreux*] is consonant with the Prince of Darkness already suggested by the tarot pack as well as with night deprived of light. It conjures up the melancholy person's complicity with the world of darkness and despair.

The "black sun" (line 4) again takes up the semantic field of "saturnine," but pulls it inside out, like a glove: darkness flashes as a solar light, which nevertheless remains dazzling with black invisibility.

"Bereft" [Nerval's word: *veuf*=widower] is the first sign pointing to mourning. Would the saturnine mood then be the consequence of his having lost a wife? At this spot the Eluard manuscript adds a note, "in the past: Mausolus?" which replaces words that have been crossed out, "the Prince/dead/" or "the poem." Mausolus was the fourth-century B.C. king of Caria who married his sister Artemisia and died before she did. If the widower were Mausolus, he would have been incestuous—married to his sister, his mother, . . . to an erotic, familiar, and domestic Thing. That figure's ambivalence is yet further muddled by what Nerval does with him; having died first he cannot be a widower but leaves *a widow,* his sister Artemisia. Nerval makes her name masculine in the sonnet "Artémis" and perhaps plays with the two members of the couple as if each were the *double* of the other—interchangeable but also, consequently, imprecise in their sexuality, nearly androgynous. We are here at an extremely compact stage of Nerval's poetic process: the widow Artemisia identifies with her dead double (brother + husband), *she* is *he,* hence a widower, and this identification, the encrypting of the other, installing the other's vault in oneself, would be the equivalent of the poem. (There are indeed commentators who believe they can read the word "poem" under the obliteration.) The text as mausoleum?

Using the word "disconsolate" [*inconsolé*] as opposed to "inconsolable" suggests a paradoxical temporality: the one who speaks has not been solaced in the past, and the effect of that frustration lasts up to the present. While "inconsolable" would anchor us in the present, "disconsolate" turns the present into the past when the trauma was experienced. The present is beyond repair, without the slightest hope of solace.

Imaginary Memory

The "Prince of Aquitaine" is doubtless Waifer (or Guaifer) of Aquitaine who, pursued by Pepin III, the Short, hid in the forests of Périgord. In his mythical genealogy, partially published by Aristide Marie and then fully by Jean Richer,[5] Nerval assumed a prestigious lineage and had his own Labrunie family descend from the knights of Odo [also called Eudon or Eudes]; one of its branches supposedly came from Périgord, just like the Prince of Aquitaine. He also specified that Broun or Brunn means tower and grain-drying structure. The coat of arms of the Labrunies, who were said to have owned three châteaux on the banks of the Dordogne, would bear three silver towers, and also stars and crescents evoking the East, somewhat like the "star" and "bespangled lute" that appear in the next line of the text.

To the polyvalency of Aquitaine as a symbol—the land of waters [according to folk etymology, though the word actually derives from Auscetani]—one can add the note sent by Nerval to George Sand (quoted by Richer) in which one reads, "GASTON PHOEBUS D'AQUITAINE," whose esoteric meaning would be that of solar initiate. It will be noted more simply, following Jacques Dhaenens,[6] that Aquitaine is the land of troubadours, and thus, by evoking the Black Prince, the widower begins, through courtly song, his transformation into Orpheus . . . We are still, nevertheless, in the domain of despondent statement: "crumbled" [*abolie* = abolished] confirms the meaning of destruction, deprivation, and lack that has been woven since the beginning of the text. As Emilie Noulet has noted,[7] the phrase "whose tower has crumbled" [*à la tour abolie*] functions as "a single mental grouping" and endows the Prince of Aquitaine with a complex qualifier where words merge and syllables stand out, sounding a litany: "à-la-tour-a-bo-lie," which might also be seen as a loose anagram of Labrunie. There are three instances of the word "abolie" in Nerval's work, and Emilie Noulet has noted that this uncommon word seemed essential to Mallarmé, who used it at least six times in his poems.

A dispossessed prince, the glorious subject of a destroyed past, El Desdichado belongs to a history, but to a depreciated history. His past without future is not a historical past—it is merely a *memory* all the more present as it has no future.

The next line again takes up the personal trauma; the tower that has crumbled, the height that is henceforth lacking, was a "star" that is now dead. The star is the image of the muse, also that of a lofty universe, of the cosmos, which is higher still than the medieval tower or the presently wrecked destiny. We shall keep in mind, following Jacques Geninasca,[8] the proud, exalted, stellar scope of this first quatrain where the poet stands with his equally star-spangled lute, as if he were the negative version of the celestial, artistic Apollo. Probably, too, the "star" is also a theater star—the actress Jenny Colon, who died in 1842, catalyzed several of Nerval's crises. The star-spangled lute was elaborated through the identification with the "dead star," through scattering her in his song, as in a resonant replica of Orpheus' being torn to pieces by the bacchantes. The art of poetry asserts itself as the memory of a posthumous harmony, but also, through a Pythagorean resonance, as the metaphor of universal harmony.

On the Threshold of the Invisible and the Visible

As a result of the absorption of the "dead star" into the "lute," the "Black Sun" of "Melancholia" emerges. Beyond its alchemical scope, the "Black Sun" metaphor fully sums up the blinding force of the despondent mood—an excruciating, lucid affect asserts the inevitability of death, which is the death of the loved one and of the self that identifies with the former (the poet is "bereft" of the "star").

This intrusive affect, however, which irrigates the celestial realm with a hidden Apollo, or one who is not conscious of being such, attempts to find its expression. The verb "bears" points to that bursting out, that reaching the signs of darkness, while the learned word *melancholia* serves to bespeak the struggle for conscious mastery and precise meaning. Heralded in Nerval's letter to Alexandre Dumas, evoked in *Aurélia* ("A creature of enormous proportions—man or woman I do not know—was fluttering painfully through the air. . . . It was colored with ruddy hues and its wings glittered with a myriad changing reflections. Clad in a long gown of antique folds, it looked like Albrecht Dürer's *Angel of Melancholia*"),[9] *Melancholia* belongs in the celestial realm. It changes darkness into redness or into a sun that remains black, to be sure, but is nevertheless the sun, source of dazzling light. Nerval's introspection seems to indicate that *naming the sun* locates him on the threshold of a crucial experience, on the divide between appearance and disappearance, abolishment and song, nonmeaning and signs. Nerval's reference to the alchemical metamorphosis may be read as a metaphor more in keeping with the borderline experience of the psyche struggling against dark asymbolism than with

[*151*]

a para-scientific description of physical or chemical reality.

Who Are You?

The second stanza takes the reader down from celestial, star-spangled heights to the "night of the grave." The underground, nightly realm assumes the somber mood of the saturnine poet but changes gradually throughout the quatrain into a realm of consolation, of luminous and vital bond. The haughty, princely "I" of passive cosmic space (the "star" and "sun" of the first stanza) meets with a partner in the second stanza: a "you" appears for the first time, initiating solace, light, and the arrival of plant life. The star [*étoile*] of the celestial vault [*toit*] is henceforth someone the poet can speak to—a "you" [*toi*] who lies within.

The constant ambiguity, the continuous inversions of Nerval's world deserve emphasis; they increase the instability of its symbolism and reveal the object's ambiguity —and also that of the melancholy stance.

Who is this "you"? Scholars have asked the question and provided many answers—it is Aurélia, the saint, Artemisia/Artémis, Jenny Colon, the dead mother . . . The undecidable concatenation of these real and imaginary figures recedes once more toward the position of the archaic "Thing"—the elusive preobject of a mourning that is endemic with all speaking beings and a suicidal attraction for the depressive person.

Nevertheless—and this is not the least of its ambiguities—the "you" that the poet meets with only in "the night of the grave" can console only and precisely in that place. Joining her in the tomb, identifying with her dead body, but perhaps also joining her truly by means of a suicide, the "I" finds solace. The paradox in this action (suicide alone allows me to unite with the lost being, suicide alone brings me peace) can be grasped through the placidness, serenity, and that kind of happiness that veils a number of suicidal people, once they have made the fatal decision. A narcissistic fullness seems to build up in imaginary fashion; it is one that removes the disastrous anguish over loss and finally gratifies the dismayed subject: there is no need to be distressed any more, solace comes through joining the beloved being in death. Death then becomes the phantasmal experience of returning to the lost paradise. The past tense of "you who brought me solace" will be noted.

Henceforth the grave brightens; the poet finds in it the luminous bay of Naples and the Posilipo promontory (in Greek, *pausilypon* means the "cessation of sadness"), and a watery billowing, maternal expanse ("the sea of Italy"). One should add to the polyvalency of this liquid, luminous, Italian universe—as opposed to the Apollonian or medieval, interstellar, and mineral universe of the first stanza—first the fact that Nerval tried to commit suicide on Posilipo out of love for Jenny Colon.[10] Second, there is the connection made by Hoffman between "Aurélia and the picture of Santa Rosalia," which was confirmed by Nerval who, during his stay in Naples (October 1834), gazed upon the "likeness of Santa Rosalia" that embellished the abode of an anonymous mistress.[11]

A Flower, a Saint: The Mother?

The virgin Rosalia links the symbolism of feminine Christian purity with the esoteric connotations of the text that have already been mentioned. This way of thinking seems justified by the note, "Vatican Gardens," which Nerval inserted in the Eluard manuscript on line 8: "where grape-vine and rose combine" [in French, *à la rose s'al-lie* = Rosalie].

The flowery connotation of the saint's name becomes explicit on line 7, "the *flower* that so pleased my distressed heart." The dead *star* of the previous stanza (line 3) resurrects as a *flower* within the identification of the poet with the dead woman. The identification is evoked in the metaphor of the "arbor," climbing network, interpenetration of twigs and leaves, which "combines" the grapevine and the rose and moreover evokes Bacchus or Dionysus, the god of a plant-loving intoxication, as opposed to the black, astral Apollo of the first stanza. Let us note that, for some contemporary commentators, Dionysus is less a phallic deity than the one who, in his body and dancing intoxication, conveys an intimate complicity, even an identification, with femininity.[12]

The Bacchic "grapevine" and the mystical "rose," Dionysus and Venus, Bacchus and Ariadne . . . one can imagine a series of mystical couples implicitly evoked in this funereal *and* resurrectional grouping. Let us recall Nerval's naming of the Virgin Mary as "white Rose" and, among others, "Les Cydalises": "Where are our lovers? / They are in the grave / They are far happier / In a more beautiful region! . . . Oh white betrothed! / Oh blossoming young virgin!"[13]

The "flower" can be interpreted as being the flower into which the melancholy Narcissus was changed—finally solaced by his drowning in the reflection-spring. It is also the "myosotis":[14] this foreign-sounding word evokes the artifice of the poem ("An answer is heard in a soft foreign tongue") at the same time as it invokes the memory of those who will love the writer ("Forget me not!"). Let me finally suggest a semantic possibility for this flowery universe appended to the evocation of the other: Nerval's mother, who died when he was two years old, was named Marie-Antoinette-*Marguerite-Laurent* and usually called Laurence—a saint and a flower (marguerite [daisy], laurel), while Jenny Colon's real first name was . . . Marguerite. Enough to nourish a "mystical rose."

Ancholia and Hesitation: Who Am I?

There is a merging that is consoling but also lethal—the luminous fulfillment arrived at by uniting with the rose, but also the darkness of the grave; temptation to commit suicide, but also flowery resurrection . . . Did such a mingling of opposites appear to Nerval, as he reread his text, as "madness"?

On line 7 (refering to "flower") he noted in the Eluard manuscript: "ancholia"—symbol of sadness for some, emblem of madness for others.★ *Melancholia/ancholia.* The rhyme leads me once again to read both similitude and opposition between the first two stanzas. Mineral sadness (first stanza) is superimposed on a death-bearing merger that is also madly attractive, like the promise of an other life, beyond the grave (second stanza).

The first tercet clarifies the uncertainty of the "I." Triumphant at first, then linked with "you," he now ponders the question, "Am I?" It is the turning point of the sonnet, a moment of doubt and lucidity. The poet searches, precariously, for his specific identity, on a level one can assume to be neutral, neither Apollonian nor Dionysian, neither dismayed nor exhilarated. The inter-

★*Ancolie* is the common French name for a flower of the Aquilegia genus—the columbine, which does not convey the symbolic connotation and rhyme of the French word. The neologism "ancholia," which preserves the link with "melancholia," may be thought of as refering to an imaginary flower—LSR.

rogative removes us, for a while, from the almost hallucinatory world of the two quatrains, their changeable, undecidable connotations and symbolisms. It is the time for
choice: are we dealing with Cupid, in other words Eros,
psyche's lover (reminder of the second quatrain), or with
Phoebus/Apollo (reminder of the first quatrain) who, according to Ovid's *Metamorphoses,* pursued the nymph
Daphne? She escapes by being changed into a laurel tree—
and one will recall the flowery transformation suggested
in the second quatrain. Is this the case of a gratified lover
or a frustrated one?

As to Lusignan d'Agenais, he would be one of the
Labrunie's forebears, according to Nerval's imaginary fi-
liation, who was crushed by the desertion of his serpent-
wife Melusina. Biron takes us back to an ancestor of the
Dukes of Biron, the crusader Elie de Gontaut in the Third
Crusade; or perhaps to Lord Byron, for Nerval confused
the spellings Biron/Byron.[15]

What is the precise logical relation within those two
pairs (Cupid and Phebus, Lusignan and Biron) and between them as well? Are we dealing with a listing of more
or less unhappy lovers in quest of an always elusive mistress? Or with two kinds of lovers, gratified and dis-
heartened? Exegeses pile up and diverge, some favoring
the idea of a listing, others the chiasmus.

Nonetheless, the basic polyvalency of Nerval's seman-
tics (thus, among others, "Fair-haired or dark / Must we
choose? / The Lord of the World / Is called Pleasure")[16]
leads one to believe that here, too, logical relationships are
doubtful. Perhaps in the image of that butterfly whose
fascinating uncertainty the writer describes in this fashion:
"The butterfly, stemless flower, / That flutters about, /
That one harvests in a net; / Within infinite nature, / It
provides harmony / Between plants and birds! . . ."[17]

Ultimately, the proper names gathered in this tercet perhaps work more as signs of various identities (see 'Names as Clues" below). If the "persons" that have been named belong to the same world of love and loss, they suggest— through the poet's identification with them—a dispersal of the "I," loving as well as poetic, among a constellation of elusive identities. It is not certain that those figures had for Nerval the semantic fullness of their mythological or medieval source. The litaneutical, hallucinatory gathering of their names allows one to suppose that they might merely have the value of signs, broken up and impossible to unify, of the lost Thing.

An Underlying Violence

The question as to the speaker's own identity has barely been suggested when line 10 recalls his dependency on the queen; the questioning "I" is not supreme, he has a sovereign ("My brow is still red from the kiss of the queen"). With the alchemical evocation of the king and queen and their union and redness as sign of infamy and murder ("I sometimes bear Cain's inexorable redness!"), we are once more steeped in an ambiguous world. The brow bears the memory of the loved one's kiss and thus signifies loving joy at the same time as redness recalls the blood of a murder and, beyond Cain and Abel, signifies the destructive violence of archaic love, the hatred underlying lovers' passion, the revenge and the persecution that underlie their romance. The powerful Anteros of the melancholy person seethes behind a dashing Eros: "You ask me why my heart is raging so / . . . Yes, I am one of those whom the Avenger drives, / He has scarred my forehead with his angry lip, / And sometimes, alas, Abel's pallor is covered with blood, / For I carry from Cain that inexorable red."[18]

Does the despairer's paleness hide the avenging and to himself unavowed anger of the murderous violence directed at his loved one? While such aggressiveness is heralded on line 10, the speaker does not assume it. It is projected: not I but the kiss of the queen wounds, cuts, bloodies. Then, immediately, the outburst of violence is suspended, and the dreamer appears in a protected haven —uterine refuge or swinging cradle. The red queen is changed into a siren who swims or "turns green" (*Le Mousquetaire* version). The floral, vital, resurrectional value of the second quatrain has been pointed out, as well as the frequent oppositions of red and green with Nerval. Red asserts itself as metaphor of revolt, of insurrectional fire. It is Cainish, diabolical, infernal, while green is saintly, and Gothic stained glass assigned it to John [the Divine].[19] Need I emphasize once more the mistress' royal function, the more dominating as she is undominated, filling the entire space of authority and fatherhood and for that very reason enjoying an insuperable ascendency over the saturnine poet?—she is the queen of Sheba, Isis, Mary, queen of the Church . . . Facing her, the act of writing alone is implicitly master and avenger: let us remember that the sonnet was written in *red ink*.

We thus find only a simple, slight allusion to sexual desire and its ambivalence. The erotic connection does, in fact, bring to their climax the conflicts of a subject who experiences both sexuality and the discourse that refers to it as destructive. One understands why the melancholy withdrawal is a fugue in the face of the dangers of eroticism.

Such an avoidance of sexuality and its naming confirms the hypothesis according to which the "star" of *El Desdichado* is closer to the archaic Thing than to an object of desire. Nevertheless, and although such an avoidance seems

necessary for the psychic balance of some, one could wonder if, by thus blocking the way toward the *other* (threatening, to be sure, but also insuring the conditions for
setting up the boundaries of the self), the subject does not
sentence itself to lie in the Thing's grave. Sublimation
alone, without elaborating the erotic and thanatoid con-
tents, seems a weak recourse against the regressive tendencies that break up bonds and lead to death.

The Freudian way, on the contrary, aims at planning
(in all circumstances and no matter what difficulties there
might be with so-called narcissistic personalities) for the
advent and formulation of sexual desire. Such a design,
often disparaged as reductionist by detractors of psychoanalysis, is imperative—in the perspective of considera-
tions on melancholy imagination—as an ethical option,
for *named* sexual desire insures securing the subject to the
other and, consequently, to meaning—to the meaning of
life.

I Narrate

The poet, however, returns from his descent into hell. He
goes "twice" across the Acheron, remaining "alive" (*Le
Mousquetaire* version) or being a "conqueror" (*Les Filles du
feu* version), and the two crossings recall the two previous
major attacks of madness suffered by Nerval.

Having assimilated an unnamed Eurydice into his song
and the chords of his lyre, he adopts the pronoun "I" as
his own. Not as strict as in the first line and beyond the
uncertainties of the ninth, this "I" is, at the conclusion of
the sonnet, an "I" who narrates a story. The untouchable,
violent past, black and red, and also the verdant dream of
a lethal resurrection have been modulated into an artifice
that includes temporal distance ("I've . . . been across")

and belongs to another reality, that of the lyre. The beyond of melancholy hell would thus be a modulated, sung narrative, an integration of prosody into a narration that has only been started here.

Nerval does not specify the cause, the motive, or the reason that lead him to this miraculous modification ("I've twice, as a conqueror, been across the Acheron"), but he unveils the economy of his metamorphosis, which consists in transposing into his melody and song "the sighs of the saint and the screams of the fay." The figure of the loved one is divided at first: ideal *and* sexual, white and red, Rosalia and Melusina, the virgin and the queen, spiritual and carnal, Adrienne and Jenny, and so forth. Besides and even more so, these women are henceforth *sounds* borne by characters in a *story* that narrates a past. Neither unnameable beings resting in the depths of polyvalent symbolism nor mythical objects of destructive passion, they attempt to turn into the imaginary protagonists of a cathartic narrative that endeavors to name, by differentiating them, ambiguities and pleasures. The "sighs" and the "screams" connote jouissance, and one distinguishes idealizing love (the "saint") from erotic passion (the "fay").

By means of a leap into the orphic world of artifice (of sublimation), the saturnine poet, out of the traumatic experience and object of mourning, remembers only a gloomy or passional tone. He thus comes close, through the very components of language, to the lost Thing. His discourse identifies with it, absorbs it, modifies it, transforms it: he takes Eurydice out of the melancholy hell and gives her back a new existence in his text/song.

The rebirth of the two, the "bereft" and the "star"-"flower," is nothing but the poem strengthened by the start of a narrative stance. That particular imagination is granted with the economy of a resurrection.

Nevertheless, Nerval's narrative is simply suggested in "El Desdichado." In the other poems it remains scattered and always incomplete. In the prose texts, in order to maintain their difficult linear motion toward a limited goal and message, he resorts to the subterfuge of the voyage or the biographic reality of a literary character whose adventures he takes up. *Aurelia* is the very instance of a narrative dispersal, replete with dreams, splittings, musings, incompletions . . .

One should not speak of a "failure" faced with that dazzling narrative kaleidoscope foreshadowing contemporary experiments in novelistic fragmentation. Just the same, narrative continuity, which, beyond the certainty of syntax, builds space and time and reveals the mastery of an existential judgment over hazards and conflicts, is far from being Nerval's favorite realm. Any narrative already assumes that there is an identity stabilized by a completed Oedipus and that, having accepted the loss of the Thing, it can concatenate its adventures through failures and conquests of the "objects" of desire. If such be the narrative's internal logic, one can understand why the telling of a story seems too "secondary," too schematic, too unessential to capture the "black sun's" incandescence with Nerval.

Prosody will then be the basic, fundamental sieve that will sift the "black prince's" sorrow and joy into language. A fragile filter but often the only one. Does one not, when all is said and done, and beyond the multifarious and contradictory meanings of words and syntactic structures, hear the vocal gesture? With the very first alliterations, rhythms, melodies, the transposition of the speaking body asserts itself through a glottic and oral presence. T: *téné-breux* (saturnine), *Aquitaine*, *tour* (tower), *étoile* (star), *morte* (dead), *luth* (lute), *constellé* (bespangled), *porte*

(bears); BR–PT–TR: Ténébreux (saturnine), prince, tour
(tower), morte (dead), porte (bears); S: suis (am), inconsolé
(disconsolate), prince, seule (lone), constellé (bespangled),
soleil (sun); ON: inconsolé (disconsolate), mon (my), constellé (bespangled) . . .

Repetitive, often monotonous, such a prosody[20] forces
on the affective flow a grid that is as rigorous to decipher
(it presupposes precise knowledge of mythology or eso-
terics) as it is flexible and unsettled on account of its very
allusiveness. Who are the Prince of Aquitaine, the "lone
dead star," Phebus, Lusignan, Biron . . . ? We can find
out, we do find out, interpretations pile up or differ . . .
But the sonnet can also be read by ordinary readers who
know nothing about such referents, if they will simply
allow themselves to be caught up in the sole phonic and
rhythmic coherence, which at the same time limits and
permits the free associations inspired by each word or
name.

It can thus be understood that the triumph over melancholia resides as much in founding a symbolic family
(ancestor, mythical figure, esoteric community) as in con-
structing an independent symbolic object—a sonnet. At-
tributable to the author, the construction becomes a substitute for the lost ideal in the same way as it transforms
the woeful darkness into a lyrical song that assimilates
"the sighs of the saint and the screams of the fay." The
nostalgic focus—"my lone star is dead"—turns into feminine voices incorporated into the symbolic cannibalism
constituted by the poem's composition, into the prosody
created by the artist. One is to interpret in analogous
fashion the massive presence of proper nouns in Nerval's
texts, particularly in his poetry.

Names as Clues: It Is

The series of names attempts to fill the space left empty by the lack of a sole name. Paternal name, or Name of God. "Oh father! Is it you that I sense within myself? / Do you have the power to live and to conquer death? / Might you have succumbed after a final effort / From that angel of darkness who was anathematized . . . / For I feel completely alone, crying and suffering, / Alas! And if I die, it is because everything is going to die!"[21]

This first person Christly lament is very much like the biographical complaint of an orphan or one lacking paternal support (Mme Labrunie died in 1810, Nerval's father, Etienne Labrunie, was wounded at Vilna in 1812). Christ forsaken by his father, Christ's passion as he descends into hell alone, attract Nerval who interprets this as a signal, at the very heart of Christian religion, of the "death of God" proclaimed by Jean Paul [Richter], whom Nerval quotes in the epigraph. Abandoned by his father who thus renounces his almightiness, Christ dies and drags every creature down into the abyss.

The melancholy Nerval identifies with Christ forsaken by the Father; he is an atheist who seems no longer to believe in the myth of "this madman, this sublime demented person . . . This forgotten Icarus who ascended back into heaven."[22] Is Nerval afflicted with the same nihilism that shook Europe from Jean Paul to Dostoyevsky and Nietzsche and echoes Jean Paul's well-known utterance all the way to the epigraph of *Christ at the Mount of Olives:* "God is dead! The sky is empty . . . / Weep! Children, you no longer have a father!"? Identifying with Christ, the poet appears to suggest it: " 'No, God does not exist!' / They were asleep. 'Friends, have you heard *the news?* / With my brow I touched the eternal vault; / I am covered in blood, exhausted, I shall suffer for many days! / Brethren, I misled you. Abyss! Abyss! Abyss! / God is missing from the altar where I am the victim . . . / God is no more! God is no more!' / But they were still asleep!"[23]

His philosophy, however, is perhaps more of an immanent Christianity coated with esoterica. For the dead God he substitutes the hidden God—the God not of Jansenism but of a diffuse spirituality, the ultimate refuge of a psychic identity in catastrophic anguish: "Often, in an obscure being, lives a hidden God; / And, like a new-born eye covered by its lids, / A pure spirit grows under the covering of stones."[24]

The amassing of names (which refer to historical, mythical, and above all esoteric figures) achieves first this impossible naming of the One, then its pulverizing, finally its reversal toward the dark region of the unnameable Thing. This means that we are not engaged here in a debate internal to Jewish or Christian monotheism, about the possibility or impossibility of naming God, about the oneness or mutiplicity of his names. Within Nerval's subjectivity the crisis of naming and that of the authority answerable for subjective oneness went deeper.

Since the One or His Name is deemed dead or negated, there looms the possibility of replacement through a series of imaginary filiations. Such mythical, esoteric, or historical families or brotherhoods or doubles that Nerval feverishly imposes in place of the One, however, seem finally to be endowed with incantatory, conspiratorial, ritual value. Instead of pointing to their concrete referent, those names indicate, rather than mean, a massive, uncircumventable, unnameable presence, as if they were the anaphora of the unique object; not the mother's "symbolic equivalence," but the shifter "this," empty of meaning. Names are the gestures that point to the lost being out of which the "black sun of melancholia" first breaks out, before the erotic *object* separated from the mournful subject settles in, along with the linguistic *artifice of signs* that transposes that object to the symbolic level. In the final analysis, and beyond the anaphoras' ideological value, the poem integrates them as signs without signifieds, as *infra* or *supra*-signs, which, beyond communication, attempt to reach the dead or untouchable object, to take over the unnameable being. Thus the sophistication of polytheist knowledge has the ultimate aim of taking us to the threshold of naming, to the edge of the unsymbolized.

By representing that unsymbolized as a maternal object, a source of sorrow and nostalgia, but of ritual veneration as well, the melancholy imagination sublimates it and gives itself a protection against collapsing into asymbolism. Nerval formulates the temporary triumph of that genuine arbor of names hauled up from the abyss of the lost "Thing" in the following fashion: "I cried out at length, invoking my mother under the names given to ancient divinities."[25]

Commemorating Mourning

Thus the melancholy past does not pass. Neither does the poet's past. He is the continuous historian less of his real history than of the symbolic events that have lead his body toward significance or threatened his consciousness with foundering.

A poem by Nerval thus has a highly mnemonic function ("a prayer to the goddess Mnemosyne," he writes in *Aurélia*),[26] in the sense of a commemoration of the genesis of symbols and phantasmal life into texts that become the artist's only "true" life: "Here began what I shall call the overflowing of the dream into real life. From that moment on, everything took on at times a double aspect" (p. 120). One can follow, for instance, in a section of *Aurélia,* the concatenation of the following sequences: death of the loved woman (mother), identifying with her and with death, setting up a space of psychic solitude buttressed by the perception of a bisexual or asexual form, and finally bursting forth of the sadness that is summed up by the mention of Dürer's *Melancholia.* The following excerpt can be interpreted as a commemoration of the "depressive position" dear to the disciples of Melanie Klein (see chapter 1): "I saw in front of me a woman with deathly pale complexion, hollow eyes, whose features seemed to me like Aurélia's. I said to myself: 'I am being warned of either her *death* or mine.' . . . I was wandering about a vast building composed of several rooms. . . . A creature of enormous proportions—man or woman I do not know —was fluttering painfully through the air . . . it looked like Dürer's *Angel of Melancholia.* I could not keep myself from crying out in terror and this woke me up with a start" (p., 118). The symbolics of language and, more markedly, of the text takes over from terror and triumphs, for a while, through the death of the other or of the self.

Variations of the "Double"

Widower or poet, stellar or funereal being, identifying with death or Orphic conqueror—such are merely a few of the ambiguities that a reading of "El Desdichado" reveals, and they require us to view *doubling* as the central image of Nerval's imagination.

Far from repressing the trouble that the loss of the object entails (whether archaic or present loss), melan-

choly persons settle the lost Thing or object within themselves, identifying with the loss's beneficial features on the
one hand, with its maleficent ones on the other. This
presents us with the first state of the self's doubling, which
initiates a series of contradictory identifications that the
work of the imagination will attempt to reconcile—tyrannical judge and victim, unreachable ideal or sick person
beyond recovery, and so forth. Figures follow one upon
another, meet, pursue or love one another, love, look
after, reject one another. Brothers, friends, or enemies,
doubles might be involved in a true dramatic staging of
homosexuality.

Nevertheless, when one of the figures becomes identified with the female sex of the lost object, the attempt at
reconciliation beyond the splitting leads up to a feminiza-
tion of the speaker or to androgyny. "From that moment
on, everything took on at times a double aspect" (p. 120).
Aurélia, "a woman whom I had loved for a long while,"
is dead. But "I said to myself: 'I am being warned of
either her *death* or mine'!" (pp. 115, 118). Having found
Aurélia's funereal bust, the narrator recounts the melancholy state caused by the knowledge of his illness: "I
believed that I myself had only a short while longer to
live. . . . Besides, she belonged to me much more in her
death than in her life" (p. 132). She and he, life and death,
here are entities that reflect each other in mirrorlike fashion, interchangeable.

After evoking the process of creation, prehistoric animals, and various cataclysms ("Everywhere the suffering
image of the eternal Mother was dying, weeping, or lan-
guishing"; p. 136), he sees another double. It is an oriental
prince whose face is that of the narrator: "It was my own
face, my whole form magnified and idealized" (p. 138).

Having been unable to unite with Aurélia, the narrator

changes her into an idealized and, this time, masculine double: " 'Every man has a double,' I said to myself. 'I feel two men in myself' " (p. 139). Spectator and actor, speaker and respondent, all nevertheless rediscover the projective dialectic of good and evil: "In any case, my *other* is hostile to me." Idealization turns into persecution and entails a "double meaning" in everything the narrator hears. Because he is being visited by this bad double, by "an evil genius [who] had my place in the soul world," Aurélia's lover gives in to a greater despair. To crown it all, he imagines that his double "was going to marry Aurélia"—"Immediately a mad rage seized me," while all around him they laughed at his impotence. As a result of this dramatic doubling, women's screams and foreign words— other signs of doubling, this time sexual and verbal— pierce Nerval's dream (p. 142). Meeting, under an arbor, a woman who is Aurélia's physic double, he is again thrust into the idea that he must die in order to be with her, as if he were the dead woman's alter ego (p. 157).

The episodes of doubling follow one upon the other and vary, but they all lead up to a celebration of two fundamental figures: the universal Mother, Isis or Mary, and Christ, who is praised and of whom the narrator wishes to be the ultimate double. "A kind of mysterious choir chanted in my ears. Children's voices were repeating in chorus: *Christe! Christe! Christe!* . . . 'But Christ is no more,' I said to myself" (p. 157). The narrator descends to hell as Christ did and the text comes to a stop with that image, as if it were not sure of forgiveness and resurrection.

The theme of forgiveness asserts itself indeed in the last pages of Aurélia: guilty because he did not mourn for his old parents as strongly as he mourned for "that woman," the poet cannot hope for forgiveness. And yet, "Christ's pardon was pronounced for you also!" (p. 175). Thus the longing for forgiveness, an attempt to belong to the religion that promises an afterlife, haunts the struggle against melancholia and doubling. Confronting the "black sun of melancholia" the narrator asserts, "God is the Sun" (p. 156). Is this a resurrectional metaphor or a reverse with respect to a solidary obverse seen as the "black sun"?

Speaking the Breakup

At times, the doubling becomes a "molecular" breakup that is metaphorized by currents crisscrossing a "sunless day." "I felt myself carried painlessly along on a current of molten metal, and a thousand similar streams, the colors of which indicated different chemicals, criss-crossed the breast of the world like those blood-vessels and veins that writhe in the lobes of the brain. They all flowed, circulated and throbbed just like that, and I had a feeling that their currents were composed of living souls in a molecular condition, and that the speed of my own movement alone prevented me from distinguishing them" (p. 124).

Strange insight, admirable knowledge of the accelerated dislocation subtending the process of melancholia and its underlying psychosis. The language of that breathtaking acceleration assumes a combinatory, polyvalent, and totalizing aspect, dominated by primary processes. Such a symbolic activity, often not lending itself to representation, "nonfigurative," "abstract," is brilliantly perceived by Nerval. "The speech of my companions took *mysterious turns* whose sense I alone could understand, and *formless*, inanimate objects lent themselves to the *calculations* of my mind; from *combinations* of pebbles, from *shapes in corners*, *chinks* or openings, from the *outlines* of leaves, colors, smells, and sounds, emanated for me hitherto unknown harmonies. 'How have I been able to live so long,' I asked myself, 'outside nature and without identifying myself with it? Everything lives, moves, everything corresponds . . . it is a transparent *network* that covers the world" (pp. 166–67; see also chapter 1).

Cabalism or esoteric theories involving "correspondences" show up here. All the same, the quotation is also an extraordinary allegory of the prosodic polymorphism characteristic of a writing in which Nerval appears to favor the network of intensities, sounds, significances rather than communicating univocal information. Indeed, this "transparent network" refers to Nerval's very text, and we can read it as a metaphor of sublimation—a transposition of drives and their objects into destabilized and recombined signs that make the writer capable of "sharing my joys and sorrows" (p. 167).

Whatever allusions to freemasonry and initiation there may be, and perhaps at the same time, Nerval's writing conjures up (as in analysis) archaic psychic experiences that few people reach through their conscious speech. It appears obvious that Nerval's psychotic conflicts could favor such an access to the limits of the speaking being and of humanity. With Nerval, melancholia represented only one aspect of such conflicts, which could reach the point of schizophrenic fragmentation. Nevertheless, because of its key position in the organization and disorganization of psychic space, at the limits of affect and meaning, of biology and language, of asymbolia and breathtakingly rapid or eclipsed significance, it is indeed melancholia that governed Nerval's representations. Creating prosody and an undecidable polyphony with symbols centered in the "black spot" or the "black sun" of melancholia thus provided an antidote to depression, a temporary salvation.

Melancholia subtends the "crisis of values" that shook up the nineteenth century and was expressed in esoteric proliferation. The legacy of Catholicism became involved, but the elements pertaining to states of psychic crisis were recovered and inserted in a polymorphic and polyvalent spiritualistic syncretism. The Word was experienced less as incarnation and euphoria than as a *quest for a passion* remaining unnameable or secret, and as *presence of an absolute meaning* that seems as omnivalent as it is elusive and prone to abandon. A true melancholy experience of man's symbolic resources was then undergone on the occasion of the religious and political crisis caused by the French Revolution. Walter Benjamin has stressed the melancholy substratum of the imagination that has been deprived of both classical and religious stability but is still anxious to give itself a new meaning (as long as we speak, as long as artists create), which nevertheless remains basically disappointed, racked by the evil or the irony of the Prince of Darkness (so long as we live as orphans but creating, creators but forsaken . . .).

"El Desdichado," however, like all Nerval's poetry and poetic prose, attempted a tremendous *incarnation* of the unbridled significance that leaps and totters within the polyvalence of esoterisms. By accepting the dispersal of meaning — the text's replica of a fragmented identity — the themes of the sonnet relate a true archeology of affective mourning and erotic ordeal, overcome by assimilating the archaic state into the language of poetry. At the same time, the assimilation is also accomplished through oralization and musicalization of the signs themselves, thus bringing meaning closer to the lost body. At the very heart of the value crisis, poetic writing mimics a resurrection. "I've twice, as a conqueror, been across the Acheron . . ." There would be no third time.

Sublimation is a powerful ally of the Disinherited, provided, however, that he can receive and accept another one's speech. As it happened, the other did not show up at the appointment of him who went to join—without a lyre this time, but alone in the night, under a street lamp —"the sighs of the saint and the screams of the fay."

7

Dostoyevsky, The Writing of Suffering, and Forgiveness

Claude Lorrain, *Acis and Galatea*. Staatliche Kunstsammlunger,
Gemaldegalerie Alte Meister (Sempergalerie), Dresden.
Photograph © Viollet collection.

In Praise of Suffering

The tormented world of Dostoyevsky (1821–1881) is ruled more by epilepsy than by melancholia in the clinical sense of the term.[1] While Hippocrates used the two words interchangeably and Aristotle distinguished them while comparing them, present clinical practice views them as basically separate entities. Nonetheless, one should keep in mind the despondency that precedes or above all follows, in Dostoyevsky's writings, the attack as he himself describes it; one should also take note of the hypostasis of suffering, which, without having any explicit, immediate relation to epilepsy, compels recognition throughout his work as the essential feature of his outlook on humanity.

Oddly enough, Dostoyevsky's insistence on locating the presence of a precocious or at least primordial suffering on the fringe of consciousness brings to mind Freud's thesis concerning a primal "death drive," bearing desires, and "primary masochism" (see chapter 1). Whereas with Melanie Klein projection most frequently precedes introjection, aggression comes before suffering, and the paranoid-schizoid position subtends the depressive position, Freud stresses what one might call a zero degree of psychic life where noneroticized suffering ("primary masochism," "melancholia") would be the primordial psychic inscription of a break (remembering the leap from inorganic to organic matter; affect of the separation between body and ecosystem, child and mother, etc.; but also death-bearing effect of a permanent, tyrannical superego).

Dostoyevsky seems very close to such an insight. He views suffering as a precocious, primary affect, reacting to a definite but somehow preobject traumatism, to which one cannot assign an agent distinct from the subject and thus liable to attract energies, psychic inscriptions, representations, or outward actions. As if under the impact of an equally precocious superego that recalls the melancholy superego seen by Freud as a "cultivation of death drive," the drives of Dostoyevsky's heroes turn back on their own space. Instead of changing into erotic drives, they are inscribed as a suffering mood. Neither inside nor outside, in between, on the threshold of the self/other separation and before the latter is even possible, that is where Dostoyevsky's brand of suffering is set up.

Biographers point out that Dostoyevsky preferred the company of those who were prone to sorrow. He cultivated it in himself and exalted it in both his texts and his correspondence. Let me quote from a letter to Maikov, dated May 27, 1869, written in Florence: "The main thing is sadness, but if one talks about it or explains it more, so much more would have to be said. Just the same, sorrow is such that if I were alone, I should perhaps have become ill with grief. . . . At any rate sadness is dreadful, and worse yet in Europe, I look at everything here as an animal might. No matter what, I have decided to return to Petersburg next spring. . . ."

Epileptic fits and writing are in the same way the high points of a paroxysmal sadness that reverses into a mystical jubilation outside time. Thus, in the *Notebooks of the*

Possessed (the novel was published in 1873): "Attack at six in the morning (the day and almost the hour of Tropmann's torture). I did not hear it, woke up at eight with the consciousness of an attack. My head hurt, my body was exhausted. Generally, the repercussions of the attack, that is, nervousness, shortening of the memory, now persist longer than in preceding years. Before, it was over in three days, and now it was not over in six. Evenings especially, by candlelight, a *hypochondriac sadness without object, and a shade of red, blood-red* (not a color) covered everything. . . ."[2] Or, "nervous laughter and mystical sadness,"[3] he repeats in implicit reference to the medieval monks' *acedia.* Or still, *"How can one write?* One must suffer, suffer a lot. . . ."

Suffering, here, seems to be an "excess," a power, a sensual pleasure. The "black spot" of Nerval's melancholia has given way to a torrent of passion, a hysterical affect if you wish, whose fluid overflow carries away the placid signs and soothed compositions of "monological" literature. It endows Dostoyevsky's text with a breathtaking polyphony and imposes as ultimate truth of his characters a rebellious flesh that delights in not submitting to the Word. A sensual pleasure in suffering that has "no coldness and no disenchantment, nothing of what was made fashionable by Byron," but has an "inordinate, insatiable thirst for sensual delights," an "inextinguishable thirst for life," including "delight in theft, in crime, sensual delight in suicide."[4] Such an exaltation of moods, which can revert from suffering to immeasurable jubilation, is admirably described by Kirillov for the moments that precede suicide or an attack:

> There are seconds—they come five or six at a time—
> when you suddenly feel the presence of the eternal
> harmony perfectly attained. It's something not earthly

—I don't mean in the sense that it's heavenly—but in that sense that man cannot endure it in his earthly aspect. He must be physically changed or die. The feeling is clear and unmistakable; . . . it's not being deeply moved. . . . It's not that you love—oh, there's something in it higher than love—what's most awful is that it's terribly clear and such joy. If it lasted more than five seconds, the soul could not endure it and must perish. . . . To endure ten seconds one must be physically changed. . . .
—Don't you have fits, perhaps?
—No.
—Well, you will. Be careful, Kirillov. I've heard that's just how [epileptic] fits begin.

And concerning the slow duration of this state:

Remember Mahomet's pitcher from which not a drop of water was spilt while he circled Paradise on his horse. That was a case of five seconds too; that's too much like your eternal harmony, and Mahomet was an epileptic. Be careful, it's epilepsy!"[5]

Irreducible to feelings, the affect in its twofold aspect of energy flow *and* psychic inscription—lucid, clear, harmonious, even though outside language—is translated here with an extraordinary faithfulness. The affect does not go through language, and when referring to it language is not bound to it as it is to an idea. The verbalization of affects (unconscious or not) does not use the same economy as the verbalization of ideas (unconscious or not). One may suppose that the verbalization of unconscious affects does not make them conscious (the subject knows no more than before wherefrom and how joy or sadness emerges and modifies neither one), but causes them to work differently. On the one hand, affects *redistribute the order of language* and give birth to a style. On the other, they *display* the unconscious through characters and actions that represent the most forbidden and transgressive drive motions. Literature, like hysteria, which Freud saw as a "distorted work of art," is a *staging* of affects both on the intersubjective level (characters) and on the intralinguistic level (style).

It is probably because of such an intimacy with affect that Dostoyevsky was led to a vision according to which man's humanity lies less in the quest for pleasure or profit (an idea that subtends even Freudian psychoanalysis in spite of the prominence finally granted a "beyond the pleasure principle") than in a longing for voluptuous suffering. Such suffering differs from animosity or rage, it is less objectal, more withdrawn into its own person, and beyond it there would be only the loss of self within the darkness of the body. It is an inhibited death drive, a sadism hampered by a guarding consciousness, turned back on a self that is henceforth painful and inactive. "Again, in consequence of those accursed laws of consciousness, my spite is subject to chemical disintegration. You look into it, the object flies off into air, your reasons evaporate, the criminal is not to be found, the insult becomes fate rather than an insult, something like the toothache, for which no one is to blame. . . ."[6] Finally, there is a plea in favor of suffering that is worthy of the medieval *acedia* or even of Job: "And why are you so firmly, so triumphantly convinced that only the normal and the positive—in short, only prosperity—is to the advantage of man? Is not reason mistaken about advantage? After all, perhaps man likes something besides prosperity? Perhaps he likes suffering just as much? Perhaps suffering is just as great an advantage to him as prosperity? Man is sometimes fearfully,

passionately in love with suffering and that is a fact."
Quite typical of Dostoyevsky is the definition of suffering
as asserted freedom, as *caprice:*

> After all, I do not really insist on suffering or on pros-
> perity either. I insist on my caprice, and its being guar-
> anteed to me when necessary. Suffering would be out
> of place in vaudevilles, for instance; I know that. In the
> crystal palace it is even unthinkable; suffering means
> doubt, means negation. . . . Why, after all, suffering is
> the sole origin of consciousness . . . consciousness, in
> my opinion, is the greatest misfortune for man, yet I
> know man loves it and would not give it up for any
> satisfaction.[7]

The transgressor, that Dostoyevskian "overman" who
searches for his identity through an apologia for crime
with Raskolnikov, for instance, is not a nihilist but a man
of values.[8] His suffering is the proof of that, and it results
from a permanent quest for meaning. He who is conscious
of his transgressive act is by the same token punished, for
he suffers on account of it—"he will suffer for his mistake. That will be his punishment—as well as the prison";[9]
"Pain and suffering are always inevitable for a large intelligence and a deep heart. The really great men must, I
think, have great sadness on earth. . . ."[10] Thus, after
Nikolay confesses to having committed a crime although
he is innocent, Porfiry thinks he can detect in that zealous
self-accusation the old Russian mystical tradition that glo-
rifies suffering as a sign of one's humanity: "Do you know
. . . the force of the word 'suffering' among some of these
people! It's not a question of suffering for someone's benefit, but simply, 'one must suffer.' If they suffer at the
hands of the authorities, so much the better."[11] "Suffer!
Maybe Nikolay is right in wanting to suffer."[12]

Suffering would be an act of consciousness; consciousness (for Dostoyevsky) says: suffer.

> Conscious implies suffering, but I do not wish to suffer, since why should I consent to suffering? Nature, through the medium of my consciousness, proclaims to me some sort of harmony of the whole. Human consciousness has produced religions out of this message. . . . abase myself, accept suffering because of the harmony of the whole, and consent to live. . . . And why should I bother about its preservation after I no longer exist— that is the question. It would have been better to be created like all animals—*i.e.,* living but not conceiving myself rationally. But my consciousness is not harmony, but, on the contrary, precisely disharmony, because with it I am unhappy. Look: who is happy in the world and what kind of people *consent* to live?—Precisely those who are akin to animals and come nearest to their species by reason of their limited development and consciousness.[13]

In such a view, nihilistic suicide would itself be a fulfillment of man's condition—of man endowed with consciousness but . . . deprived of forgiving love, of ideal meaning, of God.

A Suffering That Precedes Hatred

Let us not too hastily interpret those remarks as an acknowledgment of pathological masochism. Is it not by *signifying* hatred, the destruction of the other, and perhaps above all his own execution, that the human being survives as a symbolic animal? An inordinate but checked violence opens onto the execution of the self by itself in order that the subject be born. From a diachronic standpoint, we are there at the lower threshold of subjectivity, before an *other* stands out who might be the *object* of a hateful or loving attack. Now, this same checking of hatred also allows for the mastery of signs: I do not attack you, I *speak* (or write) *my* fear or *my* pain. My suffering is the lining of my speech, of my civilization. One can imagine the masochistic risks of that civility. As far as writers are concerned, they can extract jubilation out of it through the manipulation they are able, on that basis, to inflict upon signs and things.

Suffering and its solidary obverse, jouissance or "voluptuousness," in Dostoyevsky's sense, are essential as the ultimate indication of a break that immediately precedes the subject's and the Other's becoming autonomous (chronologically and logically). It can involve an internal or external bioenergetic break or a symbolic one caused by an abandonment, a punishment, a banishment. One cannot overemphasize the harshness of Dostoyevsky's father who was held in contempt by his muzhiks and perhaps even killed by them (according to some biographers, now disproved). Suffering is the first or the last attempt on the part of the subject to assert his "own and proper" at the closest point to threatened biological unit and to narcissism put to the test. Consequently this humoral exaggeration, this pretentious swelling of one's "own and proper" states an essential given of the psyche in the process of being set up or collapsing under the sway of an already dominant Other, although still unrecognized in its powerful otherness, under the gaze of the ego ideal riveted to the ideal ego.

Erotization of suffering seems to be secondary. Indeed, it shows up only by becoming integrated into the flow of a sadomasochistic aggressiveness turned against the other who tinges it with voluptuousness and caprice; the whole can then be rationalized as a metaphysical experience of freedom or transgression. Nevertheless, at a logically and chronologically earlier stage, suffering appears as the ultimate threshold, the primary affect, of distinction or separation. In this perspective one needs to consider recent remarks according to which the feeling of harmony or joy caused by the coming of an epileptic fit would be only an aftereffect of the imagination, which, following the fit, attempts to appropriate in positive fashion the blank, disruptive moment of that suffering caused by discontinuity (violent energy discharge, break in symbolic order during the fit). Dostoyevsky would thus have misled doctors who, in his wake, thought they noticed, with epileptics, euphoric periods preceding the fit, whereas the moment of rupture would actually be marked only by the painful experience of loss and of suffering, and this according to the secret experience of Dostoyevsky himself.[14]

One might argue that, within *masochistic economy,* the psychic experience of discontinuity is experienced as trauma or loss. The subject represses or repudiates the paranoid-schizoid violence that, from this standpoint, would be subsequent to the painful psychic inscription of discontinuity. It then logically or chronologically regresses to the level where separations as well as bonds (subject/object, affect/meaning) are threatened. In *melancholy* persons this stage is revealed by the dominance of mood over the very possibility of verbalization, before an eventual affective paralysis.

One might, however, consider the *epileptic symptom* as another variation on the subject's withdrawal when, threatened with a lapse into the paranoid-schizoid position, it effects by means of motor discharge a silent acting out of the "death drive" (break in neural transmissibility, interruption of symbolic bonds, preventing the homeostasis of the living structure).

From this standpoint, *melancholia* as a mood-breaking

symbolic continuity but also *epilepsy* as motor discharge represent, on the subject's part, dodges with respect to the erotic relation with the other and particularly the paranoid-schizoid potentialities of desire. On the other hand, one can interpret idealization and sublimation as attempts to elude the same confrontation while signifying regression and its sadomasochistic ambivalences. In this sense *forgiveness*, coextensive with sublimation, diseroticizes beyond Eros. The Eros/Forgiveness pair is substituted for Eros/Thanatos, so that the potential melancholia is not frozen as an affective withdrawal from the world but *traverses the representation* of aggressive and threatening bonds with the other. Within representation, to the extent that it is shored up by the ideal and sublimational economy of forgiveness, the subject is able not to act but to shape—*poiein*—its death drive as well as its erotic bonds.

Dostoyevsky and Job

The suffering being, with Dostoyevsky, reminds one of Job's paradoxical experience, which had, moreover, made such a deep impression on the writer: "I am reading the Book of Job and it gives me a curiously painful delight: I stop reading and I walk about my room for an hour, almost weeping. . . . It is strange, Anya, but that book was one of the first to impress me in my life—I was almost an infant then."[15] Job, a prosperous man, faithful to Yahweh, was suddenly stricken—by Yahweh or by Satan?—with various misfortunes . . . But this "depressed" person, the object of mockery ("If one should address a word to you, will you endure it?" Job 4:2), is sad, when all is said and done, only because he values God. Even if that God is ruthless, unjust with the faithful, generous with the ungodly, that does not induce Job to break his divine contract. On the contrary, he lives constantly under the eyes of God and constitutes a striking acknowledgment of the depressed person's dependency on his superego blended with the ideal ego: "What is man that you (God) should make so much of him?" (7:17); "Turn your eyes away, leave me a little joy" (10:20). And yet Job does not recognize God's true power ("Were he to pass me, I should not see him"; Job 9:11), and God himself will have to sum up before his depressed creature the whole of Creation, to assert his position as Lawmaker or superego susceptible of idealization, in order for Job to feel hopeful again. Would suffering persons be narcissistic, overly interested in themselves, attached to their own value, and ready to take themselves for an immanence of transcendence? After having punished him, however, Yahweh finally rewards him and places him above those who disparaged him. "I burn with anger against you . . . for not speaking truthfully about me as my servant Job has done" (42:8).

Likewise, with Dostoyevsky the Christian, suffering—a major evidence of humanity—is the sign of man's dependency on a divine Law, as well as of his irremediable difference in relation to that Law. The coincidence of bond and lapse, of faithfulness and transgression are to be found again on the very ethical plane where Dostoyevsky's character is an idiot through holiness, an enlightener through criminality.

Such a logic postulating interdependence of law and transgression cannot be extraneous to the epileptic fit being triggered by what is very often a strong contradiction between love and hatred, desire for the other and rejection of the other. One might wonder, on the other hand, whether or not the well-known *ambivalence* of Dostoyevsky's heroes, which led Bakhtin to postulate a "dialogism" at the foundation of his poetics,[16] was an attempt to *represent,* through the ordering of discourses and the conflicts between characters, the opposition, without a synthetic solution, of the two forces (positive and negative) specific to drive and desire.

Nevertheless, if the symbolic bond were broken, Job would turn into Kirillov, a suicidal terrorist. Merezhkovsky is not completely wrong to see in Dostoyevsky the precursor of the Russian revolution.[17] Certainly he dreads it, he rejects and denounces it, but it is he who experiences its underhanded advent in the soul of his suffering man, ready to betray Job's humility in favor of the manic excitement of the revolutionary who thinks he is God (such, according to Dostoyevsky, is the socialist faith of atheists). The depressed person's narcissism becomes inverted in the mania of atheistic terrorism: Kirillov is the man without God who has taken God's place. Suffering ceases so that death might assert itself; was suffering a dam against suicide and against death?

Suicide and Terrorism

One will recall at least two solutions, both fatal, to suffering in Dostoyevsky—the ultimate veil of chaos and destruction.

Kirillov is convinced that God does not exist but, in abiding by divine authority, he wants to raise human freedom to the level of the absolute through the utterly free, negating act that suicide constitutes for him. *God does not exist—I am God—I do not exist—I commit suicide—* such would be the paradoxical logic of the negation of an absolute paternity or divinity, which is nevertheless maintained so that I might take hold of it.

Raskolnikov, on the other hand, and as if in a manic

defense against despair, redirects his hatred not on himself but on another disavowed, denigrated person. Through his gratuitous crime, which involves killing an insignificant woman, he breaks the Christian contract ("You must love your neighbor as yourself"). He disavows his love for the primal object ("Since I do not love my mother my neighbor is insignificant, and this allows me to suppress him without bother," is what he seems to say) and, on the basis of such implicitness he takes it upon himself to actualize his hatred against a family circle and a society experienced as persecuting.

We know that the metaphysical meaning of such behavior is the nihilistic negation of the supreme value, which also reveals an inability to symbolize, think, and assume suffering. With Dostoyevsky, nihilism arouses the believer's revolt against transcendental erasing. The psychoanalyst will take note of the ambiguous, to say the least, fascination of the writer with certain manic defenses set up against suffering, and with the exquisite depression he otherwise nurtures as well, as necessary and antinomical linings of his writing. Such defenses are contemptible, as the relinquishment of morality, the loss of the meaning of life, terrorism, or torture, so frequent in current events, do not cease reminding us. As far as the writer is concerned, he has chosen to support religious orthodoxy. Such "obscurantism," so violently denounced by Freud, is, all thing considered, less harmful to civilization than terrorist nihilism. With and beyond ideology, writing remains—a painful, continuing struggle to compose a work edge to edge with the unnameable sensuous delights of destruction and chaos.

Are religion or mania, daughter of paranoia, the only counterbalances to despair? Artistic creation integrates and expends them. Works of art thus lead us to establish relations with ourselves and others that are less destructive, more soothing.

A Death Without Resurrection: Apocalyptic Time

In front of Holbein's "Dead Christ" Myshkin and Ippolit as well, in *The Idiot* (1869), have doubts as to the Ressurection. This body's death, so natural, so implacable, seems to leave no room for redemption: "[Christ's] swollen face is covered with bloody wounds, and it is so terrible to behold" Anna Grigorievna Dostoyevskaya wrote in her reminiscences.

> The painting had a crushing impact on Fyodor Mikhailovich. He stood there as if stunned. And I did not have the strength to look at it—it was too painful for me, particularly in my sickly condition—and I went into other rooms. When I came back after fifteen or twenty minutes, I found him still riveted to the same spot in front of the painting. His agitated face had a kind of dread in it, something I had noticed more than once during the first moments of an epileptic seizure.
>
> Quietly I took my husband by the arm, led him to another room and sat him down on a bench, expecting the attack from one minute to the next. Luckily this did not happen. He calmed down little by little and left the museum, but insisted on returning once again to view this painting which had struck him so powerfully.[18]

A sense of time abolished weighs on that picture, the inescapable prospect of death erasing all commitment to a project, continuity, or resurrection. This is an apocalyptic time that Dostoyevsky is familiar with: he evokes it before the mortal remains of his first wife Marya Dimitriyevna ("There should be time no longer"), referring to the Book of Revelation (10:6), and Prince Myshkin speaks of it in the same terms to Rogozhin ("At this moment I feel that I understand those peculiar words, *There should be time no longer*"), but, like Kirillov, he contemplates, Mohammad-like, a happy version of that temporal suspension. With Dostoyevsky, to suspend time means to suspend faith in Christ: "Everything thus depends on this: does one accept Christ as the definitive ideal on earth? This amounts to saying that everything depends on one's faith in Christ. If one believes in Christ one also believes in life eternal."[19] And yet what forgiveness can there be, what salvation in the face of the irremediable void of the lifeless flesh, the absolute solitude of Holbein's picture? The writer is disturbed, as he was before the corpse of his first wife in 1864.

What Is Tact?

The meaning of melancholia? Merely an abyssal suffering that does not succeed in signifying itself and, having lost meaning, loses life. That meaning is the weird affect that the analyst will be looking for with utmost empathy, beyond the motor and verbal retardation of the depressed, in the tone of their voice or else in cutting up their devitalized, vulgarized words—words from which any appeal to the other has disappeared—precisely attempting to get in touch with the other through syllables, fragments, and their reconstruction (see chapter 2). Such an analytic hearing implies *tact*.

What is tact? To hear true, along with forgiveness. *Forgiveness:* giving in addition, banking on what is there in order to revive, to give the depressed patient (that stranger withdrawn into his wound) a new start, and give him the possibility of a new encounter. The solemnity of

that forgiveness is best displayed in the conception Dostoyevsky elaborates in connection with the meaning of
melancholia: between suffering and acting out, aesthetic
activity constitutes forgiveness. This is where one notices
the imprint of Dostoyevsky's orthodox Christianity, which
thoroughly imbues his work. This is also where—more
so than at the place of his imaginary complicity with the
criminal—the feeling of discomfort aroused by his texts
builds up in the contemporary reader who is caught up in
nihilism.

Indeed, any modern imprecation against Christianity—
up to and including Nietzsche's—is an imprecation against
forgiveness. Such "forgiveness," however, understood as
connivance with degradation, moral softening, and refusal
of power is perhaps only the image one has of decadent
Christianity. On the other hand, the *solemnity* of forgiveness—as it functions in theological tradition and as it is
rehabilitated in aesthetic experience, which identifies with
abjection in order to traverse it, name it, expend it—is
inherent in the economy of psychic rebirth. At any rate,
that is how it appears under the benevolent impact of
analytic practice. In that locale, the "perversion of Christianity" that Nietzsche denounced in Pascal[20] but that is
also forcefully displayed in the ambivalence of aesthetic
forgiveness with Dostoyevsky is a powerful fight against
paranoia, which is hostile to forgiveness. An example of
this is the path followed by Raskolnikov, who went through
melancholia, terrorist negation, and finally gratitude, which
proved to be a rebirth.

Death: An Inability to Forgive

The notion of forgiveness fully occupies Dostoyevsky's
work.

In *The Insulted and Humiliated* (1861) we meet, in the very first pages, a living corpse. This body, resembling that of a dead man but actually on the threshold of death, haunts Dostoyevsky's imagination. When he saw Holbein's picture in Basel in 1867, his feeling was doubtless that of having met an old acquaintance, an intimate ghost:

> Another thing that amazed me was his extraordinary emaciation: he had hardly any flesh left, it seemed there was nothing but skin stretched over his bones. His large, but lustreless eyes, set as they were in blue circles, always stared straight before him, never swerving, and never seeing anything—of that I feel certain. . . . What is he thinking about? I went on wondering. What goes on in his mind? And does he still think of anything at all? His face is so dead that it no longer expresses anything.[21]

That was a description not of Holbein's painting but of an enigmatic character who appears in *The Insulted and Humiliated*. He is an old man named Smith, the grandfather of Nelly, the little epileptic, the father of a "romantic and unreasonable" daughter whom he never forgave her relationship with Prince P. A. Valkovsky, a relationship that was to wipe out Smith's fortune, destroy the young woman and Nelly herself, the prince's illegitimate child.

Smith displays the rigid, death-bearing dignity of one who does not forgive. In the novel, he is the first in a series of deeply humiliated and insulted characters who cannot forgive and, at the hour of death, curse their tyrant with an impassioned intensity that leads one to suspect that at the very threshold of death it is the persecutor who is desired. Such was the case with Smith's daughter and with Nelly herself.

That series contrasts with another—the narrator's, a writer like Dostoyevsky, and the Ikhmenev family who, in circumstances similar to those of the Smith family, are humiliated and insulted but end up forgiving not the cynic but the young victim. (I shall return to that difference when emphasizing the crime's statute of limitations, which does not erase it but allows the forgiven person to "start a new life.")

Allow me to stress, for the time being, the impossibility of forgiving. Smith forgives neither his daughter nor Valkovsky; Nelly forgives her mother but not Valkovsky; the mother forgives neither Valkovsky nor her own embittered father. As in a dance of death, humiliation without forgiveness calls the tune and leads the "selfishness of suffering" to sentence everyone to death within and through the narrative. A hidden message seems to emerge: he who does not forgive is condemned to death. The body demeaned by old age, disease, and solitude, all the physical signs of inescapable death, illness, and sadness itself would in that sense point to an inability to forgive. Consequently, the reader infers that the "Dead Christ" himself would be a Christ viewed as one to whom forgiveness is unknown. In order to be so "truly dead," such a Christ could not have been forgiven and will not forgive. On the contrary, the Resurrection appears as the supreme expression of forgiveness: by bringing his Son back to life the Father becomes reconciled with Him but, even more so, in coming back to life Christ indicates to the faithful that He is not leaving them. "I come to you," he seems to say, "understand that I forgive you."

Unbelievable, uncertain, miraculous, and yet so basic to Christian faith as well as to Dostoyevsky's aesthetics and morals, forgiveness is almost madness in *The Idiot,* a *deus ex machina* in *Crime and Punishment.*

Indeed, apart from his convulsive fits, Prince Myshkin is an "idiot" only because he holds no grudges. Made ridiculous, insulted, jeered at, even threatened with death by Rogozhin, the prince forgives. Mercy finds in him its literal psychological fulfillment: having suffered too much, he takes upon himself the miseries of others. As if he had had an inkling of the suffering that underlies aggressions, he ignores them, withdraws, and even gives solace. The scenes of arbitrary violence he is subjected to and that Dostoyevsky evokes with tragic and grotesque power cause him pain, to be sure. Let us remember his compassion for the Swiss peasant girl, who was held in contempt in her village following a sexual transgression and whom he taught the children to love; or the childish and lovingly edgy mocking on Aglaya's part, which does not fool him in spite of his absentminded, goodnatured appearance; or Nastasya Filippovna's hysterical aggressions against this fallen prince, who she knows is the only one to have understood her; or even Rogozhin lunging at him with a knife on the dark stairs of that hotel where Proust saw Dostoyevsky's genius displayed as fashioner of new spaces. The prince is shocked by such violence, evil causes him pain, horror is far from being forgotten or neutralized within him, but he takes a hold on himself, and his benevolent uneasiness shows how fine "the essential part of [his] mind" is, as Aglaya put it: "For although you really are ill mentally (you will not, of course, be angry with me for saying this, for I don't mean it at all derogatively), yet the most essential part of your mind is much better than in any of them. Indeed, it's something they never dreamed of. For there are two sorts of mind—one that is essential and one that isn't. Isn't that so?"[22] That sort of mind leads him to soothe his aggressor and to harmonize the group of which he consequently appears to be not a minor element, a "stranger," an "outcast,"[23] but a spiritual leader, discreet and unmasterable.

The Object of Forgiveness

What is the object of forgiveness? Insults, of course, any moral and physical wound, and, eventually, death. Sexual lapse is at the heart of *The Insulted and Humiliated* and it goes with many of Dostoyevsky's feminine characters (Nastasya Filippovna, Grushenka, Natasha), and it is also signaled in masculine perversions (Stavrogin's rape of minors, for instance) in order to represent one of the principal grounds for forgiveness. Absolute evil, however, is still death, and whatever the delights of suffering or the reasons that lead his hero to the limits of suicide and murder, Dostoyevsky implacably condemns murder, that is, the death that the human being is capable of inflicting. He does not seem to distinguish the senseless murder from murder as moral punishment imposed by men's justice. If he were to set up a distinction between them, he would favor torture and pain, which, through erotization, seem to "cultivate" and thus humanize murder and violence in the eyes of the artist.[24] He does not, on the other hand, forgive cold, irrevocable death, the very "clean" death inflicted by the guillotine: there is "no greater agony." "Who says that human nature is capable of bearing this without madness?"[25] Indeed, for one condemned to the guillotine, forgiveness is impossible. "The face of a condemned man a minute before the fall of the guillotine blade, when he is still standing on the scaffold and before he lies down on the plank"[26] reminds Prince Myshkin of the picture he had seen at Basel. "It was of agony like this and of such horror that Christ spoke."[27]

Dostoyevsky, who was himself sentenced to death, was

pardoned. Did forgiveness, in his vision of the beautiful and the just, draw its importance from such a tragedy, resolved at the last moment? It is possible that forgiveness, coming as it did after an already imagined death, a lived death if one may say so, and which necessarily kindled a sensitivity as excitable as Dostoyevsky's, might actually put death *in abeyance:* erasing it and reconciling the condemned man with the condemning power? A great surge of reconciliation with the deserting power, which has again become a desirable ideal, is doubtless necessary for the life given again to continue and for contact with newly found others to be established.[28] Below this surge, however, there remains the often unquenched melancholy anguish of the subject who has already died once, even though miraculously resurrected . . . The writer's imagination is then beset with an alternation between the unsurpassability of suffering and the flash of forgiveness, and their eternal return articulates the whole of his work.

Dostoyevsky's dramatic imagination, his tormented characters, particularly suggest the difficulty, even the impossibility of such forgiveness/love. The most compact statement of the turmoil triggered by the necessity *and* the impossibility of forgiveness/love may perhaps be found in the writer's notes jotted down on the death of his first wife, Marya Dmitriyevna: "To love man *as oneself* according to Christ's instruction, that is impossible. Is one bound by the law of the individual on earth? The *Self* prevents it."[29]

The illusoriness of forgiveness and resurrection, imperative as they nevertheless are for the writer, explodes in *Crime and Punishment* (1866).

From Sorrow to Crime

Raskolnikov described himself as a sad person: "Listen, Razumuhin . . . I gave them all my money . . . I am so sad, so sad . . . like a woman."[30] And his own mother senses his melancholia: "Do you know, Dounia, I was looking at you two. You are the very portrait of him, and not so much in face as in soul. You [Raskolnikov and his sister Dounia] are both melancholy, both morose and hot-tempered, both haughty and both generous" (p. 236).

How does such sadness become inverted into crime? Here Dostoyevsky probes an essential aspect of depressive dynamics—the seesawing between self and other, the projection on the self of the hatred against the other and, vice versa, the turning against the other of self-depreciation. What comes first, hatred or depreciation? Dostoyevsky's praise of suffering suggests, as we have seen, that he gives greater place to self-depreciation, self-humiliation, or even a sort of masochism under the stern gaze of a precocious and tyrannical superego. From that standpoint, crime is a defense reaction against depression: murdering the other protects against suicide. Raskolnikov's "theory" and criminal act demonstrate that logic perfectly. The gloomy student who allows himself to go on living like a bum constructs, as one will recall, a "division of people into ordinary and extraordinary": the first serve only to procreate and the second "have the gift or the talent to utter *a new word.*" In "the second category all transgress the law; they are destroyers or disposed to destruction according to their capacities" (pp. 255–56). Does he himself belong in that second category? Such is the fateful question the melancholy student will try to answer by *daring or not* to take action.

The murderous act takes the depressive out of passivity and despondency by confronting him with the only desirable object, which, for him, is the prohibition embodied by the law and the master. To act like Napoleon, "the real *Master* to whom all is permitted" (pp. 268–69; trans. modified). The correlative of the tyrannical and desirable law that is to be challenged is but an insignificant thing, a louse. Who is the louse? It is the murderer's victim, or the melancholy student himself, temporarily glorified as murderer, but who knows he is basically worthless and abominable? The confusion persists, and Dostoyevsky thus brilliantly brings to the fore the identification of the depressed with the hated object: "The old woman was a mistake perhaps. . . . I was in a hurry to overstep . . . I didn't kill a human being, but a principle" (p. 269). "There is only one thing, one thing needful: one has only to dare! . . . to go straight for it and send it flying to the devil! I . . . I wanted *to have the daring* . . . and I killed her. . . . I went into it like a wise man, and that was just my destruction . . . or that if I asked myself whether a human being is a louse it proved that it wasn't so *for me,* though it might be for a man who would go straight to his goal without asking questions. . . . I wanted to murder without casuistry, *to murder for my own sake, for myself alone! . . .* I wanted to find out then and quickly whether I was a louse like everybody else or a man. Whether I can step over barriers or not . . ." (pp. 405–6). And finally, "I murdered myself, not her" (p. 407). "And what shows that I am utterly a louse . . . is that I am perhaps viler and more loathsome than the louse I killed" (p. 270). His friend Sonia reaches the same conclusion: "What have you done—what have you done to yourself!" (p. 399).

Mother and Sister: Mother or Sister

Between the two reversible focuses of depreciation and hatred, the self and other, taking action asserts not a subject but a paranoid position that repudiates suffering at the same time as the law. Dostoyevsky considers two antidotes for that catastrophic motion: recourse to suffering, and forgiveness. The two movements take place at the same time and, perhaps thanks to an underground, dark revelation, difficult to grasp in the tangle of Dostoyevsky's narrative, are nevertheless perceived with sleepwalking lucidity by the artist . . . and the reader.

The tracks of that "illness," that insignificant thing or "louse," converge on the despondent student's mother and sister. Loved and hated, attractive and repulsive, these women meet the murderer at the crucial moments of his actions and reflections, and, like two lightning rods, draw to themselves his ambiguous passion, unless they be its origin. Thus: "Both rushed to him. But he stood like one dead; a sudden intolerable sensation struck him like a thunderbolt. He did not lift his arms to embrace them, he could not. His mother and sister clasped him in their arms, kissed him, laughed and cried. He took a step, tottered and fell to the ground, fainting" (p. 191). "Mother, sister —how I loved them! Why do I did hate them now? Yes, I hate them, I feel a physical hatred for them, I can't bear them near me. . . . H'm. *She* [his mother] must be the same as I am. . . . Ah, how I hate the old woman now! I feel I should kill her again if she came to life!" (p. 270). In those last words, which he utters in his frenzy, Raskolnikov indeed reveals the confusion between his debased self, his mother, the old murdered woman . . . Why such a confusion?

The Svidrigailov-Dounia episode throws a little light on the mystery. The "debauched" man who recognizes Raskolnikov as the old woman's murderer desires his sister Dounia. The gloomy Raskolnikov is again ready to kill, but this time in order to defend his sister. To kill, to transgress, in order to protect his unshared secret, his impossible incestuous love? He almost knows it: "Oh, if only I were alone and no one loved me and I too had never loved anyone! *Nothing of all this would have happened*" (p. 504).

The Third Way

Forgiveness appears as the only solution, the third way between dejection and murder. It arises in the wake of erotic enlightenment and appears not as an idealizing movement repressing sexual passion, but as its working through. The angel of the paradise reached after the apocalypse is called Sonia, a prostitute out of compassion to be sure and concern for her unfortunate family, but a prostitute just the same. When she follows Raskolnikov to Siberia in a burst of humility and abnegation, the prisoners call her "our dear, good little mother" (p. 528). Reconciliation with a loving mother, though she might be unfaithful or even a prostitute, beyond and in spite of her "lapses," thus appears as a condition for reconciliation with one's self. The "self" finally becomes acceptable because henceforth placed outside the tyrannical jurisdiction of the master. The forgiven and forgiving mother becomes an ideal sister and replaces . . . Napoleon. The humiliated, warring hero can then calm down. We have reached the pastoral scene at the end; a clear, mild day, a land flooded with sunlight, time has stopped. "There time itself seemed to stand still, as though the age of Abraham and his flocks had not passed" (p. 530). And even if seven years of penal servitude remain, suffering is henceforth linked to happiness. "But [Raskolnikov] had risen again and he knew it and felt in all his being, while [Sonia]—she only lived in his life" (p. 531).

Such an outcome could seem contrived only if one ignored the fundamental importance of idealization in the sublimational activity of writing. Through Raskolnikov and other interposed devils, does the writer not relate his own unbearable dramatic scheme? Imagination is that strange place where the subject ventures its identity, loses itself down to the threshold of evil, crime, or asymbolia in order to work through them and to bear witness . . . from elsewhere. A divided space, it is maintained only if solidly fastened to the ideal, which authorizes destructive violence to be *spoken* instead of being *done*. That is sublimation, and it needs *for-giving*.

The Timelessness of Forgiving

Forgiveness is ahistorical. It breaks the concatenation of causes and effects, crimes and punishment, it stays the time of actions. A strange space opens up in a timelessness that is not one of the primitive unconscious, desiring and murderous, but its counterpart—its sublimation with full knowledge of the facts, a loving harmony that is aware of its violences but accommodates them, elsewhere. Confronted with that stay of time and actions within the timelessness of forgiving, we understand those who believe that God alone can forgive.[31] In Christianity, however, the stay, divine to be sure, of crimes and punishment is *first* the work of men.[32]

Let me emphasize this timelessness of forgiving. It does not suggest the Golden Age of ancient mythologies. When

Dostoyevsky considers that Golden Age, his musing is introduced by Stavrogin *(The Possessed)*, by Versilov *(A Raw Youth)*, and in "The Dream of a Ridiculous Man" *(The Diary of a Writer*, 1877) his presentation is done through the medium of Claude Lorrain's *Acis and Galatea.*

In a true counterpoint to Holbein's "Dead Christ" the representation of the idyll between the river-god Acis and the sea-nymph Galatea, under the wrathful but, for the time being, subdued gaze of Polyphemus who was then her lover, depicts the Golden Age of incest, the preoedipal narcissistic paradise. The Golden Age is outside time because it avoids the desire to put the father to death by basking in the fantasies of the son's almightiness within a "narcissistic Arcadia."[33] This is how Stavrogin experiences it:

In the Dresden gallery there is a painting by Claude Lorrain, called in the catalogue *Acis and Galatea,* if I am not mistaken, but which I always called *The Golden Age,* I don't know why. . . . It was this picture that appeared to me in a dream, yet not as a picture but as though it were an actual scene. . . . As in the picture, I saw a corner of the Greek archipelago the way it was some three thousand years ago: caressing azure waves, rocks and islands, a shore in blossom, afar a magic panaroma, a beckoning sunset—words fail one. European mankind remembers this place as its cradle, and the thought filled my soul with the love that is bred of kinship. Here was mankind's earthly paradise, gods descended from heaven and united with mortals, here occurred the first scenes of mythology. Here lived beautiful men and women! They rose, they went to sleep, happy and innocent; the groves rang with their merry songs, the great overflow of unspent energies poured itself into love and simple-hearted joys, and I sensed all that, and at the same time I envisaged as with second sight, their great future, the three thousand years of life which lay unknown and unguessed before them, and my heart was shaken with these thoughts. Oh, how happy I was that my heart was shaken and that at last I loved! The sun poured its rays upon these isles and this sea, rejoicing in its fair children. Oh, marvelous dream, lofty illusion! The most improbable of all visions, to which mankind throughout its existence has given its best energies, for which it has sacrificed everything, for which it has pined and been tormented, for which its prophets were crucified and killed, without which nations will not desire to live, and without which they cannot even die! . . . But the cliffs, and the sea, and the slanting rays of the setting sun, all that I still seemed to see when I woke up and opened my eyes, for the first time in my life literally wet with tears. . . . And all of a sudden I saw clearly a tiny red spider. I remembered it at once as it had looked on the geranium leaf when the rays of the setting sun were pouring down in the same way. It was as if something had stabbed me. . . . That is the way it all happened![34]

The Golden Age dream is actually a negation of guilt. Indeed, immediately following Claude Lorrain's picture, Stavrogin sees the little creature of remorse, the spider, which maintains him in the web of a consciousness unhappy to be under the sway of a repressive and vengeful law, against which precisely he had reacted by a crime. The spider of guilt brings forth the image of little Matryosha who was raped and committed suicide. Between *Acis and Galatea* or the spider, between flight into regression or the eventually guilt-provoking crime, Stavrogin is as if cut off. He is without access to the mediation of love, he is a stranger to the world of forgiveness.

Of course it is Dostoyevsky who hides behind the masks of Stavrogin, Versilov, and the ridiculous man dreaming of the Golden Age. But he no longer puts on a mask when describing the scene of forgiveness between Raskolnikov and Sonia: as artist and Christian, it is he, the narrator, who assumes responsibility for that strange device that informs the forgiveness epilogue in *Crime and Punishment*. The scene between Raskolnikov and Sonia, while recalling that of *Acis and Galatea* because of the pastoral joy and heavenly radiance that imbues it, refers neither to Claude Lorrain's work nor to the Golden Age. A strange "Golden Age" indeed, lying at the very heart of hell, in Siberia, near the prisoner's shed. Sonia's forgiveness evokes the narcissistic regression of the incestuous lover but does not merge with it: Raskolnikov crosses the break in loving happiness by plunging into the reading of Lazarus' story from the New Testament that Sonia lent him.

The time of forgiveness is not the time of the chase nor that of the mythological cave "Under the living rock, where midsummer sun, / Midwinter cold, do never come."[35] It is that of the deferment of crime, the time of its *limitation*. A limitation that knows the crime and does not forget it but, without being blinded as to its horror, banks on a new departure, on a renewal of the individual.[36]

> Raskolnikov came out of the shed on to the river bank, sat down on a heap of logs by the shed and began gazing at the wide deserted river. From the high bank a broad landscape opened before him, the sound of singing floated faintly audible from the other bank. In the vast steppe, bathed in sunshine, he could just see, like

black specks, the nomad's tents. There there was freedom, there other men were living, utterly unlike those
here; there time itself seemed to stand still, as though
the age of Abraham and his flocks had not passed.
Raskolnikov sat gazing, his thoughts passed into daydreams, into contemplation; he thought of nothing, but
a vague restlessness excited and troubled him. Suddenly
he found Sonia beside him; she had come up noiselessly
and sat down at his side. . . . She gave him a joyful
smile of welcome, but held out her hand with her usual
timidity. . . . How it happened he did not know. But
all at once something seemed to seize him and fling him
at her feet. He wept and threw his arms round her
knees. For the first instant she was terribly frightened
and she turned pale. She jumped up and looked at him
trembling. But at the same moment she understood,
and a light of infinite happiness came into her eyes. She
knew and had no doubt that he loved her beyond
everything and that at last the moment had come . . .
[pp. 530–31][37]

According to Dostoyevsky, forgiveness seems to say:
Through my love, I exclude you from history for a while,
I take you for a child, and this means that I recognize the
unconscious motivations of your crime and allow you to
make a new person out of yourself. So that the unconscious might inscribe itself in a new narrative that will not
be the eternal return of the death drive in the cycle of
crime and punishment it must pass through the love of
forgiveness, be transferred to the love of forgiveness. The
resources of narcissism and idealization imprint their stamps
upon the unconscious and refashion it. For the unconscious is not structured like a language but like all the
imprints of the Other, including and most particularly so

those that are most archaic, "semiotic," it is constituted by preverbal self-sensualities that the narcissistic or amorous experience restores to me. Forgiveness *renews the unconsious* because it inscribes the right to narcissistic regression within History and Speech.

These turn out to be modified by it. They are neither linear flight forward nor eternal return of the revenge/death recurrence, but a spiral that follows the path of death drive *and* of renewal/love.

By staying the historical quest in the name of love, forgiveness discovers the regenerative potential peculiar to narcissistic satisfaction and idealization, both intrinsic to the loving bond. It thus simultaneously takes into account two levels of subjectivity—the *unconscious level,* which stops time through desire and death, and the *love level,* which stays the former unconscious and the former history and begins a rebuilding of the personality within a new relation for an other. *My unconscious is reinscribable beyond the gift that an other presents me by not judging my actions.*

Forgiveness does not cleanse actions. It raises the unconscious from beneath the actions and has it meet a loving other—an other who does not judge but hears my truth in the availability of love, and for that very reason allows me to be reborn. Forgiveness is the luminous stage of dark, unconscious timelessness—the stage at which the latter changes laws and adopts the bond with love as a principle of renewal of both self and other.

Aesthetic Forgiveness

One grasps the seriousness of such forgiveness with and through the unacceptable horror. Such seriousness is perceivable in analytical listening that neither judges nor calculates but attempts to untangle and reconstruct. Its spiraled temporality is accomplished within the time of writing. Because I am *separated* from my unconscious through a new transference to a new other or a new ideal I am able to *write* the dramatic unfolding of my nevertheless unforgettable violence and despair. The time of that separation and renewal, which underlies the very act of writing, does not necessarily show up in the narrative themes, which might reveal only the inferno of the unconscious. But it can also display itself through the device of an epilogue, like the one in *Crime and Punishment,* that stays a novelistic experience before causing it to be reborn by means of another novel. The crime that is not forgotten but signified through forgiveness, the written horror, is the requirement for beauty. There is no beauty outside the forgiveness that remembers abjection and filters it through the destabilized, musicalized, resensualized signs of loving discourse. *Forgiveness is aesthetic* and the discourses (religions, philosophies, ideologies) that adhere to the dynamics of forgiving precondition the birth of aesthetics within their orbit.

Forgiveness at the outset constitutes a will, postulate, or scheme: *meaning exists.* This is not necessarily a matter of a disavowal of meaning or a manic exaltation in opposition to despair (even if, in a number of instances, this motion may be dominant). Forgiveness, as a gesture of assertion and inscription of meaning, carries within itself, as a lining, erosion of meaning, melancholia, and abjection. By including them it displaces them; by absorbing them it transforms them and binds them for someone else. "There is a meaning": this is an eminently transferential gesture that causes a third party to exist for and through an other. *Forgiveness emerges first as the setting up of a form.* It has the effect of an acting out, a doing, a *poiesis.* Giving

shape to relations between insulted and humiliated individuals—group harmony. Giving shape to signs—harmony of the work, without exegesis, without explanation, without understanding. Technique and art. The
"primary" aspect of such an action clarifies why it has the
ability to reach, beyond words and intellects, emotions
and bruised bodies. That economy, however, is anything
but primitive. The logical possibility for taking over
(Aufhebung) that it implies (nonmeaning and meaning,
positive burst integrating its potential nothingness) follows upon a sound fastening of the subject to the oblatory
ideal. Whoever is in the realm of forgiveness—who forgives and who accepts forgiveness—is capable of identifying with a loving father, an imaginary father, with whom,
consequently, he is ready to be reconciled, with a new
symbolic law in mind.

Disavowal is fully involved in this process of taking
over or identifying reconciliation. It provides a perverse,
masochistic pleasure in going through suffering toward
the new bonds constituted by forgiveness as well as the
work of art. Nevertheless, in opposition to the disavowal
of negation that voids the signifier and leads to the empty
speech of melancholia (see chapter 2), another process now
comes into play in order to insure the life of the imagination.

This involves the forgiveness that is essential to sublimation, that leads the subject to a complete identification
(real, imaginary, and symbolic) with the very agency of
the ideal.[38] It is through the miraculous device of that
identification, which is always unstable, unfinished, but
constantly threefold (real, imaginary, and symbolic), that
the suffering body of the forgiver (and the artist as well)
undergoes a mutation—Joyce would say, a "transubstan-
tiation." It allows him to live a second life, a life of forms

and meaning, somewhat exalted or artificial in the eyes of outsiders, but which is the sole requisite for the subject's survival.

East and West: Per Filium or Filioque

The clearest source for the notion of forgiveness, which Christian thought has elaborated upon for centuries, goes back in the New Testament to Paul and Luke.[39] Like all basic principles of Christianity it was expanded by Augustine. It is, however, in the works of John of Damascus (in the eighth century) that one finds a hypostasis for the "benevolence of the father" *(eudoxia)*, "affectionate mercy" *(eusplankhna)*, and condescension (the Son lowers himself to our level—*synkatabasis*). Contrarily, such notions may be interpreted as paving the way for the uniqueness of orthodox Christian thought up to the schism of *Per Filium/Filioque*.

There is one theologian who seems to have deeply determined the orthodox faith that is so powerfully expressed with Dostoyevsky and gives to the inner experience specific to his novels that emotional intensity and that mystical pathos that are so surprising to the West. He is Symeon the New Theologian (999–1022).[40] The account of this *agrammatos*' conversion to Christianity bears a style that has been termed Paulian: "Weeping without cease, I went in quest of you. Unknown, I would forget everything. . . . Then you appeared, you, invisible, elusive. . . . It seems to me, oh Lord, that you, motionless, moved me, you, unchanging, you changed, you, featureless, assumed features. . . . You were excessively radiant and seemed to appear before me fully, completely. . . ."[41] Symeon understands the Trinity as a merging of the differences constituted by the three persons and expresses it intensely through the metaphor of light.[42]

Light and hyspostases, unity and visions—such is the logic of Byzantine Trinity.[43] It at once finds, with Symeon, its anthropomorphic equivalent: "As it is impossible that there be a man endowed with speech and spirit but without soul, thus is it impossible to think the Son with the Father without the Holy Spirit. . . . For your own spirit, like your soul, lies within your intellect, and all your intellect is in all your speech, and all your speech is in all your spirit, without separation and without confusion. It is the image of God within us."[44] Along this path, the believer becomes deified by merging with the Son *and* with the Spirit: "I give you thanks for having, without confusion, without change, become a single Spirit with me, although you are God above all, become for me everything in everything."[45]

Here we touch upon the "originality of orthodoxy." It led, by way of many institutional and political controversies, to the schism broached in the ninth century and completed with the fall of Constantinople to the crusaders in 1204. On a strictly theological level, it was Symeon, more so than Photius, who formulated the Eastern doctrine of *Per Filium* as opposed to the Latin's *Filioque*. Emphasizing the Spirit, he asserted the identity of life in the Spirit with life in Christ, and he set the origin of that powerful pneumatology within the Father. Nonetheless, such a paternal agency is not merely an authority principle or a simple mechanical cause: in the Father the Spirit loses its immanence and identifies with the kingdom of God as defined through germinal, floral, nutritional, and erotic metamorphoses that imply, beyond the cosmic energy theory often viewed as specific to the East, the openly sexual fusion with the Thing at the limits of the nameable.[46]

Within such a dynamics, the Church itself appears as a *soma pneumatikon,* a "mystery," more than an institution made in the image of monarchies.

The ecstatic identification of the three hypostases with one another and of the believer with the Trinity does not lead to the concept of the Son's (or the believer's) *autonomy,* but to a pneumatological *belonging* of each to the other; this is expressed through the phrase *Per Filium* (the Spirit descends from the Father *through* the Son) as opposed to *Filioque* (the Spirit descends from the Father *and* the Son).[47]

It was impossible at the time, to find the rationalization for that mystical motion, internal to the Trinity and to faith, in which, without losing its value as a person, the Spirit merges with the two other centers and, by the same token, endows them, beyond their value as distinct identities or authorities, with an abyssal, breathtaking, and certainly also sexual depth, where the psychological experience of loss and ecstasy finds its place. The Borromean knot that Lacan used as metaphor of the unity *and* the difference between the Real, the Imaginary, and the Symbolic perhaps allows one to think out this logic, assuming that it is necessary to rationalize it. Now, precisely, this did not seem to have been the intention of Byzantine theologians from the eleventh to the thirteenth century, preoccupied as they were with describing a new postclassical subjectivity rather than subjecting it to the reason then in existence. On the other hand, the Fathers of the Latin Church, more logically inclined, and who had just discovered Aristotle (while the East had been nurtured on him and sought only to differentiate itself from him), logicized the Trinity by seeing God as a simple intellectual essence that could be articulated as dyads—the Father engenders the Son; Father and Son as a set cause the Spirit to come forth.[48] Developed through the syllogistic of Anselm, Archbishop of Canterbury, at the council of Bari in 1098, the argumentation concerning the *Filioque* was taken up again and expanded by Thomas Aquinas. It had the advantage of providing a basis for the political and spiritual authority of the papacy on the one hand, and on the other for the autonomy and rationality of the believer's person, identified with a Son having power and prestige equal to that of the Father. What had thus been gained in equality and therefore in performance and historicity had perhaps been lost at the level of the experience of *identification,* in the sense of a permanent instability of identity.

Difference and identity, rather than autonomy and equality, did on the contrary build up the Eastern Trinity, which consequently became the source of ecstasy and mysticism. Orthodoxy nurtured it by adoring, beyond oppositions, a sense of fullness where each person of the Trinity was linked to and identified with all others—an erotic fusion. In that "Borromean" logic of Orthodox Trinity, the psychic space of the believer opened to the most violent movements of passion for rapture or death, distinguished merely to be joined in the unity of divine love.[49]

It is against that psychological background that one needs to understand the daring of Byzantine imagination in representing the death and Passion of Christ in iconic art, as well as the propensity of Orthodox discourse to explore suffering and mercy. Unity may be lost (that of Christ on Golgotha, of the believer in humiliation or death), but in the motion of the Trinitarian knot it may recover its temporary consistency thanks to benevolence and mercy, before resuming the eternal cycle of disappearance and reappearance.

"I" Is Son and Spirit

Let me recall, with that in mind, some of the theological, psychological, and pictorial events that prefigure the schism as well as, later, the Russian Orthodox spirituality, which is at the basis of Dostoyevsky's discourse. For Symeon, the New Theologian, light was inseparable from the "painful affection" *(katanyxis)* that opened up to God through humility and a flood of tears, for it knew right away that it was forgiven. Moreover, the pneumatic conception of the Eucharist, expounded for instance by Maximus the Confessor (twelfth century), leads one to believe that Christ was *at the same time* deified *and* crucified, that death on the cross is innate in life and living. On that basis painters permitted themselves to present Christ's death on the Cross—because death was living, the dead body was an incorruptible body that could be kept by the Church as image *and* reality.

As early as the eleventh century the simplicity of ecclesiastical architecture and iconography became enriched with a representation of Christ surrounded by apostles, offering them goblet and bread—a Christ "who offers and is being offered," according to John Chrisostom's expression. As Olivier Clement emphasized, the very art of mosaic imposes the presence of light, the gift of grace and splendor, at the same time as the iconic representation of the Marian cycle and Christ's Passion calls for having individual believers identify with characters in the scriptures. Such a subjectivism, in the light of grace, finds one of its privileged expressions in Christ's Passion: just like man, Christ suffers and dies. And yet the painter can show it, and the believer can see it, his humiliation and suffering being submerged in the affection of mercy for the Son within the Spirit. As if resurrection made *death visible* and at the same time even more moving. Scenes from the Passion were added to the traditional liturgical cycle in 1164 at Nerez, in a Macedonian church founded by the Comneni.

The progressiveness of Byzantine iconography compared with the classical or Judaic tradition was nevertheless to be stalled later on. The Renaissance was Latin, and it is likely that political and social causes or foreign invasions were not alone in contributing to the decline of Orthodox pictorial art into oversimplicity. The Eastern conception of the Trinity definitely gave less autonomy to individuals when it did not subject them to authority, and it surely did not encourage them to turn into "artistic individualities." Nevertheless, through meanderings that were less spectacular, more intimate, and therefore less restrainable—those of the verbal arts—a blossoming did indeed take place in spite of the delay one knows, with, as a bonus, a refinement of the alchemy of suffering, particularly in Russian literature.

Coming late after the Byzantine expansion and that of the southern Slavs (Bulgarians, Serbs), the Russian church intensified its pneumatologic and mystic tendencies. Pagan, Dionysiac, Eastern, the pre-Christian tradition imprinted on the Byzantine Orthodoxy as it passed into Russia a heretofore unattained paroxysm. There were the *khlysti,* a mystic sect of Manichean inspiration, who favored excesses in suffering and eroticism, in order to achieve a complete fusion of their followers with Christ; the theophany of the earth (which led to the notion of Moscow as the "third Rome," after Constantinople . . . but also, according to some, to the Third International); the praise of salvation/love and especially the hypostasis of affection *(oumilienie),* at the intersection of suffering and joy and within Christ; the movement of "those who have undergone the Passion" *(strastotierptsy)*, that is, those who have actually been brutalized or humiliated but respond to evil only with forgiveness. Such are some of the most paroxysmal and concrete expressions of Russian Orthodox logic.

It would be impossible to understand Dostoyevsky without it. His dialogism, his polyphony[50] undoubtedly spring from multiple sources. It would be a mistake to neglect that of Orthodox faith whose Trinitarian conception (difference and unity of the three Persons within a generalized pneumatology inviting any subjectivity to a maximal display of its contradictions) inspires the writer's "dialogism" as well as his praise of suffering *at the same time* as forgiving. In that view, the image of the tyrannical father, present in Dostoyevsky's universe and in which Freud saw the source of epilepsy as well as play dissipation (the addiction to gambling),[51] needs to be balanced—in order to understand not the neurotic Dostoyevsky but Dostoyevsky the artist—with that of the benevolent father specific to Byzantine tradition, his affection and forgiveness.

The Spoken Forgiveness

The writer's position is one of speech: a symbolic configuration absorbs and replaces forgiveness as emotional impulse, mercy, anthropomorphic compassion. To say that the work of art is a forgiving already implies leaving psychological forgiveness (but without ignoring it) for a singular act—that of naming and composing.

One will thus be unable to understand why art is forgiveness without examining all the levels at which forgiveness functions and is exhausted. One should begin with that of psychological, subjective identification, with suffering, and the affection of others, the "characters" and

oneself, supported in Dostoyevsky's writings with Orthodox faith. One should next and necessarily go on to examine the logical formulation of the effectiveness of forgiving as an undertaking of transpersonal creation, as
Thomas Aquinas understands it (inside the *Filioque* this
time). Finally, one should observe the shifting of forgiveness, beyond the work's polyphony, to the morals of
aesthetic performance alone, to the jouissance of passion
as beauty. Potentially immoralistic, the third moment of
the performance/forgiveness returns to the point of departure of that circular motion—to the suffering and affection
of the other for the stranger.

The Act of Giving Reduces the Affect

Thomas Aquinas linked "God's mercy" with his justice.[52]
After having stressed that "[God's] justice observes a divine decency and renders to himself what is due to himself," Aquinas takes care to establish the truth of that
justice, it being understood that "the order of things
matching the exemplar of his wisdom, namely his law, is
appropriately called truth." As to mercy itself he does not
fail to mention the very anthropomorphic, and therefore
psychological opinion of John the Damascene, who said,
"mercy is a sort of sorrow." Aquinas dissociates himself
from that opinion; he deems, "Above all is mercy to be
attributed to God, nevertheless in its *effect,* not in the affect
of *feeling.*" "To feel sad about another's misery is no
attribute of God, but to drive it out is supremely his, and
by misery we mean here *any sort of defect.*"[53] By remedying
the defect with perfection in mind, mercy would be a
donation. "For a pardon is a sort of present; St. Paul calls
forgiving a giving, forgiving one another as God in Christ
forgave you" (one can translate, "Render thanks to one

another" as well as "Forgive one another"). Forgiveness makes up for the lack, it is an additional, free gift. I give myself to you, you welcome me, I am within you. Neither justice nor injustice, forgiveness would be a "fullness of justice" beyond judgment. This is what causes James to say, "Mercy triumphs over judgment."[54]

While it is true that human forgiveness does not equal divine mercy, it attempts to mold itself after the latter's image; a gift, an oblation distancing itself from judgment, forgiveness assumes a potential identification with that effective and efficient merciful divinity of which the theologian speaks. Nevertheless, and in contrast to divine mercy, which excludes sadness, forgiveness gathers on its way to the other a very human sorrow. Recognizing the lack and the wound that caused it, it fulfills them with an ideal gift —promise, project, artifice, thus fitting the humiliated, offended being into an order of perfection, and giving him the assurance that he belongs there. Love, all in all, beyond judgment, takes over from sadness, which is nevertheless understood, heard, displayed. It is possible to forgive ourselves by releasing, thanks to someone who hears us, our lack or our wound to an ideal order to which we are sure we belong—and we are now protected against depression. How can one be sure, however, of joining that ideal order by going through the lack, without once more negotiating the narrow pass of identification with flawless ideality, loving fatherhood, primitive guarantor of our safeties?

Writing: Immoral Forgiveness

Whoever creates a text or an interpretation is more than anyone else drawn to accept the fully *logical* and *active* agency of Thomistic mercy beyond emotional effusion. He accepts its value of justice in the act, and even more so of the act's appropriateness. It is by making his words suitable to his commiseration and, in that sense, accurate that the subject's adherence to the forgiving ideal is accomplished and effective forgiveness for others as well as for oneself becomes possible. At the boundaries of emotion and action, writing comes into being only through the moment of the negation of the affect so that the effectiveness of signs might be born. Writing causes the *affect* to slip into the *effect—actus purus,* as Aquinas might say. It conveys affects and does not repress them, it suggests for them a sublimatory outcome, it transposes them for an other in a threefold, imaginary, and symbolic bond. Because it is forgiveness, writing is transformation, transposition, translation.

From that moment on, the world of signs lays down its own logic. The jubilation it affords, that of performance as well as reception, intermittently erases the ideal as well as any possibility of external justice. Immoralism is the fate of that process, which Dostoyevsky is well acquainted with: writing is bound to evil not only at the outset (in its pre-text, in its objects) but also at the end, in the absoluteness of its universe that excludes all otherness. Dostoyevsky is also conscious of the aesthetic effect being locked in an exteriorless passion—with the risk of a deathly as well as joyful closure through imaginary self-consumption, through the tyranny of the beautiful; that is perhaps what prompts him to cling violently to his religion and its principle—forgiveness. The eternal return of a threefold motion thus gets under way: affection tied to suffering, logical justice and appropriateness of the work, hypostasis, and finally unease over the final, masterful accomplishment. Then, once again, in order to forgive himself, he resumes the threefold logic of forgiveness . . . Do we not need it in order to give a live—erotic, immoral— meaning to the melancholy hold?

8

The Malady of Grief: Duras

Grief is one of the most important things in my life.
—*Grief*

I told him that during my childhood my mother's misfortune took up the space of dreams.
—*The Lover*

The Blank Rhetoric of the Apocalypse

We, as civilizations, we now know not only that we are mortal, as Paul Valéry asserted after the war of 1914;[1] we also know that we can inflict death upon ourselves. Auschwitz and Hiroshima have revealed that the "malady of death," as Marguerite Duras might say, informs our most concealed inner recesses. If military and economic realms, as well as political and social bonds, are governed by passion for death, the latter has been revealed to rule even the once noble kingdom of the spirit. A tremendous crisis of thought and speech, a crisis of representation, has indeed emerged; one may look for analogues in past centuries (the fall of the Roman empire and the dawning of Christianity, the years of devastating medieval plagues and wars) or for its causes in economic, political, and juridical bankruptcies. Nonetheless, never has the power of destructive forces appeared as unquestionable and unavoidable as now, within and without society and the individual. The despoliation of nature, lives, and property is accompanied by an upsurge, or simply a more obvious display, of disorders whose diagnoses are being refined by psychiatry—psychosis, depression, manic-depressive states, borderline states, false selves, etc.

While political and military cataclysms are dreadful and challenge the mind through the monstrosity of their violence (that of a concentration camp or of an atomic bomb), the shattering of psychic identity, whose intensity is no less violent, remains hard to perceive. That fact already struck Valéry as he compared the disaster affecting the spirit (following on the First World War but also, earlier, on the nihilism stemming from the "death of God") to what a physicist observes "in a kiln heated to incandescence: if our eyes endured, they would see *nothing*. No luminous disparity would remain, nothing would distinguish one point in space from another. This tremendous, trapped energy would end up in invisibility, in *imperceptible equality*. An equality of that sort is nothing else than *a perfect state of disorder*."[2]

One of the major stakes of literature and art is henceforth located in that invisibility of the crisis affecting the identity of persons, morals, religion, or politics. Both religious and political, the crisis finds its radical rendering in the crisis of signification. From now on, the difficulty in naming no longer opens onto "music in literature" (Mallarmé and Joyce were believers and aesthetes) but onto illogicality and silence. After Surrealism's rather playful and yet always politically committed interlude, the actuality of the Second World War brutalized consciousness through an outburst of death and madness that no barrier, be it ideological or aesthetic, seemed able to contain any longer. This was a pressure that had found its intimate, unavoidable repercussion at the heart of psychic grief. It was experienced as an inescapable emergency, without for that matter ceasing to be invisible, nonrepresentable—but in what sense?

If it is still possible to speak of "nothing" when attempting to chart the minute meanderings of psychic grief and death, are we still in the presence of nothing when confronting the gas chambers, the atomic bomb, or the gulag? Neither the spectacular aspect of death's eruption in the universe of the Second World War nor the falling apart of conscious identity and rational behavior ending in institutional aspects of psychosis, often equally spectacular, are at stake. What those monstrous and painful sights do damage to are our systems of perception and representation. As if overtaxed or destroyed by too powerful a breaker, our symbolic means find themselves hollowed out, nearly wiped out, paralyzed. On the edge of silence the word "nothing" emerges, a discreet defense in the face of so much disorder, both internal and external, incommensurable. Never has a cataclysm been more apocalyptically outrageous; never has its representation been assumed by so few symbolic means.

Within some religious movements there was a feeling that in the presence of so much horror silence alone was appropriate; death should be removed from living speech and be called to mind only in indirect fashion in the rifts and unspoken bits of a concern bordering on contrition. A fascination with Judaism—one would rather not call it a flirtation—was conspicuous along those lines, revealing the guilt of an entire generation of intellectuals in the presence of antisemitism and the collaboration [with the Germans] that existed during the early years of the war.

A new rhetoric of apocalypse (etymologically, *apocalypso* means de-monstration, dis-covering through sight, and contrasts with *aletheia,* the philosophical disclosure of truth) seemed necessary for a vision of this nevertheless monstrous nothing to emerge—a monstrosity that blinds and compels one to be silent. Such a new apocalyptic rhetoric was carried out in two seemingly opposite, extreme fashions that complement each other: a wealth of images and a holding back of words.

On the one hand, the art of imagery excels in the raw display of monstrosity. Films remain the supreme art of the apocalypse, no matter what the refinements, because the image has such an ability to "have us walk into fear," as Augustine had already seen.[3] On the other hand, verbal and pictorial arts have turned to the "uneasy, infinite quest of [their] source."[4] Beginning with Heidegger and Blanchot respectively evoking Hölderlin and Mallarmé, and including the Surrealists, commentators have noticed that poets—doubtless diminished in the modern world by the ascendancy of politics—turn back to language, which is their own mansion, and they unfold its resources rather than tackle innocently the representation of an external object. Melancholia becomes the secret mainspring of a new rhetoric: what is involved this time is to follow ill-being step by step, almost in clinical fashion, without ever getting the better of it.

Within this image/words dichotomy, it falls to films to spread out the coarseness of horror or the external outlines of pleasure, while literature becomes internalized and withdraws from the world in the wake of the crisis in thought. Inverted into its own formalism, thereby more lucid than the existentialists' enthusiastic commitment and libertarian/adolescent eroticism, contemporary postwar literature sets out nevertheless on a difficult course. Its quest of the invisible, perhaps metaphysically motivated by the ambition to remain faithful to the intensity of horror down to the ultimate exactness of words, becomes imperceptible and progressively antisocial, nondemonstrative, and also, by dint of being antispectacular, uninteresting. Mass communication arts on the one hand, the experience of the *nouveau roman* on the other, exemplify the two alternatives.

An Aesthetics of Awkwardness

The practice of Marguerite Duras seems less that of "working toward the origin of the work," as Blanchot had hoped, than a confrontation with Valéry's "nothing" —a "nothing" that is thrust upon a perturbed consciousness by the horror of the Second World War and independently but in similar fashion by the individual's psychic unease due to the secret impacts of biology, the family, the others.

Duras' writing does not analyze itself by seeking its sources in the music that lies under the words nor in the defeat of the narrative's logic. If there be a formal search, it is subordinate to confrontation with the silence of horror in oneself and in the world. Such a confrontation leads her to an aesthetics of *awkwardness* on the one hand, to a *noncathartic literature* on the other.

The affected rhetoric of literature and even the common rhetoric of everyday speech always seem somewhat festive. How can one speak the truth of pain, if not by holding in check the rhetorical celebration, warping it, making it grate, strain, and limp?

There is some appeal, however, to her drawn-out sentences, lacking in acoustic charm, and whose verb seems to have forgotten its subject ("Her elegance, both when resting and when in motion, Tatiana tells, was worrisome"),[6] or come to a sudden end, having run out of breath, out of grammatical object or qualifier ("Then, while remaining very quiet, she again began asking for food, that the window be opened, for rest"[7] and, "Such are the last obvious pertaining facts [of her recent history]").[8]

Often one comes up against last-minute additions piled up into a clause that has made no allowance for them, but to which it brings its full meaning, a surprise ("his fond desire for girls who are not quite grown-up, sad, immodest, *and speechless*";[9] "Their union is based on insensitivity that is of a general nature and which they momentarily dread; *all predilection is excluded.*").[10] One also meets with words that are too learned and superlative, or on the contrary too ordinary and hackneyed, conveying a stilted, artificial, and sickly grandiloquence: "I don't know. I know something concerning only the *stillness of life*. Therefore, when it is shattered, I know it."[11] "When you cried, it was over yourself alone and not the *wonderful impossibility* of reuniting with her through the difference that separates you."[12]

We are not dealing with spoken discourse but with a speech that is overrated by dint of being underrated, as one can be without makeup or undressed without being slovenly but because one is compelled by some unconquerable disease that is nevertheless filled with a pleasure that enthralls and challenges. Meanwhile, and perhaps for that very reason, the distorted speech sounds strange, unexpected, and above all painful. A difficult seduction drags one into the characters' or the narrator's weaknesses, into that nothing, into what is nonsignifiable in an illness with neither tragic crisis nor beauty, a pain from which only tension remains. Stylistic awkwardness would be the discourse of dulled pain.

For such silent or precious exaggeration of speech, for its weakness tensed as if on a tightrope above suffering, films come as a substitute. Having recourse to theatrical representation, and especially to the film image, necessarily leads to an uncontrollable wealth of associations, of semantic and sentimental richness or poverty according to the viewer. If it be true that images do not make up for verbal stylistic awkwardness, they do nevertheless plunge it into the inexpressible—the "nothing" becomes undecidable and silence inspires one to muse. As a collective art, even when the scriptwriter manages to control it, the cinema adds something to the Spartan indications of the author (who ceaselessly protects a sickly secret at the heart of a more and more elusive plot); what it adds are the inevitably spectacular volumes and aggregates of bodies, gestures, actors' voices, setting, lighting, producers and all those whose task is to show. If Duras uses the screen in order to burn out its spectacular strength down to the glare of the invisible by engulfing it in elliptical words and allusive sounds, she also uses it for its excess of fascination, which compensates for verbal constriction. As the characters' seductive power is thus increased, their invisible malady becomes less infectious on the screen because it can be performed: filmed depression appears to be an alien artifice.

We now understand why Duras' books should not be put into the hands of oversensitive readers. Let them go see the films and the plays; they will encounter the same malady of distress but subdued, wrapped up in a dreamy charm that softens it and also makes it more feigned and made up—a convention. Her books, on the contrary, bring us to the verge of madness. They do not point to it from afar, they neither observe it nor analyze it for the sake of experiencing it at a distance in the hope of a solution, like it or not, some day or other . . . To the contrary, the texts domesticate the malady of death, they fuse with it, are on the same level with it, without either distance or perspective. There is no purification in store

[*227*]

for us at the conclusion of those novels written on the brink of illness, no improvement, no promise of a beyond, not even the enchanting beauty of style or irony that might provide a bonus of pleasure in addition to the revealed evil.

Without Catharsis

Lacking recovery or God, having neither value nor beauty other than illness itself seized at the place of its essential rupture, never has art had so little cathartic potential. Undoubtedly and for that very reason it falls more within the province of sorcery and bewitchment than within that of grace and forgiveness traditionally associated with artistic genius. A complicity with illness emanates from Duras' texts, a complicity that is somber and at the same time light because absentminded. It leads us to X-ray our madness, the dangerous rims where identities of meaning, personality, and life collapse. "The mystery in full daylight" is how Maurice Barrès described Claude Lorrain's paintings. With Duras what we have is madness in full daylight: "I went mad in the full light of reason."[13] We are in the presence of the nothing of meaning and feelings as lucidity accompanies them to their dying out, and we bear witness to the neutralization of our own distress, with neither tragedy nor enthusiasms, with clarity, in the frigid insignificance of a psychic numbness, both the minimal and also ultimate sign of grief and ravishment.

Clarice Lispector (1924–1977), too, offered a revelation of suffering and death that does not share in the aesthetics of forgiveness. Her *A maçã no escuro (The Apple in the Dark)*[14] seems opposed to Dostoyevsky. Lispector's hero has murdered a woman, as Raskolnikov has (but here she happens to be his own wife), and then meets two others, a voluptuous one and a platonic one. While they free him of the murder—as Sonia does for the prisoner in *Crime and Punishment*—they neither save nor forgive him. Worse yet, they turn him over to the police. Nevertheless, such an outcome is neither the reverse of forgiveness nor a punishment. The inescapable stillness of destiny closes in on the protagonists and bounds the novel with an implacable, perhaps feminine, gentleness, not unlike Duras' disenchanted tone, a truthful mirror of the sorrow that permeates the subject. While Lispector's universe, in contrast to Dostoyevsky's, is not one of forgiveness, it still exudes complicity among protagonists; their bonds outlast their separation and, once the novel is ended, weave a friendly, invisible environment.[15] One might add that beyond sinister display of evil, so much humor runs through the writer's fierce novellas that it acquires a purifying value and shields the reader from the crisis.

There is nothing like that in Duras. Death and pain are the spider's web of the text, and woe to the conniving readers who yield to its spell: they might remain there for good. The "crisis in literature" that Paul Valéry, Roger Caillois, or Maurice Blanchot discussed reaches here a kind of apotheosis. Literature is neither self-criticism, nor criticism, nor a generalized ambivalence cleverly blending man and woman, real and imaginary, true and false, within the disillusioned celebration of the seeming, dancing on the volcano of an impossible object or lost time. . . . Here, the crisis leads writing to remain on the near side of any warping of meaning, confining itself to baring the malady. Lacking catharsis, such a literature encounters, recognizes, but also spreads the pain that summons it. It is the reverse of clinical discourse—very close to it, but as it enjoys the illness' secondary benefits cultivates and tames it without ever exhausting it. Considering such faithfulness to discomfort, it is understandable that an option may be found in films' neoromanticism or in the concern for sending ideological or metaphysical messages and meditations. Between *Détruire, dit-elle* (1969; *Destroy, She Said,* 1986) and *La Maladie de la mort* (1982; *The Malady of Death,* 1986), which brings to the utmost degree of condensation the death-love theme, there extend thirteen years of films, plays, explanations.[16]

The exotic eroticism of *L'Amant* (1984; *The Lover,* 1985) then takes over from those beings and words that have been prostrated by tacit death. It displays the same painful, deadly passion (a constant with Duras), conscious of itself and held back ("She might answer that she doesn't love him. She says nothing. Suddenly she knows, right here, at that moment, knows he doesn't understand her, knows he never will, knows he hasn't the means to understand so much perversity").[17] But geographic and social realism, the journalistic account of colonial destitution and of the discomforts of the Occupation, the naturalistic presentation of the mother's failures and hatreds—all that shrouds the smooth, sickly pleasure of the prostituted child who gives herself over to the tearful sensuality of a wealthy Chinese grownup, sadly and yet with the perseverence of a professional narrator. While it remains an impossible dream, feminine jouissance becomes rooted in local color and in a story, a distant one to be sure, but one that the Third World's irruption, on the one hand, and the realism of family carnage on the other, make henceforth plausible and strangely close, intimate. With *L'Amant* suffering gains a social and historical neoromantic congruity that has insured its place among bestsellers.

The whole of Duras' work does perhaps not correspond to the aescetic faithfulness to madness that precedes *L'Amant.* A few texts, however, among others, will allow us to observe the high points of that madness.

Hiroshima of Love

Because of what took place in history, there can be no artifice involving Hiroshima. Neither tragical nor pacifist artifice facing the atomic explosion, nor rhetorical artifice facing the mutilation of feelings. "All one can do is to speak of the impossibility of speaking of Hiroshima. The knowledge of Hiroshima is something that must be set down, a priori, as being an exemplary delusion of the mind."[18] Hiroshima itself, and not its repercussions, is the sacrilege, the death-bearing event. The text sets out to "be done with description of horror through horror, for that has been done by the Japanese themselves" and to "have the horror rise from its ashes by having it inscribed into a love that will inevitably be distinctive and 'wonder-filling.' "[19] The nuclear explosion therefore permeates love itself, and its devastating violence makes love both impossible and gorgeously erotic, condemned and magically alluring—as is the nurse, portrayed by Emmanuelle Riva, at one of the high points of passion. The text and the film open not with the image of the nuclear mushroom as initially planned, but with parts of clasping bodies belonging to a couple of lovers who might be a couple of dying people. "In their place and stead mutilated bodies are seen —at the level of the head and hips—moving—preys either to love or to the pangs of death—successively covered with ashes, dew, atomic death—and the sweat of love fulfilled."[20] Love stronger than death? Perhaps. "Always their personal history, brief as it might be, will prevail over Hiroshima." But perhaps not. For, if He comes from Hiroshima, She comes from Nevers where "she has been mad with meanness." Her first lover was German, he was killed during the Liberation, her hair was shorn. A first love destroyed by the "utterness and dreadfulness of stupidity." On the other hand, the horror of Hiroshima somehow liberated her from her French tragedy. The recourse to the atomic weapon seems to prove that horror is not limited to one side; it knows neither place nor party but can rage absolutely. Such a transcendence of horror frees the loving woman of mistaken guilt. The young woman henceforth wanders with her "purposeless love" all the way to Hiroshima. Beyond their wedding, which they term a happy one, the new love of the two protagonists—although powerful and strikingly authentic—will also be "strangled": sheltering a disaster on either side, Nevers here, Hiroshima there. However intense it may be in its unnameable silence, love is henceforth in suspense, pulverized, atomized.

To love, from her point of view, is to love a dead person. The body of her new lover merges with the corpse of her first love, which she had covered with her own body, a day and a night, and whose blood she savored. Furthermore, passion is intensified by a taste for the impossible forced on her by the Japanese lover. In spite of his "international" appearance and Western face as per the scriptwriter's directions, he remains if not exotic at least other, from an other world, a beyond, to the extent of merging with the image of the German who was loved and who died in Nevers. But the very dynamic Japanese engineer is also marked by death because he necessarily bears the moral scars of the atomic death of which his countrymen were the first victims.

A love crippled by death or a love of death? A love that was made impossible or a necrophilic passion for death? *My love is a Hiroshima,* or else, *I love Hiroshima for its suffering is my Eros? Hiroshima mon amour* preserves that ambiguity, which is, perhaps, the postwar version of love. Unless that historical version of love reveals the profound ambiguity of love with respect to death, the death-bearing halo of all passion . . . "His being dead does not keep her from desiring him. She can no longer help herself wanting him, dead as he might be. Her body is drained, breathless. Her mouth is moist. Her posture is that of a desiring woman, shameless to the point of crudeness. More shameless than anywhere else. Disgusting. She desires a dead man."[21] "The purpose of love is to die more comfortably into life."[22]

The implosion of love into death and of death into love reaches its highest expression in the unbearable grief of madness. "They pretended I was dead . . . I went mad. With meanness. I would spit, so I was told, in my mother's face."[23] Such a madness, bruised and deadly, might be no more than the absorption, on Her part, of His death. "One might think her dead, so fully is she dying of his own death."[24] The identification of the protagonists with each other as they fuse their borders, their words, their being, is a standing metaphor with Duras. While she does not die as he does, while she outlasts their dead love, she nevertheless becomes *like* a dead woman—severed from others and from time, she has the endless, animal stare of cats, she is mad—"Having died of love in Nevers." ". . . I couldn't manage to find the slightest difference between that dead body and mine . . . Between that body and mine I could find only similarities . . . such that I could scream, do you understand?"[25] Frequent, even permanent, identification with the object of mourning is nonetheless absolute and inescapable. Because of that very fact, mourning becomes impossible and changes the heroine into a crypt inhabited by a living corpse . . .

Private and Public

Duras' entire work is perhaps contained in the 1960 text that sets the plot of Resnais' film in the year 1957, fourteen

years after the atomic explosion. Everything is there—
suffering, death, love, and their explosive mixture within
a woman's mad melancholia; but above all the combination of sociohistorica¹ *realism* adumbrated in *Un Barrage
contre le Pacifique* (1950; *The Sea Wall,* 1986), which resur-
faced in *L'Amant,* with the *X-ray of depression* that was
inaugurated in *Moderato cantabile* (1958; Eng. tr. 1960) and
would become the favorite ground, the exclusive area of
the subsequent intimist texts.

While history is unobtrusive and later disappears, it is
here cause and setting. This drama of love and madness
appears to be independent of the political drama as the
power of passion outstrips political events, atrocious as
they may be. What is more, this mad, impossible love
seems to triumph over the events—if one may speak of
triumph when eroticized suffering or love in suspense hold
sway.

Nevertheless, Duras' melancholia is *also* like an explosion in history. Private suffering absorbs political horror
into the subject's psychic microcosm. The French woman
in Hiroshima might have come out of Stendhal; perhaps
she is even eternal and yet she nonetheless exists because
of the war, the Nazis, the bomb . . .

Because of its integration into private life, however,
political life loses the autonomy that our consciousness
persists in setting aside for it, religiously. The different
participants in the global conflict do not disappear, for all
that, through a global condemnation that would amount
to a remission of the crime in the name of love. The young
German is an enemy, the Resistance's severity has its logic,
and nothing is said that could justify the Japanese interven-
tion on the side of the Nazis any more than the violence
of the belated American counterattack. Political events
having been acknowledged by an implicit political con-

sciousness that belongs to the left (the Japanese man should unquestionably appear as a leftist), the aesthetic stake just the same remains that of love and death. It therefore sets public events in the light of madness.

Today's milestone is human madness. Politics is part of it, particularly in its lethal outbursts. Politics is not, as it was for Hannah Arendt, the field where human freedom is unfurled. The modern world, the world of world wars, the Third World, the underground world of death that acts upon us, do not have the civilized splendor of the Greek city state. The modern political domain is massively, in totalitarian fashion, social, leveling, exhausting. Hence madness is a space of antisocial, apolitical, and paradoxically free individuation. Confronting it, political events, outrageous and monstrous as they might be—the Nazi invasion, the atomic explosion—are assimilated to the extent of being measured only by the human suffering they cause. Up to a point, considering moral suffering, there is no common ground between a shorn lover in France and a Japanese woman scorched by the atom. In the view of an ethic and an aesthetic concerned with suffering, the mocked private domain gains a solemn dignity that depreciates the public domain while allocating to history the imposing responsibility for having triggered the malady of death. As a result, public life becomes seriously severed from reality whereas private live, on the other hand, is emphasized to the point of filling the whole of the real and invalidating any other concern. The new world, necessarily political, is unreal. We are living the reality of a new suffering world.

Starting with that imperative of fundamental uneasiness, the various political commitments appear identical and disclose their strategies for flight and mendacious weakness: "Collaborators, the Fernandezes. And myself,

[235]

two years after the war, a member of the communist party. An absolute, final equivalence. It's the same thing, the same call for help, the same judgment deficiency, let's say the same superstition, which consists in believing there is a political solution to a personal problem."[26]

One might, on that basis, defer the examination of political matters and scrutinize only the spectrum of suffering. We are survivors, living dead, corpses on furlough, sheltering personal Hiroshimas in the bosom of our private worlds.

It is possible to imagine a form of art that, while acknowledging the weight of contemporary suffering, would drown suffering in the conquerors' triumph, or in metaphysical sarcasms and enthusiasms, or yet in the fondness of erotic pleasure. Is it not also true, is it not especially true, that contemporary man succeeds, better than ever, in defeating the grave, that life prevails in the experience of the living, and that, from a military and political standpoint, the destructive forces of the Second World War appear to have been arrested? Duras chooses or yields to the appeal of another path—the conniving, voluptuous, bewitching contemplation of death within us, of the wound's constancy.

The publication of *La Douleur* in 1985—a strange secret diary kept during the war and whose main narrative relates the return of Robert L. from Dachau—reveals one of the essential biographical and historical roots of such suffering. The struggle of man against death in the face of the Nazi-imposed extermination. The survivor's struggle in the midst of normal life to recapture for what is close to a corpse the elemental forces of life. The narrator—both witness and fighter in this life-and-death venture—explains it as if from within, from within her love for the renascent dying man.

The struggle with death began very soon. One had to deal softly with it, with delicacy, tact, diplomacy. It surrounded him on all sides. But there was still one way of reaching him, there was an opening, it was not too wide, through which one could communicate, but life was yet in him, hardly a splinter, but a splinter just the same. Death would launch an attack—a temperature of 103 the first day. Then 104. Then 106. Death was out of breath—106: the heart quivered like a violin string. Still 106, but it quivers. The heart, we thought, the heart is going to stop. Still 106. Death strikes, as with a battering ram, but the heart is deaf. It isn't possible, the heart is going to stop.[27]

The narrator is meticulously fastened to the minute, essential details of the body's struggle against death, of death's against the body; she scrutinizes the "distraught but sublime" head, the bones, the skin, the intestines, even the "inhuman" or "human" shit . . . At the heart of her love, her dying love for this man, she yet regains, through and thanks to suffering, her passion for the singular, unique, hence loved forever, being—Robert L., the survivor. Death rekindles dead love.

At the mere mention of that name, Robert L., I weep. I weep again. I shall weep all my life . . . during his mortal agony . . . I had known this man, Robert L., best . . . I had registered forever what made him himself, and himself alone, and nothing or no one else in the world, and I spoke of the distinctive gracefulness of Robert L.[28]

Would suffering enamored of death be the supreme individuation?

What was perhaps necessary was the strange experience

of having been uprooted, a childhood on the Asian continent, the stress of a difficult existence next to her courageous, harsh mother (who was a teacher), the precocious encounter with her brother's mental illness and the prevailing poverty—all of which may have led her personal sensitivity to suffering to espouse with such eagerness the drama of our times, a drama that imprints the malady of death at the heart of the psychic experience of most of us. Add a childhood where love, already scorched by the fire of restrained hatred, and hope were displayed only in the depths of misfortune. "I am going to spit in his face. She opened the door and the spittle weighed in her mouth. It wasn't worth it. It was bad luck, Mister Jo was bad luck, like the sea walls, the horse that kicked the bucket, it was nobody's fault, just bad luck."[29] Such a childhood of hatred and fear became the source and blazon of a vision of contemporary history. "We are a family of stone, petrified in a mass that affords no access. Every day we try to kill ourselves, to kill. We not only don't speak with one another, we don't look at one another. . . . Because of what was done to our mother, who was so kind, so trusting, we hate life, we hate one another."[30] "The remembrance is that of a crucial fear."[31] "I believe I am already able to admit it, I vaguely feel I would like to die."[32] ". . . I am immersed in a sadness that I expected and comes from me alone. I have always been sad."[33]

With a thirst for suffering to the point of madness Duras reveals the mercy that comes with our most persistent despondencies, those that are most resistant to faith, the most contemporary.

Woman as Sadness

"By what means does one take a woman? the vice-consul asks. The manager laughs. . . . I would use sadness with her, the vice-consul says, if I were allowed to do so."[34]

Sadness would be the basic illness, if it were not, for Duras, women's sickly core: Anne-Marie Stretter *(The Vice-Consul)*, for instance, Lol V. Stein *(The Ravishing of Lol V. Stein)*, or Alissa *(Destroy, She Said)*, to mention only three. It is a nondramatic, wilted, unnameable sadness. A mere nothing that produces discreet tears and elliptical words. Suffering and rapture flow together somewhat discreetly. "I have heard it said . . . her heaven is made of tears," the vice-consul notes with respect to Anne-Marie Stretter. The peculiar ambassadress to Calcutta seems to wander about with a kind of death buried in her pale, thin body. "Death in the course of life, the vice-consul finally said, but which would never catch up with you? That's it."[35] She wanders about the world, and beyond her shattered loves, bearing the melancholy charm of the Venice of her childhood and a musician's unfulfilled destiny. She is the walking metaphor of a glaucous green Venice, an end-of-the-world city, while for others the city of the Doges remains a source of excitement. Anne-Marie Stretter, however, is the embodied suffering of any ordinary woman "from Dijon, Milan, Brest, Dublin," vaguely English perhaps, or rather no, she is universal: "In other words, it is rather simplistic to think one comes only from Venice; it is also possible to come from other places one has gone through along the way, it seems to me."[36]

Suffering is her sex, the high point of her eroticism. When she brings together her set of lovers, on the sly at the *Blue Moon* or at her secret home, what do they do?

They look at her. She is thin in her black dressing gown, her eyelids are taut, her beauty has vanished. What is her unbearable well-being?

And suddenly what Charles Rossett didn't know he was expecting happened. Is it really so? Yes. There are tears. They come out of her eyes and roll down her cheeks, they are very small, they sparkle."[37]

. . . They look at her. Her broad eyelids tremble, the tears do not flow . . . I weep without any reason that I could explain to you, it is like a sorrow that goes through me, someone has to weep, it's as if it were me.

She knows they are there, very close, without a doubt, the men of Calcutta, she doesn't move at all, if she did . . . no . . . she gives one the impression that she is now trapped in a pain that is too old still to cause tears.[38]

Such a suffering expresses an impossible pleasure; it is the heartrending sign of frigidity. Holding back a passion that could not flow, suffering is nevertheless and more profoundly so the prison where mourning is locked in; it is the impossible mourning for an old love entirely made up of sensations and *autosensations* that is inalienable, inseparable, and for that very reason, unnameable. The unfulfilled mourning of the autosensual preobject determines feminine frigidity. Hence the pain that goes with it grips a woman unknown to the one who lives on the surface—a stranger. To a narcissism deprived of melancholy appearances, suffering opposes and adds deep narcissism, the archaic autosensuality of wounded affects. One therefore discovers an unacceptable renunciation at the source of such suffering. That is why suffering is revealed through the interplay of reduplications where one's own body recognizes itself in the image of another provided it is the replica of his own.

"Not I" or Abandonment

Abandonment represents the insuperable trauma inflicted by the discovery—doubtless a precocious one and for that very reason impossible to work out—of the existence of a *not-I*.[39] Indeed, abandonment structures the remains of history in Duras' texts: the woman is deserted by her lover, the German lover of the Nevers Frenchwoman dies (*Hiroshima Mon Amour*, 1960); Michael Richardson openly abandons Lol V. Stein (*The Ravishing of Lol V. Stein*, 1964); again Michael Richardson, an impossible lover, articulates a series of disasters in the life of Anne-Marie Stretter (*The Vice-Consul*, 1965); Elizabeth Alione has lost her stillborn child, and beforehand there was the young doctor's love for her, the doctor who attempts to kill himself when she shows his letter to her husband (*Destroy, She Said*, 1969); as to the man and the young woman in *The Malady of Death* (1982), they seem possessed of an inherent mourning that makes their physical passion morbid, distant, always already dismissed; finally, the young French girl and her Chinese lover are from the start convinced of the impossibility and condemnation of their affair, and as a result the girl convinces herself that she does not love him and allows herself to be disturbed by an echo of her neglected passion only by a Chopin melody on the ship that takes her to France *(The Lover)*.

The feeling of unavoidable abandonment that reveals the separation or the actual death of the lovers also seems immanent and as if predestined. It is formed about the maternal figure. The mother of the young woman of Nevers was separated from her husband . . . or else (the

narrator hesitates) she was Jewish, and left for the unoc-
cupied area. As for Lol V. Stein, the night of the fateful
dance when Michael Richardson abandoned her, she noticed the arrival of Anne-Marie Stretter accompanied by
her daughter. That woman, who thus introduces the theme
of the mother, had a graceful, bony figure, and she bore
"the emblems of a vague denial of nature."[40] Her thinness
was elegant, mortuary, and inaccessible, and she turned
out to be Lol's successful rival. More dramatically, the
mad bonzian woman in *The Vice-Consul* who, pregnant
and gangrened, unconsciously travels from Indochina to
India, struggles against death but above all against her
mother who had driven her out of her native house. "She
says a few words of Cambodian: hello, good night. To
the child, she would speak. And now, to whom? To her
old mother in Tonle-Sap, the source, the cause of all evils,
of her crooked destiny, her pure-hearted love."[41]

Like an archetype of the madwomen who fill Duras'
universe, the madness of the girl's mother, in *The Lover,*
towers with dismal Gothic force. "I see that my mother is
clearly mad. . . . From birth. It's in the blood. She wasn't
ill with it, she lived with it as if it were healthy."[42] Hatred
grips daughter and mother in a passion-driven vise that
turns out to be the source of the mysterious silence that
striates writing: "she should be locked up, beaten, killed."[43]
". . . I believe I have spoken of the love we bore our
mother but I don't know if I spoke of the hatred we also
bore. . . . She is the place on the threshold of which
silence begins. What happens there is precisely silence, that
slow labor for my entire life. I am still there, before these
possessed children, at the same distance from mystery. I
have never written, although I thought I did, I have never
loved, although I thought I loved, I have never done
anything except wait before the closed door."[44] Fear of

maternal madness leads the novelist to have the mother disappear, to free herself from her through a violence no less deadly than that of the mother herself as she beat her prostitute daughter. Destroy, the narrating daughter in *The Lover* seems to say, but in erasing the mother's image she simultaneously takes her place. The daughter acts as a substitute for maternal madness; rather than killing her mother she continues her through the negative hallucination of an always faithfully loving identification. "Suddenly there was, next to me, someone sitting in my mother's place, she wasn't my mother . . . the identity that could not be replaced with any other had disappeared, and I had no means to make her come back, to have her begin to come back. Nothing offered itself that might fill the figure. I became mad in full possession of my senses."[45]

While pointing out that the bond to the mother constitutes the previous history of suffering, the text names it neither as cause nor as origin. Suffering is sufficient unto itself; it transcends effects as well as causes and sweeps away all entities, that of the subject as well as of the object. Would suffering be the ultimate threshold of our objectless states? It does not lend itself to description, but it is accessible through inspirations, tears, blank spaces between words. "I get carried away over suffering in India. It happens to all of us, more or less, right? One cannot speak of that suffering unless one insures that it breathes within us. . . ."[46] Both massive and exterior, suffering merges with indifference or some deep splitting of the female being; such a splitting is experienced as the *emptiness of a boredom* that would be insuperable if it emerged at the very site of subjective division:

She spoke merely to say that it was impossible for her to express how boring and time-consuming it was being

Lol V. Stein. They asked her to make an effort. She didn't understand why, she would say. The difficulty she encountered when searching just for one word appeared insurmountable. She appeared to expect nothing more.

Was she thinking of something, of herself? they would ask. She didn't understand the question. One might have said that she took herself for granted, and the infinite weariness of not being able to relinquish such an attitude need not even come to mind; she had become a desert into which a nomadic power had propelled her in a never-ending quest for what? One didn't know. She didn't answer.[47]

On Ravishment: Lacking Pleasure

One should doubtless not assume that the women in Duras' fiction represent *all* there is in woman. Nevertheless, a few common features of feminine sexuality show up. One is led to postulate, in such a being racked by sadness, not a *repression* but an *exhaustion of erotic drives*. Appropriated by the object of love—by the lover or, behind him, the mother whose mourning remains impossible—the drives are blank, so to speak, emptied of their ability to provide a bond of sexual pleasure or of symbolic complicity. To be sure, the lost Thing has left its mark on its disused affects and on a discourse relieved of its meaning—but this is the mark of an absence, of a *basic disconnection*. It can cause ravishment—but not pleasure. If one were to identify that woman and her love one would have to look for her in the secret cellar where there is no one, except for the sparkling eyes of Nevers' cats and the catastrophic anguish of the young woman who merges with them.

"Shall I come back and go with her? No. Is it tears that deprive one of a person?"[48]

Would such a ravishment, hidden and anerotic (in the sense of being deprived of bonds, detached from the other, and turning only toward the hollow of one's own proper body that nevertheless at once is disappropriated of jouissance and sinks into the fondness of death for one's self), would it be if not the secret at least one aspect of feminine jouissance? That is what *The Malady of Death* gives us to understand. The man savors the young woman's open body like a blissful discovery of the otherwise inaccessible sexual difference, but which nevertheless appears to him as death-bearing, engulfing, dangerous. He defends himself against the pleasure of lying in his partner's moist sex by imagining that he kills her. "You discover that it is there, within her, that the malady of death is aroused, that it's this figure arrayed before you that decrees the malady of death."[49] On the other hand, she is on friendly terms with death. Aloof, unconcerned about sex and yet loving love and compliant to pleasure, she is fond of the death she believes she bears within herself. Even more so, such a complicity with death gives her the feeling that she is beyond death: a woman neither gives nor undergoes death because *she is part of it* and because she imposes it. He is the one who *catches* the malady of death; she *is* part of it, therefore she moves on, elsewhere: "she looks at you through the green filter of her eyes. She says, you herald the realm of death. One cannot love death if it is imposed on you from outside. You think you are weeping on account of not loving. You weep because you cannot impose death."[50] She goes away, inaccessible, deified by the narrator because she brings death to others through a love that is an "admirable impossibility" for herself as for him. A certain truth of feminine experience involving the

jouissance of suffering verges, with Duras, on the mythi-
fication of the inaccessible feminine.

Nonetheless, the no man's land of aching affects and
devalued words that comes close to being the height of
mystery, dead as it may be, is not lacking expression. It
has its own language—it is called *reduplication*. It creates
echoes, doubles, kindred beings who display a passion or
a destruction such as the aching woman is not up to
putting into words and suffers for being deprived of.

Couples and Doubles: A Reduplication

Reduplication is a jammed repetition. While what is repeated is rippled out in time, reduplication lies outside
time. It is a reverberation in space, a play of mirrors
lacking perspective or duration. A double may hold, for a
while, the instability of the same, giving it a temporary
identity, but it mainly explores the same in depth, opening
up an unsuspected, unfathomable substance. The double
is the unconscious substance of the same, that which
threatens it and could engulf it.

Produced by the mirror, reduplication precedes the
specular identification specific to the "mirror stage." It
refers to the outposts of our unstable identities, blurred by
a drive that nothing could defer, deny, or signify.

The unnameable power of such a gaze in addition to
sight asserts itself as a privileged universe, unfathomable
as to desire: "He merely looked at Suzanne with blurred
eyes, he looked at her again, he heightened his gaze with
additional sight, as one usually does when choked by
passion."[51] On the far or near side of sight, hypnotic
passion sees doubles.

Anne Desbaresdes and Chauvin in *Moderato cantibile* construct their love story as a reflection of what they imagine

to be the story of the passionate couple where the woman wanted to be killed by the man. Would the two protagonists exist without the imaginary reference to the masochistic jouissance of the couple who preceded them? The framework is laid for another reduplication to be played out, "moderato cantabile," that of the mother and her son. Mother and child carry out the crisis of the imaginative thought process in which the identity of a woman is buried in the love for her young. If mother and daughter can be rivals and enemies *(The Lover)*, the mother and her small boy appear in *Moderato cantabile* as pure devouring love. Like wine, and even before she drinks, her son engrosses Anne Desbaresdes; she accepts herself, lenient and delighted, only through him; he is the hinge that substitutes for implied amorous disappointments and reveals her insanity. The son is the visible form of a disappointed mother's madness. Without him, perhaps, she would be dead. With him, she is caught in the whirlwind of love, of practical and educational concerns, but also of solitudes; she is forever exiled from others and from herself. As daily, banal replica of the woman who, at the beginning of the novel, desired to be killed by her lover, Anne Desbaresdes as mother lives her ecstatic death in the love for her son. While revealing the masochistic chasms of desire, this complex figure (mother-son/male lover–female lover/passionate dead woman–passionate killer) shows by what narcissistic and autosensuous delights feminine suffering is supported. The son of course is his mother's resurrection, but, conversely, her own deaths survive in him—her humiliations, her nameless wounds that are now living flesh. The more motherly love hovers over a woman's suffering, the more the child is painfully and subtly affectionate . . .

The Japanese and the German in *Hiroshima Mon Amour*

are also doubles. In the amorous experience of the young woman from Nevers, the Japanese man revives the memory of her dead lover, but the two male images fuse into a hallucinatory jigsaw puzzle that suggests that the love for the German is present without any possibility of being forgotten and, conversely, the love-for the Japanese man is destined to die. Reduplication and exchange of complements. Through that strange osmosis, the vitality of a survivor of the Hiroshima catastrophe comes to be dimmed by a gruesome fate, while the other's definitive death lives on, translucently, in the young woman's bruised passion. Such a reverberation of her objects of love shatters the heroine's identity: she belongs to no time period but to the space of the contamination of entities where her own being wavers, dejected and delighted.

The Criminal Secret

The technique of reduplication reaches its height in *The Vice-Consul*. Anne-Marie Stretter's decadent melancholia corresponds to the expressionistic madness of the Savannakhet bonzian woman—who takes up again the theme of the Asian woman with a diseased foot in *The Sea Wall*.[52] Facing the heartrending poverty and rotting flesh of the Asian woman, Anne-Marie Stretter's Venetian tears seem a luxurious, unbearable caprice. Nevertheless, the contrast between the two fades away when suffering intervenes. Against a backdrop of illness the images of the two women merge, and Anne-Marie Stretter's ethereal universe aquires a measure of madness that would not be as strong without the imprint of the other wanderer. Two musicians—the pianist, the raving singer; two exiles—one from Europe, the other from Asia; two wounded women—one with an invisible wound, the other gan-

grened by social, family, human violence . . . The duet
becomes a threesome with the addition of another replica,
this time a masculine one: the Vice-Consul from Lahore.
He is a strange figure, supposedly bearing a never acknowledged archaic distress; all that is known of him are
his sadistic acts—stinkbombs in school, shooting human
beings in Lahore . . . Is it true, is it false? The Vice-
Consul, whom every one fears, becomes Anne-Marie
Stretter's accomplice and a lover condemned to suffer her
coldness alone, for even the tears of this charmer are in-
tended for others. Could the Vice-Consul be a corrupted,
possible metamorphosis of the melancholy ambassadress,
her masculine replica, her sadistic variant, the expression
of taking action—something she precisely does not do,
not even through intercourse? He may be homosexual,
loving with an impossible love a woman who, in her
sexual distress, haunted by a desire without satisfaction,
would very much have liked to be like him—beyond the
law, beyond reach. The unbalanced threesome—the bonzian woman, the Vice-Consul, the depressed ambassadress
—weave a world that is beyond the other characters in the
novel, even when they are most attached to the ambassadress. They provide the narrator with a rich soil for her
psychological search—uncovering the insane, criminal secret that lies beneath the surface of our diplomatic behavior, of which the sadness of a number of women bears
discreet witness.

The act of love is often the occasion for such a reduplication, as each partner becomes the other's double. Thus,
in *The Malady of Death,* the man's death-bearing obsession
merges with his mistress' deathful thoughts. The tears of
the man, as he joys in the woman's "abominable frailty,"
correspond to her languid, detached silence and reveal its
meaning: suffering. What she believes to be the falseness

of his discourse, which would not fit the subtle reality of things, becomes abreacted in her own flight when, indifferent to his passion, she leaves the room of their love-making. As a result, the two characters end up appearing as two voices, two waves "between the whiteness of the sheets and that of the sea."[53]

A suffering that has faded (as a color does) fills these men and women, doubles and replicas, and, gratifying them, deprives them of any other psychology. Those carbon copies are henceforth individuated only through their *names*—black, matchless diamonds, unfathomable, that harden over the expanse of suffering. Anne Desbaresdes, Lol V. Stein, Elisabeth Alione, Michael Richardson, Max Thorn, Stein . . . The names seem to condense and retain a story of which their bearers are perhaps as much unaware as the reader, a story that almost ends up revealing itself to our own unconscious uncanniness by becoming suddenly incomprehensible but in a familiar fashion.

Event and Hatred: Among Women

As an echo to death-bearing symbiosis with the mothers, passion between two women represents one of the most intense images of doubling. When Lol V. Stein becomes deprived of her fiancé by Anne-Marie Stretter (who does not, however, benefit, and whose inconsolable sadness will become known to us in *The Vice-Consul*), she confines herself in a bored and inaccessible isolation: "To know nothing about Lol was already to know her."[54] Nevertheless, years later, while everyone thinks she is healed and peaceably married, she watches the love-making of her former friend Tatiana Karl with Jacques Hold. She is in love with the couple, especially with Tatiana— she would like to take her place, in the same sheets, in the same bed. Such an absorption of the other woman's passion—Tatiana being here the substitute for the first rival. Anne-Marie Stretter, and, in the last instance, for the mother—also works the other way. Tatiana, who until then has been careless and playful, begins to suffer. The two women are henceforth carbon copies of each other, replicas in the script of suffering, which, in Lol V. Stein's delighted eyes, controls the world's merry-go-round:

> things are becoming clearer around her and she suddenly sees their sharp edges, the remains that lie around all over the world, revolving, there is a scrap already half-eaten by rats, it is Tatiana's suffering, she sees it, she is ill-at-ease, always those feelings, one slips on that grease. She believed that time was possible, a time that was alternately filled and emptied, that fills and drains, and then is yet, always, ready for use, she still believes it, she believes it always, never will she be cured.[55]

Doubles are multiplied in the mirror of *Destroy, She Said* and drift over the theme of destruction, which, once it is named in the body of the text, rises to the surface to clarify the title and make one understand all the relations that the novel presents. Elisabeth Alione, who is depressed following an unhappy love affair and the stillbirth of her baby girl, is resting in a bleak hotel, full of sick people. There she meets Stein and his double, Max Thor, two Jews ceaselessly about to become writers: "How strongly it compels one sometimes not to write it down."[56] Two men bound by an inexpressible passion that one assumes is homosexual, and which precisely does not succeed in inscribing itself, except through the medium of two women. He loves/they love Alissa and are fascinated by Elisa. Alissa Thor discovers that her husband is happy to know Elisa, who captivates Stein; therefore she herself allows the same Stein to get close to her and love her (the reader is free to make up dyads within that suggestive web). She is amazed to discover that Max Thor is happy here in the kaleidoscopic world of doubles—with Stein, possibly on account of Elisa? But he also asserts that it is due to Alissa herself—" 'Destroy,' she says."[57] As fully obsessed as she is by that destruction, Alissa gazes at herself in Elisa and reveals, through the ambiguity of identification and decomposition, a true madness under the appearance of a fresh-looking young woman. "I am someone who is afraid, Alissa goes on, afraid of being deserted, afraid of the future, afraid to love, afraid of violence, of crowds, afraid of the unknown, of hunger, of poverty, of truth."[58]

Which truth? Hers or Elisa's? "Destroy, she said." The two women, however, get along. Alissa is Elisa's mouthpiece. She repeats her words, she bears witness to her past and prophesies about her future, in which, moreover, she sees only repetitions and doubles, the more so as the uncanniness of each one to him or herself causes each to become, in time, his/her own double and his/her own other.

> Elisabeth doesn't answer.
>
> "We knew each other when we were kids, she says. Our families were on good terms."
>
> Alissa repeats in a very low voice:
>
> "We knew each other when we were kids. Our families were on good terms."
>
> Silence.
>
> "If you loved him, if you had loved him, just once, only once, in your life, you would have loved the others," Alissa says, "Stein and Max Thor."
>
> "I don't understand . . ." Elisabeth says, "but . . ."
>
> "That will happen some other time," Alissa says,

"later. But it will be neither you nor them. Don't pay any attention to what I am saying."

"Stein says that you are mad," Elisabeth says.

"Stein says it all."[59]

The two women echo each other; one finishes the other's sentences and the other denies them while knowing that those words speak a portion of their common truth, their complicity.

Does such a duality stem from their being women, from partaking in a same, so-called hysterical malleability, each being quick to take her own image for the other's ("She experiences what the other experiences")?[60] Or does it stem from loving the same man, who is double? From not having a stable object of love, dissecting that object into a shimmering of elusive reflections, since no support is able to hold and assuage an endemic passion, perhaps a maternal one?

Indeed, the man dreams of her—of them. Max Thor is in love with his wife Alissa, but since he has not forgotten that he is Stein's double he calls her Elisa in his dreams, while Stein himself dreams and speaks Alissa's name . . . Elisa/Alissa . . . The fact remains that they "both find themselves caught in a mirror."

> "We resemble each other," Alissa says. "We would love Stein if it were possible to love.". . .
>
> "How beautiful you are," Elisabeth says.
>
> "We are women," Alissa says. "Look." . . .
>
> "I love you and I desire you," Alissa says.[61]

Homonymy notwithstanding, it is nevertheless not an identification that takes place between them. Beyond the fleeting moment of specular, hypnoidal recognition, the impossibility of being the other opens up in breathtaking fashion. Hypnosis (whose motto might be, *the one is the other*) is accompanied by the pain of seeing that the merging of their bodies is an impossibility, they will never become the mother and her inseparable daughter—Elisabeth's daughter is dead, the daughter is destroyed at birth. That is enough to unbalance each protagonist and hollow out even more her unsettled identity.

What are the ingredients of such a mixture of hypnosis and utopic passion?

Jealousy, suppressed hatred, fascination, sexual desire of the rival and her man: the entire gamut creeps into the behavior and the words of those temperamental beings who live through "a tremendous grief" and complain without saying so but "as if they were singing."[62]

The violence of drives that cannot be reduced to words is subdued particularly by behavioral restraints; it is as if behavior were already mastered in itself thanks to the effort of giving it shape, as in a preexistent writing. The scream of hatred therefore is not sounded in its wild brutality. It is changed into music, which (reminding one of the smile of the Virgin or Mona Lisa) bares the knowledge of a secret that is itself invisible, underground, uterine, and conveys to civilization a suffering that is civilized, delighted but always unquenched, and for which words are too much. It is a music both neutral and destructive— "smashing trees, bringing down walls," weakening wrath into "sublime gentleness" and "absolute laughter."[63]

Would feminine melancholia be appeased by reunion with the other woman, as soon as the latter could be imagined as man's privileged partner? Or else would it be revived, or perhaps even caused, by the impossibility of meeting—of satisfying—the other woman? Among women, at any rate, the hatred that has been harnessed, swallowed, where the archaic rival lies confined, becomes exhausted. When depression expresses itself, it becomes eroticized as destruction—unleashed violence with the mother, graceful tearing down with the friend.

The domineering, tattered, mad mother establishes herself powerfully in *The Sea Wall* and determines her children's sexuality. "She is desperate of hope itself."[64] "The doctor diagnosed the source of her attacks as being the sea wall's collapse. Perhaps he was wrong. So much resentment, year after year, day after day. There was more than one cause. There were a thousand, including the dams' collapse, injustice in the world, the sight of her children bathing in the river . . . to die of that, to die of misfortune."[65] Exhausted by "bad luck," exasperated by her daughter's wanton sexuality, the mother is subject to fits. "She was still hitting her, as if under the pressure of an unrelenting necessity. Suzanne, at her feet, half naked in her torn dress, was crying. . . . What if I want to kill her? If it suits me to kill her?"[66] That is what she says concerning her daughter. Under the influence of that passion, Suzanne gives herself without loving anyone. Except, perhaps, her brother Joseph. And that incestuous desire that the brother shares in and carries out in his own furious and nearly delinquent fashion (". . . I slept with a sister when I slept with her")[67] sets up the favored theme of the novels that followed—the impossibility of a love defined by doubles . . .

After the implosion of the mother's hatred in the mad bonzian woman *(The Vice-Consul),* the mother/daughter destruction in *The Lover* compels us to realize that the mother's outburst of fury against the daughter is the "event" that the hateful, loving daughter watches for, experiences, and restores with wonder: "In her fits my mother rushes at me, locks me up in the room, beats me with her fists, slaps me, undresses me, comes close to me, smells my body, my underwear, she says she recognizes the scent of the Chinese man . . ."[68]

Thus the elusive double reveals the staying power of an archaic object of love, one that is uncontrollable, imaginary, and which puts me to death on account of its domination and its evasions, its sisterly or motherly closeness, but also on account of its impregnable and thus malevolent, detestable exteriority. All the figures of love converge on this autosensual, harrowing object, even if they are constantly revived by the mainspring of a masculine presence. Often at the center, the man's desire is nevertheless always outflanked and carried away by the ruffled but deceitfully powerful passivity of women.

All those men are aliens—the Chinese in *The Lover,* the Japanese in *Hiroshima Mon Amour,* and the whole series of Jews or uprooted diplomats . . . Both sensuous and abstract, they are undermined by a fear that their passion never succeeds in overcoming. That passionate fear is like a mountain crest, an axis, or revival of mirror-playing among women who spread out of the flesh of suffering, of which men are the skeleton.

Beyond the Looking Glass

An unfillable lack of satisfaction, delighted nevertheless, opens up in the space that has thus been set up and which separates two women. It might be called, clumsily, feminine homosexuality. With Duras, however, we are dealing more with an ever nostalgic quest for the same as other, for the other as same, within the array of narcissistic mirage or a hypnosis that the narrator finds inevitable. She relates the psychic substratum previous to our conquests of the other sex, and which still underlies the eventual, perilous encounters between men and women. One is accustomed to pay no attention to that nearly uterine space.

And one is not wrong. For in that crypt full of reflections, identities, bonds, and feelings destroy one another. "Destroy, she said." And yet the society of women is neither necessarily wild nor simply destructive. Out of the weakness or impossibility of the inevitably erotic bonds, it erects an imaginary aura of complicity that can prove to be slightly painful and necessarily plunged into mourning because it has sunk all sexual objects, all sublime ideals into its narcissistic flow. Values do not hold in the face of that "irony of the community" (as Hegel called women), whose destructiveness, however, is not necessarily amusing.

Suffering unfurls its microcosm through the reverberation of characters. They are articulated as doubles, as in mirrors that magnify their melancholia to the point of violence and delirium. That display of reduplication recalls the child's unstable identity when, in the mirror, it finds the image of its mother only as a (soothing or terrifying) replica or echo of itself. Like an alter ego that has been frozen within the gamut of drive intensities that disturb it, detached in front of it, but never steady and on the brink of invading it through a hostile return, like a boomerang. Identity, in the sense of a stable and solid image of the self where the autonomy of the subject will be established, emerges only at the end of this process when narcissistic shimmering draws to a close in a jubilatory assumption that is the work of the Third Party.

Even the soundest among us know just the same that a firm identity remains a fiction. Suffering, in Duras' work, in a mannered way and with empty words evokes that impossible mourning, which, if its process had been completed, would have removed our morbid lining and set us up as independent, unified subjects. Thus it takes hold of us and carries us to the dangerous, furthermost bounds of our psychic life.

Modern and Postmodern

As the literature of our illness, Duras' fiction accompanies the distress that has certainly been triggered and increased by the contemporary world but proves to be essential and transhistorical.

It is a literature of limits because it also displays the limits of the nameable. The characters' elliptical speech, the obsessive conjuring up of a "nothing" that might epitomize the malady of suffering, point to a disaster of words in the face of the unnameable affect. Such a silence, as I mentioned earlier, recalls the "nothing" that Valéry's eye saw in an incandescent oven at the heart of a gruesome confusion. Duras does not orchestrate it in the fashion of Mallarmé, who sought for the music in words, nor in the manner of Beckett who refines a syntax that marks time or moves ahead by fits and starts, warding off the narrative's flight forward. The reverberation among characters as well as the silence inscribed as such, the emphasis on the "nothing" to be spoken as ultimate expression of suffering, leads Duras to a blankness of meaning. Coupled with rhetorical awkwardness, they make up a world of unsettling, infectious ill-being.

Historically and psychologically contemporary, this writing is today confronted with the postmodern challenge. The point now is to see in "the malady of grief" only one moment of the *narrative synthesis* capable of sweeping along in its complex whirlwind philosophical meditations as well as erotic protections or entertaining pleasures. The postmodern is closer to the human comedy than to the abyssal discontent. Has not hell as such, thoroughly investigated in postwar literature, lost its infernal inaccessibility and become our everyday, transparent, almost humdrum lot—a "nothing"—like our "truths" henceforth made visible, televised, in short not so secret as all that . . .? The desire for comedy shows up today to conceal—without for that matter being unaware of it—the concern for such a truth without tragedy, melancholia without purgatory. Shades of Marivaux and Crébillon.

A new amatory world comes to the surface within the eternal return of historical and intellectual cycles. Following the winter of discontent comes the artifice of seeming; following the whiteness of boredom, the heartrending distraction of parody. And vice versa. Truth, in short, makes its way amid the shimmering of artificial amenities as well as asserting itself in painful mirror games. Does not the wonderment of psychic life after all stem from those alternations of protections and downfalls, smiles and tears, sunshine and melancholia?

NOTES

[Note: All biblical references follow the text of *The Jerusalem Bible,* Reader's Edition (Garden City, N.Y.: Doubleday, 1968)—LSR.]

1. *Psychoanalysis—A Counterdepressant*

1. See my *Tales of Love* (New York: Columbia University Press, 1987).

2. See *La Melanconia dell'uomo di genio* (Genoa: Enrica Salavaneschi, 1981).

3. On melancholia in the history of art and ideas see the basic work by Raymond Klibanski, Erwin Panofski, and Fritz Saxl, *Saturn and Melancholy* (London: T. Nelson, 1964).

4. See Karl Abraham, "Préliminaires à l'investigation et au traitement psychanalytique de la folie maniaco-depressive et des états voisins" (1912), in *Oeuvres complètes* (Paris: Payot, 1965), 1:99–113; Sigmund Freud, "Mourning and Melancholia" (1917), in *The Standard Edition of the Complete Psychological Works of Sigmund Freud* (hereafter *SE*), 24 vols., James Strachey, tr. and ed. (London: Hogarth 1953–74), 14:237–58; Melanie Klein, "A Contribution to the Psychogenesis of Manic-Depressive States" and "Mourning and Its Relation to Manic-Depressive States" in *Contributions to Psychoanalysis, 1921–1945* (London: Hogarth Press, 1948), pp. 282–338. Klein's "A

Contribution" is reprinted in Peter Buckley, ed., *Essential Papers on Object Relations* (New York: New York University Press, 1986).

5. As was stressed in Pierre Fédida's "Le Cannibalisme mélancolique," in *L'Absence* (Paris: Gallimard, 1978), p. 65.

6. See Edith Jacobson, *Depression: Comparative Studies of Normal, Neurotic, and Psychotic Conditions* (New York: International University Press, 1977); B. Grunberger, "Etude sur la dépression" and "Le Suicide du mélancolique," in *Le Narcissisme* (Paris: Payot, 1975); G. Rosolato, "L'Axe narcissique des dépressions," in *Essais sur le symbolique* (Paris: Gallimard, 1979).

7. Having noted that, from the very dawn of Greek philosophy, holding on to the *thing* is bound up with the utterance of a statement and the assertion of its truth, Heidegger nevertheless throws open the matter of the "historied" aspect of the *thing:* "The question of the thing again comes into motion from its beginning" (*What Is a Thing?* trans. W. B. Barton, Jr. and Vera Deutsch [Chicago: Henry Regnery, 1967), p. 48). Without going into the history of that conception of the thing but opening it up in the between that extends from the thing to man, Heidegger notes, through a reading of Kant, "that this *between* as an anticipation *(Vorgriff)* reaches beyond the thing and similarly back behind us" (*ibid.,* p. 243).

Through the opening created by Heidegger's question, but also following upon Freud's shaking up rational certainties, I shall speak of the *Thing* as being the "something" that, seen by the already constituted subject looking back, appears as the unspecified, the unseparated, the elusive, even in its determination of actual sexual matter. I shall restrict the term *Object* to the space-time constant that is verified by a statement uttered by a subject in control of that statement.

8. Gérard de Nerval, *Aurelia,* in *Selected Writings,* trans. Geoffrey Wagner (Ann Arbor: University of Michigan Press, 1957), p. 130.

9. See Sigmund Freud, *The Ego and the Id, SE* 19:31.

10. One should differentiate my statement from that of Lacan, who discusses the notion of *das Ding* starting from Freud's *Entwurf:* "*Das Ding* is not involved with what, in a manner somewhat reflexive to the extent that it can be made explicit, leads man to challenge his words as referring to the things they have nevertheless created. There is something else in *das Ding.* What there is is the true secret.

. . . Something that wants. *The* need and not just needs, pressure, emergency. The state of *Not des Lebens* is life's state of emergency . . . , the amount of energy preserved by the body considering the response and what is necessary for the preservation of life" (*L'Ethique de la psychanalyse,* seminar of December 9, 1959 [Paris: Seuil, 1986], pp. 58ff.).

This would involve psychic inscriptions *(Niederschrift)* earlier than the fourth year of life, always "secondary" for Lacan but close to "quality," to "effort," to the "endopsychic structure." "The *Ding* as *Fremde,* as an alien and even sometimes hostile place, at any rate as the first outside space . . . is that object, *das Ding,* as the subject's absolute Other that must be recovered. It is recovered, at the most, as regret. . . . It is in the state of hoping and waiting for it that such optimal tension, on this side of which there is no more perception or effort, will be sought after in the name of the pleasure principle" (p. 65). And even more clearly: *"Das Ding is originally what we therefore call the beyond-the-signified. It is in relation to that beyond-the-signified and a pathetic link to it that the subject maintains its distance and constitutes itself in such a world of relationships, of primary affect previous to any repression.* The entire first articulation of *Entwurf* is built around that" (pp. 67–68). Nevertheless, while Freud emphasizes that the *Thing* shows up only as a "cry," Lacan translates this as *word,* playing on the ambivalent meaning of the word *mot* in French *("mot* is that which is silent"). "The things we are dealing with . . . are things insofar as they are silent. And silent things are not quite the same as things that have no connection with words" (pp. 68–69; trans. by LSR).

11. "Signifiance" refers to semantic operations that are both fluid and archaic—with the latter word restricted to its Freudian sense. It refers to the work performed in language that enables a text to signify what representative and communicative speech does not say —LSR.

12. See Sigmund Freud, *Papers on Metapsychology, SE* 14:139.

13. See Sigmund Freud, "The Economic Problem of Masochism," *SE* 19:159–70.

14. See Sigmund Freud, *An Outline of Psychoanalysis, SE* 23: 139–207.

15. "The Economic Problem of Masochism," *SE* 19:163.

16. *Papers on Metapsychology,* SE 14:139.

17. See Sigmund Freud, "Analysis Terminable and Interminable," SE 23:243.

18. See Sigmund Freud, *The Ego and the Id, SE* 19:53.

19. See Melanie Klein, *Developments in Psychoanalysis* (London: Hogarth Press, 1952).

20. See Jean-Michel Petot, *Melanie Klein, le moi et le bon objet* (Paris: Dunod, 1932).

21. Melanie Klein, *Developments in Psychoanalysis,* p. 296.

22. André Green, in *Narcissisme de vie, narcissisme de mort* (Paris: Minuit, 1983), defines the notion of "negative narcissism" thus: "Beyond the parceling that fragments the self and brings it back to autoeroticism, *absolute* primary narcissism demands the mimetic quietness of death. It seeks the non-desire of the other, nonexistence, which is another way of reaching immortality" (p. 278; trans. by LSR).

23. Concerning affect, see Jacobson's *Depression* and André Green, *Le Discours vivant* (Paris: Presses Universitaires de France, 1971).

24. See my *Revolution in Poetic Language,* trans. Margaret Waller (New York: Columbia University Press, 1984), chapter 1, secs. 2 and 5: "We understand the term 'semiotic' in its Greek sense: σημειον = distinctive mark, trace, index, precursory sign, imprint, trace, figuration. . . . This modality is the one Freudian psychoanalysis points to in postulating not only the *facilitation* and the structuring *disposition* of drives, but also the so-called primary processes which displace and condense both energies and their inscription. Discrete quantities of energy move through the body of the subject who is not yet constituted as such and, in the course of his development, they are arranged according to the various constraints imposed upon this body—always already involved in a semiotic process—by family and social structures. In this way the drives, which are 'energy' charges as well as 'psychical' marks, articulate what we call a *chora:* a nonexpressive totality formed by the drives and their stases in a motility that is as full of movement as it is regulated" (p. 25). On the other hand, the *symbolic* is identified with judgment and the grammatical sentence: "We shall distinguish the semiotic (drives and their articulation) from the realm of signification, which is

always that of a proposition or judgment, in other words, a realm of *positions*. This positionality, which Husserlian phenomenology orchestrates through the concepts of *doxa, position,* and *thesis,* is structured as a break in the signifying process, establishing the *identification* of the subject and its object as preconditions of propositionality. We shall call this break, which produces the positing signification, a *thetic* phase. All enunciation, whether of a word or of a sentence, is thetic. It requires an identification; in other words, the subject must separate from and through his image, from and through his objects. This image and objects must first be posited in a space that becomes symbolic because it connects the two separated positions, recording them or redistributing them in an open combinatorial system" (p. 43).

25. See Hanna Segal, "Notes on Symbol Formation," *International Journal of Psychoanalysis* (1957), 38:391–97.

26. See *On Narcissism* (1914), *SE* 14:73ff.; *Beyond the Pleasure Principle* (1920), *SE* 18:3ff.; and *The Ego and the Id* (1923), *SE* 19:3ff.

27. Green, *Narcissisme de vie, narcissisme de mort,* pp. 255ff.

28. Thus the murder of the father in *Totem and Taboo* (1913) or the deadly threatening vagina in *The Uncanny* (1919).

2. Life and Death of Speech

1. Let us recall the progress of pharmacology in this area: the discovery, in 1952, by Delaye and Deniker of the effect of neuroleptics on states of excitement; the use of the first major antidepressants by Kuhn and Kline in 1957; and early in the sixties, Schou's controlled use of lithium salts.

2. One should refer to Daniel Widlocher, ed., *Le Ralentissement dépressif* (Paris: Presses Universitaires de France, 1983); Widlocher takes stock of the work done in this area and proposes a new concept of the psychomotor retardation characteristic of depression: "To be depressed is to be trapped in a system of acts, to act, think, and speak according to modes of which retardation is a feature" (p. 9).

3. See R. Jouvent, in *ibid.,* pp. 41–53.

4. See Y. Lecrubier, "Une Limite biologique des états dépressifs," in *ibid.*, p. 85.

5. D. E. Redmond, Jr., as quoted by Morton Reiser in *Mind, Brain, Body* (New York: Basic Books, 1984), p. 148. Emphasis mine.

6. Michael Gazzaniga, *The Bisected Brain* (New York: Meredith, 1970). Many later studies emphasize this division of symbolic functions between the two brain hemispheres.

7. See J. D. Vincent, *Biologie des passions* (Paris: Jacob, 1986).

8. See D. Widlocher, *Les Logiques de la dépression* (Paris: Fayard, 1986).

9. Sigmund Freud, *Some Psychical Consequences of the Anatomical Distinction Between the Sexes* (1925), *SE* 19:241–58.

10. Sigmund Freud, *Fetichism* (1927), *SE* 21:147–157

11. Sigmund Freud, *Negation* (1925), *SE* 19:233–39.

12. See also M. Mahler, *On Human Symbiosis and the Vicissitudes of Identification* (New York: International University Press, 1968), vol. 1. Joyce MacDougall has analyzed denial in the playacting of the perverse in "Identifications, Neoneeds, and Neosexualities," *International Journal of Psychoanalysis* (1986) 67:19–31.

13. N. Abraham and M. Torok have published the result of considerable research on introjection and the formation of psychic "crypts" in mourning, depression, and related structures. See, among others, N. Abraham, *L'Ecorce et le noyau* (Paris: Aubier, 1978). My interpretation, which differs from theirs, starts from the same clinical observation of a "psychic void" in depressed persons, something that has also been noted by André Green.

14. Concerning this second aspect of the depressive voice lacking nervousness and anxiety, what have been noted are melodic monotony, poor tone quality, and few overtones. See, for instance, M. Hamilton, "A Rating Scale in Depression," *Journal of Neurology, Neurosurgery, and Psychiatry* (1960), 23:56–62 and P. Hardy, R. Jouvent, and D. Widlocher, "Speech and Psychopathology," *Language and Speech* (1985), 28 (1):57–79. Substantially, these writers point to a prosodic flattening that accompanies psychomotor retardation. On the other hand, in the psychoanalytical clinic, the patient we hear belongs mainly to the side of the melancholy–

depressive set that is more neurotic than psychotic and during the period following severe crises when, precisely, transference is possible; we then note a certain amount of play with monotony and lower frequencies and intensities, and also a concentration of attention to vocal values. Thus, giving significance to the suprasegmental register, as I see it, seems to "rescue" depressive persons from total acathexis in speech and endow some sound fragments (syllables or syllabic groups) with an affective meaning that has otherwise been erased from the signifying sequence (as will be seen in the example that follows). These remarks add to, without necessarily contradicting, psychiatric observations on the flat depressive voice.

15. See L. Pons, "Influence du lithium sur les fonctions cognitives," *La Presse Médicale* (1963), 12:943–46.

16. *Ibid.*, p. 945.

17. In this connection, among other more technical studies, see H. Tellenbach's psychopathological meditation, *De la mélancolie* (Paris: Presses Universitaires de France, 1979).

18. See Immanuel Kant, *Anthropologie in pragmatischer Hinsicht,* as quoted by Jean Starobinski in "Le Concept de nostalgie," *Diogène* (1966), 54:92–115. One might also refer to Starobinski's other works on melancholia and depression, which shed light on my topic from historical and philosophical points of view.

19. See Hanna Segal, "Notes on Symbol Formation," *International Journal of Psychoanalysis* (1957), 38:391–97, and chapter 1 above.

20. Concerning the distinction between the semiotic and the symbolic see my *Revolution in Poetic Language* (New York: Columbia University Press, 1984) and above, chapter 1 note 24. Jean Oury notes in "Violence et mélancolie," in *La Violence/Actes du Colloque de Milan* (Paris: 10/18, 1978) that when deprived of the Great Other melancholy persons seek for undecipherable and yet vital markings up to the "point of horror" of their meeting with the "boundless" (pp. 27 and 32).

3. Illustrations of Feminine Depression

1. One is particularly indebted to the works of André Green for having developed the notion of "psychic void." See, among

others, "L'Analyste, la symbolisation et l'absence dans la cure ana-
lytique," at the Twenty-ninth International Psychoanalytic Congress,
1975, and *Narcissisme de vie, narcissisme de mort* (Paris: Minuit, 1983).

4. Beauty: The Depressive's Other Realm

1. Sigmund Freud, "On Transience," *SE* 14:305–7.

2. See Walter Benjamin, *Origine du drame baroque allemand* (Paris:
Flammarion, 1985): "Mourning is the state of mind in which feeling
gives the deserted world a new life, a sort of mask, in order to enjoy
a mysterious pleasure when contemplating it. Any feeling is *a priori*
linked with an object, and its phenomenology is the presentation of
that object" (p. 150). One will note the bond that is established
between phenomenology on the one hand and the recovered object
of melancholy feeling on the other. We are indeed dealing with the
melancholy feeling that can be named, but what of the loss of the
object and the indifference toward the signifier with melancholy
persons? Benjamin says nothing about that. "Similar to those bodies
that flip over during their fall, the allegorical intent, bouncing from
symbol to symbol, would become prey to vertigo when facing its
unfathomable depth, if precisely the most extreme of such symbols
did not force it into such a pull up as to cause everything it contains
in the way of obscurity, affectation, and distance from God to
appear as self-delusion. . . . The transient aspect of things is not so
much signified, allegorically presented, as it is offered as being
significant in itself, as allegory. As allegory of the resurrection. . . .
That is exactly the essence of deep melancholy meditation: its ultimate objects, in which it thinks it has established itself as totally
depraved, as they change into allegory fill and negate the nothingness in which they present themselves, just as at the end the intent
does not freeze in the faithful contemplation of bones but turns
back, unfaithfully, toward resurrection" (pp. 250–51; trans. from
the French by LSR).

5. Holbein's Dead Christ

1. Fyodor Dostoyevsky, *The Idiot,* trans. David Magarshack
(New York: Viking Penguin, 1955), p. 236. Emphasis mine.

2. *Ibid.,* pp. 418–20. [On a few occasions I have modified Magarshack's rendition—LSR.]

3. "Incorporated within the present frame above the painting and running its full length is an inscription, with Angels with Instruments of the Passion, JESVS NAZARENVS REX IVDAEORVM, executed with the brush on paper, almost certainly contemporaneously with the painting. An attribution to Holbein himself, while not certain, is not to be ruled out, even though the Angels recall the work of his recently deceased brother, Ambrosius" (John Rowlands, *Holbein* [Boston: David R. Godine, 1985], p. 127.)

4. The relation of height to width is 1:7, but if the plate affixed to the lower margin of the picture is included the relation becomes 1:9.

5. See Paul Ganz, *The Paintings of Hans Holbein* (New York: Phaidon, 1950), pp. 218–20.

6. See "Der Leichnam Christi im Grabe, 1522," in Joseph Gantner, ed., *Die Malerfamilie Holbein in Basel,* Ausstellung im Kunstmuseum Basel zur Fünfhundertjahr Feier der Universität Basel (1960), pp. 188–90.

7. Before Holbein such a representation of the body fully stretched out can be seen, for instance, in Pietro Lorenzetti's *Deposition* in the lower church at Assisi. One finds the same position, but turned in the opposite direction, in the recumbent Christ in the murals of the Blansingen church near Basel dated c. 1450. About 1440 the master of the *Heures de Rohan* depicts a stiff, bloodied image of the dead Christ but accompanied by Mary's mercy. Villeneuve's *Pieta* with the Christ in profile should be compared with that series (see Walter Ueberwasser, "Holbeins Christus in der 'Grabnische,' " in *Festschrift für Werner Noack* [1959], pp. 125ff.)

One should also mention the sculpted *Christ in the Tomb* in the Freiburg cathedral and another sculpture in the Freising cathedral, dated 1430, and presenting a recumbent Christ quite similar in position and proportions to Holbein's painting, leaving aside, of course, the anatomical knowledge of the body characteristic of the Renaissance artist.

8. Concerning religious feelings in Germany at the end of the Middle Ages and their influence on painting, see Louis Réau, *Mathias Grünewald et le Retable de Colmar* (Nancy: Berger-Levrault, 1920).

9. See Wilhelm Pinder, *Holbein le Jeune et la fin de l'art gothique allemand* (Cologne, 1920).

10. See Ueberwasser, "Holbeins Christus."

11. The Death theme recurs throughout the Middle Ages and finds a particularly receptive audience in northern European countries. In his prologue to the *Decameron,* on the other hand, Boccaccio banishes all interest in such gloominess and exalts the joy of living. In contrast, Thomas More, whom Holbein met through Erasmus, speaks of death as Holbein might have done on the basis of his *Dead Christ:* "We joke and believe death to be far removed. It is hidden in the deepest secrets of our organs. For since the moment you came into this world, life and death go forward at the same pace" (see A. Lerfoy, *Holbein* [Paris: Albin Michel, 1943], p. 85). Shakespeare, as is well known, excels in the tragical and magical intertwining of death themes.

12. Martin Luther, *Tischreden in der Mathesischen Sammlung,* I, 122, p. 51, as quoted by Jean Wirth, *Luther, étude d'histoire religieuse* (Geneva: Droz, 1981), p. 130. [My translation from the French, with the help of the German text in *Tischreden,* ed. Walther Rehm (Munich, 1934), p. 324; for the subsequent quotations I have used the translation by Bertram Lee Woolf of the ninety-five theses in *Reformation Writings of Martin Luther* (London: Lutterworth Press, 1952), I, 32–43—LSR.]

13. See Erasmus' *De Libero Arbitrio* and Luther's answer, *De Servo Arbitrio.* See also John M. Todd, *Martin Luther: A Biographical Study* (Westminster, Md.: Newman Press, 1964) and R. H. Fife, *The Revolt of Martin Luther* (New York: Columbia University Press, 1957).

14. See Carl C. Christensen, *Art and the Reformation in Germany* (Athens: Ohio University Press, 1979), and Charles Garside Jr., *Zwingli and the Arts* (New Haven: Yale University Press, 1966). One should note, within the same tradition, the extensive iconoclasm of H. C. Agrippa von Nettescheim's *De Incertitudine et Vanitate Scientiarum et Artium atque Excellentia Verbi Dei Declamatio* (Antwerp, 1531; French trans., Leiden, 1726).

15. See Christensen, *Art and the Reformation,* p. 169.

16. See Fritz Saxl, "Holbein and the Reformation," in *Lectures* (London: Warburg Institute, University of London, 1957), 1:278.

17. *Ibid.*, p. 282.

18. See Erwin Panofski, "Erasmus and the Visual Arts," *Journal of the Warburg and Courtauld Institutes* (1969), 32:214–19. Like Terminus, Erasmus yields to nothing; or still, according to another interpretation, it is Death itself, like Terminus, that does not yield.

19. See Pierre Vaisse, Introduction to *Holbein le Jeune* (Paris: Flammarion, 1972).

20. See Panofski, "Erasmus," p. 220.

21. Philippe de Champaigne's dead Christ lying on a shroud resembles Holbein's painting on account of the Savior's solitude. The painter eliminated the Virgin, who was present in J. Bonasono's print, after Raphael, which is Champaigne's source. Nevertheless, while Champaigne also comes close to Holbein through the coloring's starkness and restraint, at the same time he remains more faithful to the sacred texts (showing Christ's traditional wounds, the crown of thorns, etc.), and colder, distant, even hardened. The Jansenist spirit shows in that vision, as do the recommendations of latter sixteenth-century theologians (Borthini, Paleoti, Gilio) to avoid expressing pain (see Bernard Dorival, *Philippe de Champaigne [1602–1674]*, 2 vols. [Paris: Léonce-Laguet, 1978].

22. See Ganz, *The Paintings of Hans Holbein.*

23. See Rudolf and Margot Wittkower, *Born Under Saturn; the Character and Conduct of Artists: A Documented History from Antiquity to the French Revolution* (New York: Norton, 1969).

24. Thus on the one hand: "Can you drink the cup that I must drink, or be baptized with the baptism with which I must be baptized?" (Mark 20:39); "Very well, he said, you shall drink my cup" (Matthew 20:23); "I have come to bring fire to the earth, and how I wish it were blazing already! There is a baptism I must still receive, and how great is my distress till it is over!" (Luke 12:49–50); and especially the famous quotation that signals the loss of hope, "Eli, Eli, lama sabachthani? that is, *My God, my God, why have you deserted me?*" (Matthew 27:46–47 and Mark 15:34).

There is, on the other hand, the message of glad tidings: "For the Son of Man himself did not come to be served but to serve, and to give his life as a ransom for many" (Mark 10:45); "Yet here I am among you as one who serves!" (Luke 22–27).

25. See Xavier-Léon Dufour, "La Mort rédemptrice du Christ

selon le Nouveau Testament," in *Mort pour nos péchés* (Brussels: Facultés Universitaires Saint-Louis, 1979), pp. 11–45.

26. See A. Vergote, "La Mort rédemptrice du Christ à la lumière de l'anthropologie," in *Mort pour nos péchés*, p. 68.

27. René Girard, *Des Choses cachées depuis la fondation du monde* (Paris: Grasset, 1978).

28. See Urs von Balthasar, *La Gloire et la croix*, 3:2, "La Nouvelle Alliance" (Paris: Aubier, 1975).

29. See Romans 5:8, "Christ died for us while we were still sinners"; and also, "God did not spare his own Son, but gave him up to benefit us all" (Romans 8:32), and "follow Christ by loving as he loved you, giving himself up in our place *as a fragrant offering and a sacrifice to God*" (Ephesians 5:2); similarly, see Mark 10:45, Matthew 20:28 and 26:28, Mark 14:24, Luke 22:19, and 1 Peter 2:21–25.

30. See Dufour in *Mort pour nos péchés*.

31. G. W. F. Hegel, *Lectures on the Philosophy of Religion*, trans. E. B. Speirs (New York: Humanities Press, 1962), 3:93. Emphasis mine.

32. *Ibid.*, emphasis mine. [This is basically my translation, although I have relied on Speirs' vocabulary and phrasing—LSR.]

33. Blaise Pascal. *Thoughts: An Apology for Christianity*. [My translation from "Le Sépulcre de Jésus-Chrust," no. 362, in Zacharie Tourneur, ed., *Pensées de M. Pascal sur la religion* (Paris: Cluny, 1938), 2:101—LSR.]

34. [See note 33; the text is from Pascal, "Le Mystère de Jésus," no. 297, *Pensées*, 2:12—LSR.]

6. *Gérard De Nerval, The Disinherited Poet*

1. See Jeanine Moulin, *Les Chimères, Exégèses* (Lille: Giard, 1949). During the summer of 1954, a few months before his suicide, it seems that Nerval went on a pilgrimage to his mother's tomb in Glogau, Germany [now Glogów, Poland]; this was followed by a relapse.

2. See Jacques Dhaenens, *Le Destin d'Orphée, "El Desdichado" de Gérard de Nerval* (Paris: Minard, 1972).

3. "A Alexandre Dumas," in *Oeuvres complètes* (hereafter *OC*), Bibliothèque de la Pléiade (Paris: Gallimard, 1952), 1:175–76.

4. A rather precise and striking similarity has been noted between the first three lines of "El Desdichado" and the seventh volume of Court de Gebelin's *Monde primitif, analysé et comparé avec le monde moderne* (1781). Likewise, sources have been found for the five sonnets of *Chimères* ("El Desdichado," "Myrtho," "Horus," "Antéros," and "Artémis") in *Les Fables égyptiennes et grecques* (1758) by Dom Antoine-Joseph Pernety, a Benedictine monk of the Saint Maur congregation. Nerval must also have read Pernety's *Dictionnaire mytho-hermétique*. The following excerpts from Pernety can be related to Nerval's work: "The real key for the work is this blackness at the start of its process. . . . Blackness is the true sign of a perfect solution. Matter is then dissolved into a powder more minute. . . . than the atoms that flit about in the rays of the sun, and its atoms are changed into permanent water.

"Philosophers have given that disintegration such names as death, . . . hell, Tartarus, *the shades, night . . . the grave . . . melancholia . . . overshadowed sun* or *eclipse of the sun* and moon. . . . They have finally named it by using all the words that might express or designate corruption, disintegration, and blackness. It is what furnished Philosophers the stuff for so many allegories about deaths and tombs . . ." (*Fables égyptiennes et grecques*, 1:154–55; emphasis mine). Pernety quotes Raymond Lulle on the topic of blackness: "Let the body of the sun be putrefied for thirteen days, at the end of which the dissolution becomes black as ink; but its inside will be red like a ruby, or like a carbuncle. Now take this tenebrous sun, darkened by its sister's or mother's embrace, and place it in an alembic . . ." (*ibid.*, 2:136). His definition of melancholia is as follows: "Melancholia signifies the putrefaction of matter. . . . This name has been given to matter turned black, doubtless because there is something sad about the color black, and because the human body's humor called melancholia is considered to be a black, twice-cooked bile that produces sad, lugubrious vapors" (*Dictionnaire mytho-hermétique*, p. 289). "Sadness and melancholia . . . are also names that Adepts give to their matter when it has turned black" (*Les Fables égyptiennes et grecques*, 2:300).

Those connections between Nerval's text and the alchemical corpus have been established by Georges Le Breton, "La Clé des *Chimères:* l'alchimie," *Fontaine* (1945), 44:441–60; see also "L'Alchimie dans *Aurélia:* 'Les Mémorables,' " *Fontaine* (1945), 45:687–706. Many works have dealt with Nerval and esoterism, among which Jean Richer, *Expérience et création* (Paris: Hachette, 1963); François Constant, "Le Soleil noir et l'étoile ressuscitée," *La Tour Saint Jacques* (January–April 1958), nos. 13–14, and so forth.

5. Richer, *Expérience et création,* pp. 33–38.

6. See Dhaenens, *Le Destin d'Orphée.*

7. See Emilie Noulet, *Etudes littéraires, l'hermétisme de la poésie française moderne* (Mexico: Talleres Gráficos de la Editorial Cultura, 1944).

8. Jacques Geninasca, "El Desdichado," *Archives Nervaliennes,* no. 59, pp. 9–53.

9. Nerval, *Selected Writings,* trans. Geoffrey Wagner (Ann Arbor: University of Michigan Press, 1957), pp. 118–19.

10. See "Lettres à Jenny Colon," in *OC* 1:726ff.

11. See Jean Guillaume, *Aurélia: prolégomène à une édition critique* (Namur: Presses Universitaires de Namur, 1972).

12. See Marcel Détienne, *Dionysos à ciel ouvert* (Paris: Hachette, 1986).

13. Nerval, *Selected Writings,* p. 209. [Trans. slightly modified by LSR.]

14. *Aurelia,* in *Selected Writings,* p. 173.

15. See Dhaenens, *Le Destin d'Orphée,* p. 49.

16. Nerval, "Chanson gothique," in *OC* 1:59.

17. "Les Papillons," in *OC* 1:53.

18. "Anteros," in *Selected Writings,* p. 219.

19. See Dhaenens, *Le Destin d'Orphée,* p. 59.

20. See M. Jeanneret, *La Lettre perdue: écriture et folie dans l'oeuvre de Nerval* (Paris: Flammarion, 1978).

21. Nerval, "Le Christ des Oliviers," in *OC* 1:37.

22. *Ibid.,* p. 38.

23. *Ibid.,* p. 36.

24. "Gilded Verses," in *Selected Writings,* p. 225.

25. "Fragments du manuscrit d'Aurélia," in *OC* 1:423.

26. *Aurelia,* in *Selected Writings,* p. 118. Further page references are given in the text.

7. *Dostoyevsky, the Writing of Suffering, and Forgiveness*

1. Freud's canonical text on Dostoyevsky examines the writer from the point of view of epilepsy, amoralism, parricide, and gambling, and merely alludes to the "sado-masochism" that underlies suffering. See "Dostoyevsky and Parricide," *SE* 21:175ff. For a discussion of that thesis, see Philippe Sollers, "Dostoievski, Freud, la roulette," in *Théorie des exceptions* (Paris: Gaillimard, 1986).

2. Dostoyevsky, "Carnets des Démons," in *Les Démons* (Paris: Gallimard, 1955), pp. 810–11. Emphasis mine. [Translated from the French by LSR.]

3. *Ibid.,* p. 812.

4. *Ibid.,* p. 1154.

5. *The Possessed,* trans. Constance Garnett (New York: Random House, 1936), p. 601.

6. *Notes from the Underground,* trans. Ralph E. Matlaw (New York: E. P. Dutton, 1960), p. 16.

7. *Ibid.,* p. 31.

8. Nietzsche links Napoleon and Dostoyevsky in a meditation on "the criminal and those who are like him": those two extraordinary men would reveal the presence of a "Catilinarian existence" at the basis of any exceptional experience involving a transmutation of values. "The testimony of Dostoyevsky is relevant to this problem —Dostoyevsky, the only psychologist, incidentally, from whom I had something to learn. He ranks among the most beautiful strokes of fortune in my life, even more than my discovery of Stendhal. This *profound* human being, who was ten times right in his low estimate of the superficial Germans, lived for a long time among the convicts in Siberia" (*The Twilight of the Idols,* in *The Portable Nietzsche,* ed. and trans. Walter Kaufmann [New York: Viking Press, 1954], p. 549). And according to the W. II. 6. version: "The criminal type is the type of the strong human being under unfavorable circumstances; as a consequence, all instincts, branded with scorn, fear, dishonor, are usually inextricably fused with *depressive* feelings, that

is, physiologically speaking, they *degenerate"* (Nietzsche, *Oeuvres complètes* [Paris, Gallimard, 1974], p. 478—translated from the French by LSR). While appreciating Dostoyevsky's praise for the "aesthetic" and "criminal genius," Nietzsche often rebels against what appears to him as Christianity's pathological psychology, caught in the snare of love, which the Russian writer displays: there would be an "infantile idiom" in the Gospels, as in a "Russian novel," according to the *Antichrist*. One should not emphasize Nietzsche's fascination with Dostoyevsky, who is seen as the forerunner of his own overman, without especially pointing out the discomfort aroused in the German philosopher by Dostoyevsky's Christianity.

9. Dostoyevsky, *Crime and Punishment,* trans. by Constance Garnett (New York: Random House, 1950), p. 259.

10. *Ibid.*

11. *Ibid.,* p. 441.

12. *Ibid.,* p. 445.

13. Dostoyevsky, "The Verdict," in *The Diary of a Writer,* trans. by Boris Brasol (New York: George Braziller, 1954), p. 471.

14. See J. Catteau, *La Création littéraire chez Dostoyevsky* (Paris: Institut d'Etudes Slaves, 1978), pp. 125–80.

15. Dostoyevsky, *The Letters of Dostoyevsky to His Wife,* trans. Elizabeth Hill and Doris Mudie (London: Constable, 1930), p. 181.

Concerning Dostoyevsky's interest in Job, see the essay in Russian by B. Boursov, "Dostoyevsky's Personality," in *Zvesda* (1970), 12:104: "He suffered on account of God and the universe, for he did not want to uphold the eternal laws of nature and history to the extent of refusing to acknowledge that what was in the process of being accomplished had actually been accomplished. And so he went on, as it were, counter to everything."

16. See Mikhail M. Bakhtin, *Problems of Dostoyevsky's Poetics* (Ann Arbor: University of Michigan Press, 1973).

17. See the work in Russian by Dmitri S. Merezhkovsky, *Prophet of the Russian Revolution* (1906).

18. Anna Dostoevsky, *Dostoevsky/Reminiscences,* trans. and ed. by Beatrice Stillman (New York: Liveright, 1975), p. 134. The reference is to their stay in Switzerland in 1867. In the stenographic notes of her diary, the writer's wife wrote: "In the city museum

there [Basel], Fyodor Mikhailovich saw Hans Holbein's painting. It struck him with terrible force, and he said to me then, 'A painting like that can make you lose your faith.' "

According to L. P. Grossman, Dostoyevsky would have known about this painting in his childhood from the *Letters of a Russian Traveler* by Karamzin who deems that there is "nothing divine" in Holbein's Christ. The same critic believes it is likely that Dostoyevsky had read *The Haunted Pool* by George Sand, who emphasized the impact of suffering in Holbein's work. See L. P. Grossman, *F. M. Dostoyevsky* (Molodaia Gvardia, 1962) and *A Seminar on Dostoyevsky* (1923)—both in Russian.

19. *Literary Heritage* (Moscow: Nouka, n.d.), 83:174, as quoted in Catteau, *La Création littéraire . . .* , p. 174.

20. ". . . The corruption of Pascal, who believed in the corruption of his reason through original sin when it had in fact been corrupted only by his Christianity" (*The Antichrist,* in Kaufmann, ed., *The Portable Nietzsche,* p. 572).

21. Dostoyevsky, *The Insulted and Humiliated* (Moscow: Foreign Languages Publishing House, n.d.), pp. 10–11.

22. Dostoyevsky, *The Idiot,* p. 438.

23. *Ibid.,* p. 434.

24. Eroticizing suffering along with rejecting the death penalty suggest similar attitudes by the Marquis de Sade. The parallel between the two writers was drawn, not without malice, by Dostoyevsky's contemporaries. Thus, in a letter dated February 24, 1882, addressed to Saltykov-Shchedrin, Turgenev notes that Dostoyevsky, like Sade, "describes in his novels the pleasures of sensuous people," and is indignant because "Russian bishops have celebrated mass and given praise to this superman, our own Sade! What strange times do we live in?"

25. *The Idiot,* p. 46.

26. *Ibid.,* p. 86.

27. *Ibid.,* p. 46.

28. One will recall in this connection the filial bond that Dostoyevsky established with the Procurator Constantine Probedonostsev, a despotic figure embodying tsarist obscurantism. See Tsvetan Stoyanov, *The Genius and his Guardian* (Sofia, 1978).

29. Dostoyevsky, *Literary Heritage* (1971), 83:173–74, note dated April 16, 1864. Dostoyevsky continues his thoughts: "Only Christ was able to do so, but Christ was eternal, a specular ideal to which man aspires and according to the laws of nature should aspire. In the meantime, after the coming of Christ as the ideal of man in the flesh, it appeared clear as day that the superior and supreme development of the individual must precisely come to this . . . that the supreme use to which man might put his individuality, the complete development of his *Self*—was in some way to obliterate that Self, giving it wholly to each and everyone, completely and frantically. That is supreme happiness. Thus the law of the Self becomes one with the law of humanism and, in the merging of the two, the *Self* and *All* . . . their mutual and reciprocal abolishment is accomplished, and at the same time each one in particular reaches the goal of his individual development.

"That is precisely Christ's paradise. . . .

"But it will be, in my opinion, completely absurd to reach that supreme goal if, when it is reached, everything is snuffed out and disappears, that is, if human life does not go on after that goal has been achieved. Therefore there is a future, heavenly life.

"Where is it, on which planet, in which center, is it the ultimate center, at the heart of universal synthesis, that is, in God? We know nothing about it. We know only one feature of the future nature of the future being, who perhaps may not even be called a man (hence we have no idea of the kind of beings we shall be)."

Dostoyevsky goes on by considering that this utopic synthesis where the limits of the Self were erased within an amatory merging with the others would be accomplished by suspending sexuality, which produces tensions and conflicts: "Over there we have an entirely synthetic being, eternally joying and complete, for whom it will be as if time no longer existed." The impossibility of sacrificing the Self out of love for a different being ("Me and Macha") brings about a sense of suffering and the state of sin: "Thus, man must incessantly experience a suffering that is balanced by the heavenly jouissance of the accomplishment of the Law, that is, by sacrifice."

[Translated from the French by LSR.]

30. *Crime and Punishment*, pp. 189–90. Further page references are given in the text.

31. As Hannah Arendt notes, "The only rudimentary sign of an awareness that forgiveness may be the necessary corrective . . . may be seen in the Roman principle to spare the vanquished *(parcere subiectis)*—a wisdom entirely unknown to the Greeks" (*The Human Condition* [Chicago: University of Chicago Press, 1958], p. 239).

32. Thus, among others, Matthew 6:14–15: "Yes, if you forgive others their failings, your heavenly Father will forgive you yours; but if you do not forgive others, your Father will not forgive your failings either."

33. The phrase is that of Alain Besançon, *Le Tsarévitch immolé* (Paris: Plon, 1967), p. 214.

34. *The Possessed*, pp. 715–16.

35. Ovid, *Metamorphoses*, trans. Rolfe Humphries (Bloomington: Indiana University Press, 1955), p. 332.

36. Hannah Arendt reminds us of the connotations of the Greek words corresponding to certain key words in Luke, *aphienai* and *metanoein*—"dismiss," "release," for the first, "change of mind," "return," and "trace back one's steps" for the second (*The Human Condition*, p. 240, note 78).

37. Concerning dialogue and love in Dostoyevsky see Jacques Rolland, *Dostoievski: La question de l'autre* (Paris: Verdier, 1983).

38. Concerning identification, see my *Tales of Love* (New York: Columbia University Press, 1987), pp. 24–48.

39. Ephesians 4:32: "Be friends with one another, and kind, forgiving each other as readily as God forgave you in Christ." Luke 1:78: "This by the tender mercy of our God / Who from on high will bring the rising Sun to visit us."

40. See Symeon the New Theologian, *Works* (Moscow, 1890— in Russian).

41. Quoted by O. Clément, *L'Essor du christianisme oriental* (Paris: Presses Universitaires de France, 1964), pp. 25–26.

42. "The God light, the Son light, and the Holy Spirit light— those three lights are a same eternal light that is indivisible, without confusion, uncreated, completed, immeasurable, invisible, insofar that it is the source of all light" (Sermon 57, in Symeon, *Works* 2:46); "There is no difference between God who inhabits light and light itself, which is his abode; just as there is no difference between God's light and God. But they are one and the same, the abode and

the inhabitant, the light and God" (Sermon 59, *ibid.* 2:72); "God is light, infinite light, and God's light is revealed to us indistinctly inseparable into hypostases (aspects, faces). . . . The Father is light, the Son is light, the Holy Spirit is light, and the three are a single simple light, uncomplicated, having the same essence, the same value, the same glory" (Sermon 62, *ibid* 2:105).

43. "For the Trinity is a unit of three principles and that unit is called a trinity in hypostases (faces, aspects). . . . and none of those hypostases has for a single instant existed before the others. . . . the three aspects are without origin, they are coeternal and coessential" (Sermon 60, *ibid.* 2:80).

44. Sermon 61, *ibid.* 2:95.

45. "Preface to Hymns of Divine Love," PG 612, cols. 507–9, quoted by O. Clément, *L'Essor du christianisme oriental,* p. 29.

46. "I do not speak in my own name, but in the name of the very treasure that I have just found, that is, Christ who speaks through me: 'I am the resurrection and the life' (John 11:25), 'I am the mustard seed' (Matthew, 13:31–32), 'I am the fine pearl' (Matthew, 13:45) . . . 'I am the yeast' (Matthew 13:33)" (Sermon 89, *ibid.* 2:479). Symeon confides that one day as he was in a state of "infernal excitement and discharge" he spoke to God and received his light with "warm tears," having recognized in his own experience the very heavenly kingdom that the scriptures have described as a pearl (Matthew 13:45–46), a mustard seed (Matthew 13:31–32), yeast (Matthew 13:33), living water (John 4:10), flames of fire (Hebrews 1:8), bread (Luke 22:19), a bridegroom (Matthew 25:6; John 3:29; Revelations 21:9): "What more can be said about the unspeakable. . . . While we have all that at the core of ourselves, placed there by God, we cannot understand it through reason and clarify it through speech" (Sermon 90, *ibid.* 2:490).

47. "The Holy Spirit is given and sent, not in a sense that he himself would not have wished, but in the sense in which the Holy Spirit, *through the Son who is a hypostasis of the Trinity,* accomplishes, as if it were his own will, that which is the Father's wish. For the Holy Trinity is inseparable by nature, essence, and will, even though by hypostases it is called by persons, Father, Son, and Holy Spirit, and those three names are a single God and his name is Trinity" (Sermon 62, *ibid.* 2:105).

48. Clément, *L'Essor du christianisme oriental,* p. 74.

49. At the heart of this painful and joyful osmosis of the three hypostases, the self's individuality is perceived as the necessary barrier to biological and social life, which nevertheless prevents experiencing forgiveness—love for others. See above, Dostoyevsky's thoughts in connection with the self as barrier at the time of his wife Maria's death.

50. See Bakhtin, *Problems of Dostoyevsky's Poetics.*

51. See Freud, "Dostoyevsky and Parricide."

52. Thomas Aquinas, *Summa Theologia,* Latin text and English trans. Thomas Gilby, O.P. (New York: McGraw Hill, 1963), vol. 5, question 21, p. 77.

53. *Ibid.,* pp. 79 and 81. Emphasis added.

54. Quoted by Thomas Aquinas, *ibid.,* p. 81.

8. The Malady of Grief: Duras

1. Paul Valéry, "La Crise de l'esprit," *Variété,* in *Oeuvres,* Bibliothèque de la Pléiade (Paris: Gallimard, 1957), 1:988.

2. *Ibid.,* 1:991. Emphasis added.

3. "Even though man worries to no avail, nevertheless he proceeds within the image" (Augustine, "Images," *On the Trinity,* XIV, IV, 6)

4. See Maurice Blanchot, "Où va la littérature?" in *Le Livre à venir* (Paris: Gallimard, 1959), p. 289.

5. Roger Caillois recommends, in literature, "techniques permitting the exploration of the unconscious": "accounts, with or without comments, of *depressions, confusion, anxiety,* and personal emotional experiences," in "Crise de littérature," *Cahiers du Sud* (Marseille, 1935). Emphasis added.

6. Marguerite Duras, *Le Ravissement de Lol V. Stein* (Paris: Gallimard, 1964), p. 14 [All quotations in this chapter are from the French editions of Duras' novels; trans. by LSR]

7. *Ibid.,* p. 25.

8. *Ibid.,* p. 26.

9. *Ibid.,* p. 31.

10. *Ibid.,* p. 69.

11. *Ibid.,* p. 151.

12. Duras, *La Maladie de la mort* (Paris; Minuit, 1982), p. 56.

13. Duras, *L'Amant* (Paris: Minuit, 1984), pp. 105–6.

14. Clarice Lispector, *An Apple in the Dark,* trans. from the Brazilian edition by Gregory Rabassa (New York: Knopf, 1967).

15. "They both avoided looking at one another, overwrought with themselves, as if they finally had become part of that greater thing which sometimes manages to express itself in tragedy . . . as if they had just again realized the miracle of forgiveness; embarrassed by that miserable scene, they avoided looking at each other, uneasy, there are so many unaesthetic things to forgive. But, even covered with ridicule and rags, the mimicry of the resurrection had been done. Those things which seem not to happen, but do happen" (*An Apple in the Dark,* pp. 353–54).

16. Duras has written nineteen film scripts and fifteen plays, three of which are adaptations.

17. Duras, *L'Amant,* p. 48.

18. Duras, *Hiroshima mon amour, synopsis* (Paris: Gallimard, 1960), p. 10.

19. *Ibid.,* p. 11.

20. *Ibid.,* pp. 9–10.

21. *Ibid.,* pp. 136–37.

22. *Ibid.,* p. 132.

23. *Ibid.,* p. 149.

24. *Ibid.,* p. 125.

25. *Ibid.,* p. 100.

26. Duras, *L'Amant,* p. 85.

27. Duras, *La Douleur* (Paris: POL, 1985), p. 57.

28. *Ibid.,* p. 80.

29. Duras, *Un Barrage contre le Pacifique* (Paris: Gallimard, 1950), pp. 73–74.

30. Duras, *L'Amant,* p. 69.

31. *Ibid.,* p. 104

32. *Ibid.,* p. 146.

33. *Ibid.,* p. 57.

34. Duras, *Le Vice-consul* (Paris: Gallimard, 1966), p. 80.

35. *Ibid.,* p. 174.

36. *Ibid.,* p. 111.

37. *Ibid.*, pp. 195–96.

38. *Ibid.*, p. 198.

39. Marguerite Duras' asset is that she dares to write in between the "seduction that would work by setting free" and the "suicidal shock" of a death drive where what one calls sublimation would originate." See Marcelle Marini and Marguerite Duras, *Territoires du féminin* (Paris; Minuit, 1977), p. 56.

40. Duras, *Le Ravissement de Lol V. Stein*, p. 14.

41. Duras, *Le Vice-consul*, p. 67.

42. Duras, *L'Amant*, p. 40.

43. *Ibid.*, p. 32.

44. *Ibid.*, pp. 34–35.

45. *Ibid.*, p. 105.

46. Duras, *Le Vice-consul*, p. 157.

47. Duras, *Le Ravissement de Lol V. Stein*, p. 24.

48. Duras, *Le Vice-consul*, p. 201.

49. Duras, *La Maladie de la mort*, p. 38.

50. *Ibid.*, p. 48.

51. Duras, *Un Barrage contre le Pacifique*, p. 69.

52. *Ibid.*, p. 119.

53. Duras, *La Maladie de la mort*, p. 61.

54. Duras, *Le Ravissement de Lol V. Stein*, p. 81.

55. *Ibid.*, p. 159.

56. Duras, *Détruire, dit-elle* (Paris; Minuit, 1969), p. 46.

57. *Ibid.*, p. 34.

58. *Ibid.*, p. 72.

59. *Ibid.*, pp. 102–3.

60. *Ibid.*, p. 131.

61. *Ibid.*, pp. 99–100.

62. *Ibid.*, p. 126.

63. *Ibid.*, pp. 135–37.

64. Duras, *Un Barrage contre le Pacifique*, p. 142.

65. *Ibid.*, p. 22.

66. *Ibid.*, p. 137.

67. *Ibid.*, p. 257.

68. Duras, *L'Amant*, p. 73.

INDEX

Index

Cerebral function, 38-40

Champaigne, Philippe de, *Dead Christ*, 126, 271*n*21

Chemical substances, brain function, 39

Child: as antidote to depression, 88-94; and denial, 44; depressive stage, 133; fight/flight response, 36; language acquisition, 41; psychotic, 41-42

Chinese civilization, 66-67

Choice, inability in, 59

Cholinergic transmission, 35

Chora, 264*n*24

Christ: Dostoyevsky's views, 278*n*29; in Nerval's poetry, 168; Passion of, artistic depiction, 212-13

—— death of, 107-10, 119, 130-38: artistic representations, 111-19; Nerval and, 163

Christ as the Light of the World, Holbein the Younger, 123

Christ as the Man of Sorrows, Holbein the Younger, 112, 122

Christianity: allegories of, 101, 103; and forgiveness, 190, 200, 208; and hiatus, 132; medieval, and melancholy, 8; sacrifice concept, 131-32; schism, 209-11; Trinity concepts, 208-11; *see also* Catholicism; Christ

Christ in the Tomb, Freiburg cathedral, 269*n*7

Cinema, *see* Films

Clément, Olivier, 212

Cognitive process, acceleration of, 59

Colmar altarpiece, Grünewald, 116

Colon, Jenny, 150, 155

Comedy, desire for, 259

Concatenation, 40-42; and denial, 49; loss of ability, 34

Consciousness: Dostoyevsky's

view, 180-81; negation of repressed image, 45

Contrition, Luther's views, 120

Conversion of Holbein, 123

Conveyance, 66-68

Cranach, Lucas, the Elder, 120

Creative art, *see* Art

Crime, and sadness, Dostoyevsky and, 196-97

Crime and Punishment, Dostoyevsky, 192, 195-200, 203-4, 206, 228-29

Crisis of values, nineteenth-century, 171

Crisis periods: contemporary, 221-24; and melancholia, 8

Cristo in scruto, Mantegna, 117

Crucifixion, Grünewald, 116

Cultural constructs, as erotic objects, 28

Danse Macabre, Holbein the Younger, 118, 123-25

Dante Alighieri, *Inferno*, 8

Dead Christ, Champaigne, 126, 271*n*21

Death, 9; of Christ, 107-19, 130-38, 163; Christianity and, 134-36; depressed view, 4; Dostoyevsky and, 194-95; and forgiveness, 192; Holbein the Younger and, 123-26, 128; and love, 232-33, 236-37; psychic experience, 72-73; Renaissance views, 119; representation of, 25-26; repudiation of, 12; suicidal views, 153; as theme in medieval art, 270*n*11; woman and, 245

Death anxiety, 26-27

Death-bearing mother, and feminine sexuality, 78-79

Death drive, 16-21, 175-76

Death wish, psychoanalysis and, 82

Decameron, Boccaccio, 270*n*11

Index

Index

Le Breton, Georges, 146
Left brain hemisphere, and language, 38
Lesage, Alain René, *Le Diable boiteux* (The Lame Devil), 144
Life: meaning of, 6; loss of meaning, 133; of artist, 166
Life force, 15
Limbic lobe of brain stem, 38
Lineage, assumed by Nerval, 149
Linguistics, 21, 41, 43
Lispector, Clarice, 228-29
Literary creation, 22, 24; catharsis of, 24-25, 228-30
Literature, 179, 225; crisis in, 229; postmodern, 258-59; postwar, 224-25
Lithium treatment, 59, 265n1
Locus coeruleus, 35-36
Loneliness, of Holbein's *Dead Christ*, 112-15, 137
Lorenzetti, Peitro, *Deposition*, 269n7
Lorrain, Claude, 228; *Acis and Galatea*, 201-3
Loss: allegory and, 102; and artistic activity, 129-30; and beauty, 99-100; denial of, 23; denial of negation, 43-44; and depression, 5-6; and doubling, 166-67; of erotic object, 81-83, 86; fear of, 25; of meaning of life, 133; of mother, 27-30, 63; negation of, 42; of object, 10-12; of other, 5; and sublimation, 98; symbolic elaboration, 46; of "Thing," 13-14
Love: Dostoyevsky's views, 195; and forgiveness, 204-5, 216; physical, and melancholia, 5-6; postwar version, 232-33
Loved one, divisions of, in Nerval's poetry, 160
The Lover (L'Amant), Duras, 230, 241, 242-43, 255-56
Luke, Saint, 208

Lulle, Raymond, 273n4
Luther, Martin, 119-20, 121; Holbein woodcut, 123
Lützelburger, Hans, 118

A maçã no escuro (The Apple in the Dark), Lispector, 228-29
Madness, in Duras' writings, 227-38, 243, 255-56
Madonnas, Holbein paintings, 112
The Malady of Death, Duras, 230, 241, 245, 249-50
Mallarmé, Stéphane, 150, 258
Mania, defenses against suffering, 187
Manic phase, 9, 21; actions, 81; denial, 50
Manic position, 23, 24
Mantegna, Andrea, *Cristo in scruto*, 117
Marie, Aristide, 149
Mary, Virgin, 29
Masochism, 16-17, 182
Mass communication arts, 224-25
Master of Heures de Rohan, 269n7
Maternal object, mourning for, 9, 61
Matricide, 27-30
Mausolus, king of Caria, 148
Maximus the Confessor, 212
Meaning: cerebral function, 38-40; in depression, 5-6, 43, 49, 189; in depressive speech, 55-58; and forgiveness, 206; loss of, 42, 129-30, 133; omnipotent, 62-64
Meaninglessness, 51-52
Medieval art, death theme, 270n11
Medieval notion of melancholia, 8
Melancholia, 3-5, 9-11, 14, 46, 133; and amatory passion, 5-6; and epilepsy, 183-84; Freud's explanation, 98; meaning of, 189; Nerval and, 169-72; origins of, 6-9; *see also* Depression
Melancholia, Dürer, 8

[292]

Index

Index

Nostalgia, Kant's view, 60
Notebooks of the Possessed, Dostoyevsky, 177
Nothingness, apocalyptic, 223
Not-I, 241-44
Noulet, Emilie, 149-50

Oberried, Hans, 111
Object, 262n7; beauty of, 98-99; of denial, 44; of depressed person, 48; fear of loss, 25; of forgiveness, 194-95; loss of, 10; lost, 145; maternal, and frigidity, 77-79; memory as, 60-61; nonlost, 47; primal, conveyance of, 66-68; primary ascendancy over, 63-64; in primary narcissism, 58; sadness as, 12; separation from, 63
—— erotic: loss of, 81-83, 86; loss of mother, 28; of woman, 30
—— of mourning, 13-15; depressed person and, 11
Objectal depression, 24
Offenburg, Magdalena, 128, 129
Omnipotence, 61-64; feminine, case study, 77
On the Babylonian Captivity of the Church of God, Luther, 120
"On Transience," Freud, 98
Opacity of things, 100-1
Original abode, female body as, 27
Orthodox Trinity, 209-11
Other: cannibalism of, 12; eroticization of, 28; forgiveness and, 205; hatred for, 11, 16-17; life drive and, 15; loss of, and artistic style, 129-30
Other jouissance, 78-79
Overprotective mother, case study, 90-94
Overprotective parents, 61-62
Ovid, *Metamorphoses,* 156

Pain, from denial, 49
Paradise, Golden Age, 201-2

Paranoia, and forgiveness, 190; and suffering, 198
Parcellary splitting, 18-21
Pascal, Blaise, 137; Nietzsche's view, 277n20
Passion of Christ, artistic depiction, 212-13
Passive position, 63
Past, depressed sense of, 60-61
Paternal signifier, 47
Patin, Charles, 128-29
Paul, Jean, 163
Paul, Saint, 208, 215-16
Peasant's War, 121
Pepin III, the Short, 149
Per Filium/Filioque schism, 209-11
Pernety, Antoine-Joseph, 273n4
Perversion, 81-83, 86; and depression, 47-51
Phallic identification, 23
Phallic jouissance, 78-79
Phallic mother fantasy, 45, 84
Philosophy and melancholia, 7
Phobias, 85
Pieta, Villeneuve, 269n7
Pleasure, and suffering, 177-78, 239-40
Poet, disinherited, 145-46
Poetic form, 14
Poetry, 150, 224
Poisoning, 85
Politics, and private life, 234-36
Polyvalence of sign and symbol, 97
Portrait of Benedict von Hertenstein, Holbein the Younger, 128
Portrait of Bonifacius Amerbach, Holbein the Younger, 128
Portrait of Edward, Prince of Wales, Holbein the Younger, 127
Portrait of Erasmus of Rotterdam, Holbein the Younger, 128
Portrait of His Wife and His Two Elder Children, Holbein the Younger, 122, 127

[294]

Index

and hatred, 182; and negation of
loss, 42; in Nerval's poetry, 165;
splitting, 47; writing and, 217
Silence, psychic, 87-88
Solitude, cannibalistic, 71-79
Solothurn Madonna, Holbein the
Younger, 112, 127
Speaking being, 42, 145; death
drive, 20; and language, 53
Speech, depressed, 33, 34, 38, 43,
50, 52, 53-55, 266-67n14; case
study, 77; tonal modulations, 55-
58
Spirit, disasters of, 222
Splittings, 132; Kleinian definition,
18-20; of signs, 47; of subject, 44
Spoken forgiveness, 214-15
Stimulation: integration of, 65; lan-
guage as, 36-38
Style, artistic, 129-30; affects and,
179
Stylistic awkwardness, literary, 226
Subject: depressed, 47; identification with ideal, 207; life force,
15; and lost "Thing," 145-46
Subjective identity, denial and, 48
Subjectivity, and forgiveness, 205
Sublimation, 14, 45, 98, 99-100,
159, 184; and forgiveness, 207; in
Nerval's poetry, 170-72; writing
as, 200
Suffering: art and, 236; Dostoyevsky and, 175-86, 196, 198,
278n29; Duras and, 230, 243,
257; Luther's views, 120; pleasure in, 50, 239-40
Suicide, 9, 12-13, 14, 19-20, 81,
153; Dostoyevsky's views, 181,
186-87
Superego: and denial, 49; and
depression, 196; and identification, 11; and melancholia, 17;
and moods, 22; and omnipotent
meaning, 62; and suffering, 176

Supreme value, negation of, 187
Suso, Heinrich, 115
Symbolic disposition of language,
39
Symbolic equivalents, 23-25
Symbolic processes, 65
Symbols, 23-25; child's access to,
133; language and, 36-37; in
Nerval's "The Disinherited,"
146-58
Symeon the New Theologian, 208-
9, 212

Tact, psychoanalytic, 189-90
Tarot cards, poetic symbolism,
146-47
Tauler, Johannes, 115
Telencephalon, 35
Terrorism, 187; Dostoyevsky's
views, 186-88
Theophany of the earth, 213
Thetic phase, 265n24
Thing, 13-15, 47, 262n7, 262-63n10;
and depressive language, 53; lost,
145-46; mourning for, 40-41;
value of, 51-52
Time, apocalyptic, 188-89
Timelessness of forgiveness, 200-5
Time sense, of depressed people,
60-61
Tonal modulation of depressed
speech, 55-58
Transconscious formations, 27
Transference, hatred in, 11-12
Transgressor, Dostoyevskian, 180
Transience, and beauty, 98
Translation, language as, 41-42
Transposition, 40-42
Trauerspiel, 101
Traumatic memories, 46
Traumatism, preobject, suffering
and, 176
Treschel, Melchior and Gaspard,
118

EUROPEAN PERSPECTIVES
A Series of Columbia University Press

European Perspectives